Irish Studies

Irish Studies presents a wide range of books interpreting important aspects of Irish life and culture to scholarly and general audiences. The richness and complexity of the Irish experience, past and present, deserves broad understanding and careful analysis. For this reason an important purpose of the series is to offer a forum to scholars interested in Ireland, its history, and culture. Irish literature is a special concern in the series, but works from the perspectives of the fine arts, history, and the social sciences are also welcome, as are studies which take multi-disciplinary approaches.

Irish Studies is a continuing project of Syracuse University Press and is under the general editorship of Richard Fallis, associate professor of English at Syracuse University.

Irish Studies, edited by Richard Fallis

The
Irish
Historical
Novel

JAMES M. CAHALAN

Syracuse University Press   1983

This book is published with the assistance of a grant from The Department of English and Comparative Literature at the University of Cincinnati.

A version of my article "The Making of *Strumpet City*: James Plunkett's Historical Vision," copyright 1978 © by The Irish American Cultural Institute, appears here by kind permission of the editors of *Éire-Ireland* and The Irish American Cultural Institute.

Lines from "Remorse for Intemperate Speech" are reprinted with permission of the Macmillan Publishing Company as well as Michael B. Yeats and Anne Yeats, from *The Collected Poems of W. B. Yeats.* Copyright 1933 by Macmillan Publishing Company, renewed 1961 by Bertha Georgie Yeats.

Quotations appear here with permission of Macmillan Publishing Company from *The Irish Songbook* compiled by the Clancy Brothers and Tommy Makem, with Foreword by Pete Hamill (Copyright © 1969 by Tiparm Music Publishers, Inc.)

Quotations from Seán Ó Faoláin's *The Irish: a Character Study* appear by permission of the Devin-Adair Publishers, copyright © 1949 by the Devin-Adair Company, renewed 1977.

From Francis MacManus' *Men Withering* by permission of The Mercier Press, copyright 1972.

From Francis MacManus' *The Years of the Great Test, 1926–39*, by permission of The Mercier Press, copyright 1967.

From Liam O'Flaherty's *Land*, by permission of Random House, Inc., copyright 1946.

From Walter Macken's *Seek the Fair Land*, by permission of Macmillan Publishing Company, copyright 1959.

From Donna Gerstenberger's *Iris Murdoch*, by permission of Associated University Presses, copyright 1975 by Bucknell University Press.

From James Plunkett's *Strumpet City*, copyright © 1969 by James Plunkett, with kind permission of James Plunkett.

From Georg Lukács' *The Historical Novel*, translated by Hannah and Stanley Mitchell, with permission of The Merlin Press Ltd., copyright 1962.

From Liam O'Flaherty's *Famine*, by permission of A. D. Peters and Co. on behalf of Liam O'Flaherty, copyright 1937 by Victor Gollancz Ltd.

From Daniel Corkery's *The Hidden Ireland*, by permission of Gill and Macmillan Ltd., copyright 1941 by M. H. Gill.

Library of Congress Cataloging in Publication Data

Cahalan, James M.
    Great hatred, little room.

    Bibliography: p.
    Includes index.
    1. Historical fiction, English—Irish authors—History and criticism. 2. English fiction—Irish authors—History and criticism. 3. Ireland in literature. I. Title.
PR8807.H5C3 1983   823'.081'099415   83-5095
ISBN 0-8156-2297-X

Manufactured in the United States of America

To my father and my mother,
Bill and Lee Cahalan

James M. Cahalan received the M.A. from University College, Dublin, where he studied as a Fulbright Fellow, and the Ph.D. from the University of Cincinnati. He is the author of articles in *Éire-Ireland, The Journal of Beckett Studies,* and *Hemingway Notes* and is Lecturer at the University of Massachusetts-Boston.

Contents

Acknowledgments

THIS BOOK would have been impossible without the generous help over the past few years of a number of advisors, colleagues, and friends. My interest in the subject began while studying in Dublin on a Fulbright Fellowship during 1975–76, writing a master's thesis under Professor Augustine Martin of University College, Dublin. It is fitting and pleasing here to thank three other early mentors who infected me with their knowledge and enthusiasm: David Doyle and Alan Harrison of UCD and Jim Matthews, formerly of Eckerd College; the first introduced me to Irish history, the second to the Irish language, and the third to Irish literature.

I am very grateful to Professors Hugh B. Staples, Leslie F. Chard, and Edgar M. Slotkin of the University of Cincinnati for the consistently clear, kind, yet critical advice they gave me during all of my work on the manuscript. Hugh Staples was an efficient, thoughtful, unusually prompt director; Les Chard helped me considerably with my style and my command of Scott; Edgar Slotkin contributed a unique understanding of Gaelic and folkloric materials. Professor Richard Fallis of Syracuse University added valuable editorial recommendations.

I must also record some other debts more major than footnotes suggest. Without the generous responses of the Irish novelists who replied to my letters of inquiry—Eilís Dillon, Eoghan Ó Tuairisc, and James Plunkett

x ACKNOWLEDGMENTS

— I would have been operating in the dark when considering their work. My correspondence with Jim Plunkett goes back several years. I was saddened to learn of the death last year of Eoghan Ó Tuairisc, whom I never met and whose long letter to me, a virtual autobiography, now seems all the more precious. I am also especially indebted to two colleagues whose particular areas of expertise prompted me to ask each to read and critique part of my work; each responded and saved me from small but significant error or misapprehension. Francis R. Hart, Scott scholar and Professor at the University of Massachusetts — Boston, read Chapter 1; James P. McHugh of Cincinnati, who has schooled me in Irish history over the course of a long friendship, examined Chapter 2. Finally, I would like to thank Lea Masiello, for incisive criticism and universal aid; Michael Birkel, for translations from the German; Heather Hall, for skillful typing of the manuscript; Hal White, for photographic and sartorial assistance; Bö Almqvist, Director of the Irish Folklore Commission, for help in its archives; Alf MacLochlainn, Director of the National Library of Ireland, and Denis Cotter, both of whom contributed sources from the National Library; its staff and those of the Boston Public Library, the Library of Congress, and the libraries at the University of Massachusetts — Boston, Boston College, Harvard University, and the University of Cincinnati.

Arlington, Massachusetts   James M. Cahalan
January 1983

Introduction

ISTORY IS A NIGHTMARE from which I am trying to awake." Thus
spake Stephen Dedalus in the "Nestor" chapter of James Joyce's
Ulysses. It matters that he utters the maxim to Mr. Deasy, Anglo-
Irish headmaster and spokesman of British rule: Stephen the
"Fenian" awakes neither from the bad dream of Deasy's anti-Semitism nor
from the nightmare of Irish history under British domination.[1] In "Remorse for Intemperate Speech," W. B. Yeats declared:

> Out of Ireland have we come.
> Great hatred, little room,
> Maimed us at the start.
> I carry from my mother's womb
> A fanatic heart.[2]

That is always the problem in Irish history: too great hatred, too little
room, and no exit. Try as they may, the Irish cannot escape their tortured
history. Try as he may, the Irish writer cannot escape that nightmare, that
net, that fanaticism in the deep heart's core. The Irish writer has returned
over and over again to Irish history, seeing art as a battlefield on which
to play out the conflicts contained within that history.

This theme, this obsession with nationalist history, is familiar to students of Irish literature. Yeats, Joyce, and their contemporaries have asserted their historical visions, and their myriad commentators have amply reminded us of the obsession. But left unexplored has been perhaps the most persistent genre of nationalist literary endeavor short of the popular ballad: the Irish historical novel, the novel in which the Irish writer returns to a major national crisis prior to his own experience in order to recreate the past and make sense of his own heritage. Despite the immense popularity, the sheer bulk, of historical novels in Ireland since the 1820s, no extended study of the genre there has ever before appeared. Historical novels of other countries have been thoroughly explored. There were Avrom Fleishman's excellent study of *The English Historical Novel*, several books on American historical fiction, as well as books on the genre in Italy, Spain, Russia, the Ukraine, Mexico, and Chile — but none on the Irish historical novel. Several writers have explored the influence of Walter Scott on the genre — W.C. Zellars, for example, on its development in Spain and Fleishman on the English novelists.[3] But the genre's long history in Ireland and Scott's influence there have been almost totally ignored, even though the Irish historical novel has been extremely popular and persistent and Scott's influence upon it unmistakeable. Nineteenth-century Irish historical novelists deliberately imitated his work. Those in the twentieth century, while departing from conscious imitation of Scott in favor of other inspirations, still followed many of the conventions of the kind of novel he introduced.

Thomas Flanagan included a chapter on John Banim's historical novels in his study *The Irish Novelists, 1800–1850* (1958), and Donald Davie in *The Heyday of Sir Walter Scott* (1961) had some occasionally condescending things to say about a few of Scott's nineteenth-century imitators in Ireland.[4] Flanagan and Davie did not discuss the twentieth-century Irish historical novel, but since then the American Flanagan has written his own successful Irish historical novel, *The Year of the French* (1979).

The historical novel has been a popular genre since Scott forged its essential form. Its persistent prevalence in modern Irish fiction is undeniable. In *Ireland in Fiction* (1919), Father Steven J. Brown annotated 1,713 works of Irish fiction before 1920, describing 212 of them, or more than 12 percent, as historical novels.[5] Studying Brown's book and following a narrower definition of the genre, it is evident that there were at least 116 Irish historical novels published before 1920. The number published since then cannot be determined exactly, but neither the popularity nor certainly the quality of the genre has diminished: sixteen of the twenty-five novels examined in the following chapters were published within the

past fifty years. The best among them — Seán Ó Faoláin's *A Nest of Simple Folk* (1933), Liam O'Flaherty's *Famine* (1937), Francis MacManus' *Men Withering* (1939), Eoghan Ó Tuairisc's *L'Attaque* (1962), James Plunkett's *Strumpet City* (1969) — were written well after modern Irish literature matured and flowered during the Literary Revival. Ironically, but naturally enough, their superiority is due largely to the decline of Scott's popularity, which allowed these authors to write free of the shadow that dominated his nineteenth-century imitators.

It is necessary to define the Irish historical novel, because if every Irish novel with history in it were to be included, just about every Irish novel ever written would have to be examined. Therefore, let us consider the "Irish historical novel" as one dealing with political events in modern Irish history prior to the author's own experience — usually a major upheaval or revolution such as the Jacobite-Williamite war, the Penal Age, the 1798 rising, the Famine, the Land War, the 1913 Dublin lockout, the Easter Rising of 1916 and the subsequent Anglo-Irish and Civil wars. I distinguish these novels from ancient and medieval romance (Gerald Griffin's *The Invasion*, for example, or Mervyn Wall's *The Unfortunate Fursey*), much as Scott critics distinguish *Ivanhoe* from his Jacobite novels; from novels about contemporaneous politics (Liam O'Flaherty's *The Informer*, Jimmy Breslin's *World Without End Amen*); and from novels set in a past generation but lacking a public, political focus (Sheridan Le Fanu's *The House by the Church-Yard*, Somerville and Ross's *The Big House of Inver*) or dealing with minor, internal controversies rather than famous, nationalist events (Francis MacManus' *The Greatest of These*, Thomas Kilroy's *The Big Chapel*). The novelists I examine explore neither the coming of the Danes nor the Northern Ireland crisis; they deal with "the making of modern Ireland, 1603–1923," as dated by the distinguished Irish historian J. C. Beckett. Avrom Fleishman suggests that a historical novel ought to contain at least one real historical personage, an actual "big name" from history, and this seems a reasonable additional criterion.[6]

Only those novels whose quality, significance, or typicality in the development of the genre recommended them are examined here. They are representative of a long tradition of Irish historical novels that imitated, adapted, and then reshaped the model established by Scott in his Waverley novels. Irish historical novelists in the nineteenth century closely imitate Scott; in the twentieth century they depart from his influence and achieve more original visions of Irish history. Therefore, my first chapters consider Scott's influence, while the later chapters turn away from Scott to probe the more diverse sources of twentieth-century Irish historical novelists. That Irish novelists respond to the nationalist mythos of modern

Irish history, discussed in the second chapter, does not suggest that their responses have been uniform. Sheridan Le Fanu, for example, was a reactionary Unionist; Liam O'Flaherty, a socialist and Republican. To make sense of an Irish historical novel, then, the experience of its author is examined in order to understand the response of each to Irish history and to the form of the genre, not to impose Walter Scott or Irish nationalism upon them.

There are basic patterns found in these novels: the broad sweep of events and the use of parts to represent the whole; the panorama of characters from contrasting classes, religions, and occupations; the removal of the "big names" of history to the background of a fictional if historical world; the Scott hero and the hero of the Irish historical novel, modelled on history if not literally historical, and how that hero changes from a "passive hero" to a partisan hero, and his story, from a romance to a realistic novel. These are Scottian conventions imitated in nineteenth-century Irish historical novels and transformed in those of the twentieth century. I examine the genre chronologically, with the conviction that each novel must be explained in terms of its own author and its own time and with the desire to show how literary sensibilities and political points of view changed and developed.

My hope is that an understanding of the Irish historical novel will shed significant light on the development of modern Irish fiction at large, helping to clarify how individual novelists wove their works out of the fabric of their own times and how the Irish novel matured over time.

1
The Model: *Scott's Historical Novel*

N UNDERSTANDING of the Irish historical novel must begin with Walter Scott because Irish historical novelists began with him. They sought to become an Irish Scott — to write like him and to wear a cloak of success like his. John Banim, as a youth, wrote to Scott in adulation and, as an adult, consciously imitated his work. Joseph Sheridan Le Fanu, bowing to Banim, wrote an ethereal historical romance in the mold he thought was Scott's. William Carleton, proud of his facial resemblance to Scott, wrote the Irish romance Scott himself had apparently always wanted to write. Standish O'Grady, "father of the Irish Renaissance" and even more of a Tory in Ireland than Scott was in Scotland, attempted to become, like Scott, the national bard of history. Twentieth-century Irish historical novelists did not emulate Scott so consciously or imitate him so directly, but the model for the historical novel established by Scott and followed by his imitators must serve as the starting point for understanding the later novels, too — novels that departed more from the model, achieving in the process a greater literary independence, maturity, and success.

The critical consensus is that Scott was the father of the historical novel, influencing writers in England, Scotland, France, Spain, Russia, Mexico, and several more distant countries.[1] Yet his influence in Ireland was more immediate and direct, and the Irish national experience and its legacy

1

—its history, folklore, and mythos—are similar to what Scott grew up with in Scotland, although the Irish novelists' responses increasingly departed from Scott's.

Before considering Scott's influence in Ireland, however, it is worth reminding ourselves of Ireland's influence upon Scott, for the relationship was a symbiotic one. Scott began his historical fiction partly under the inspiration of an Irish writer, Maria Edgeworth. In his "General Preface to the Waverley Novels," Scott recalled that he had completed *Waverley* impelled by "the extended and well-merited fame of Miss Edgeworth, whose Irish characters have gone so far to make the English familiar with the character of their gay and kind-hearted neighbours of Ireland, that she may be truly said to have done more towards completing the Union than perhaps all the legislative enactments by which it has been followed up."[2] Having read Thady Quirk's story, *Castle Rackrent* (1800), Scott "felt that something might be attempted for my own country, of the same kind with that which Miss Edgeworth so fortunately achieved for Ireland—something which might introduce her natives to those of the sister kingdom in a more favourable light than they had been placed hitherto, and tend to procure sympathy for their virtues and indulgence for their foibles" (xxii).

Castle Rackrent shares several features with Scott's novels, especially his first one, *Waverley* (1814). Both novels frustrate conventional, Gothic expectations. A reader, especially a reader in 1800, would expect from Edgeworth's title a thoroughly Gothic story; instead "the editor" presents Thady's pointedly realistic, amusing, and deflating tale of the decadence, downfall, and final defeat of his landlord at the hands of Thady's scheming son, Jason. Thady has a vision of an Irish landlord class as chivalric, but his vision turns out to be anachronistic; we see the cruel realities through the mist of Thady's pathetic pieties. Scott's Edward Waverley is as deluded, at first, as Thady Quirk. Lost in the old chivalric romances which he has been reading, Waverley embraces the Jacobite cause, only to learn the hard way that it too is an anachronism; he enters reality, Scott tells us, only when he rejects Jacobitism in favor of a peaceful, prosperous life of marriage and the farm. "He felt himself entitled to say firmly, though perhaps with a sigh, that the romance of his life was ended, and that its real history had now commenced" (2: 410). This, for Scott, is progress. *Waverley* is partly a departure from romance in favor of progress, a novel that frustrates traditional romantic expectations,[3] substituting a new kind of romance in which moderation is rewarded with progress and property. Edgeworth also shares with Scott her use of dialect, her attention to "local color," and her method of framing her text with an editor, footnotes, and glossary. In *Castle Rackrent*, Thady's narrative perspective is reinforced

by his dialect: this is a tale of lords told by the lower class. As in Scott, it is the common people who endure as their kings and lords come and go. Scott extends Edgeworth's use of dialect in order to set one class and one nation off from the other, and he was inspired by Edgeworth's Irish example to make full use of the long literary tradition of Scots English already available to him. Linked to the particular dialect is a faithfulness to a specific setting and to particular local traditions, noted and footnoted by a scholarly, antiquarian author/editor. In these ways, Scott pursues the literary regionalism that Edgeworth introduced. But *Castle Rackrent*, dealing with the private world of Edgeworth's youth, was not a historical novel, and seems a brilliant anomaly in early Irish fiction. Other Irish novelists in the nineteenth century turned much more to Scott than to Edgeworth.

Scott was interested not only in Maria Edgeworth specifically, but in Ireland generally. As early as 1810, four years before the publication of *Waverley*, Scott noted with pride the good reception his poetry had been given in Ireland: "I am much honoured by the good opinion of the Irish nation, whose praise must be always most valuable to a poet, because they are not only a people of infinite genius, but of a warmth of heart and feeling not perhaps generally appreciated."[4] In 1825, Scott fulfilled a long-standing desire to travel to Ireland, where he visited Edgeworth, with whom he had been carrying on a cordial correspondence for several years, and who had previously visited him at Abbotsford, his home south of Edinburgh, in Melrose. The details of Scott's trip were later compiled by D. J. O'Donoghue, drawing upon Scott's biographer, John Gibson Lockhart. He published them in 1905 as *Sir Walter Scott's Tour in Ireland in 1825, Now First Fully Described*, a slim volume complete with a frontispiece portrait of Scott kissing the Blarney Stone.

O'Donoghue notes at the outset that "naturally, some of the great novelist's views will hardly appeal to the majority of Irishmen, but they are worthy of consideration as coming from one who was a good friend of Ireland and the Irish people" (6). Presumably, O'Donoghue refers to "the great novelist's views," expressed in his letters about his trip to Ireland, about "the bigotry of the Catholic religion" and "Popery" as well as his descriptions of the stereotypical Irishman, "Paddy" or "Pat." "Pat's mind is always turned to fun and ridicule. They are terribly excitable, to be sure, and will murther you on slight suspicion, and find out next day that it was all a mistake, and that it was not yourself they meant to kill at all, at all" (93). Elsewhere Scott betrays his social bias in favor of his Scots-Irish neighbors in the north of Ireland: "It is rare to see the Catholic rise above the position he is born in. The Protestant part of the

country is as highly improved as many parts of England" (74). Lockhart recorded that Scott visited the scene of the Battle of the Boyne, the great Protestant victory over King James in 1690, touring the battlefield with a British dragoon and, O'Donoghue relays, "rejoicing the veteran's heart by his vigorous recitation of the famous [Protestant] ballad ('The Crossing of the Water') as we proceeded to the ground" (28). Such enthusiasms would have been antipathetic to Scott's earliest and closest Irish imitator, John Banim.

Scott does surmount stereotype and bias when pondering the broader outlines of the Irish past, present, and future, in a letter to Thomas Moore recorded by O'Donoghue:

> In Ireland I have met with everything that was kind, and have seen much which is never to be forgotten. What I have seen has, in general, given me great pleasure; for it appears to me that the adverse circumstances which have so long withered the prosperity of this rich and powerful country are losing their force, and that a gradual but steady spirit of progressive improvement is effectually, though tacitly, counteracting their bad effects. The next twenty-five years will probably be the most impor- tant in their results that Ireland ever knew. So prophecies a sharp-sighted *seannachie* from the land of mist and snow. (71).

Scott did not allow his bias against Catholicism to blind him to the justice of Catholic Emancipation, the campaign to free Catholics from the shackles of the Penal Age and to obtain political rights for them. Lockhart wrote, according to O'Donoghue, "though no man disapproved of Romanism as a system of faith and practice more sincerely than Sir Walter always did, he had long before this period formed the opinion that no good could come of further resistance to the claim in question" (70). Scott noted that "the Catholic is holding up his head now in a different way from what they did in former days, though still with a touch of the savage about them" (74). And he admitted that "the Protestants of the old school, the determined Orangemen," while "a very fine race," were "dangerous for the quiet of a country; they reminded me of the Spaniard in Mexico, and seemed still to walk among the Catholics with all the pride of the conquerors of the Boyne and the captors of Limerick. Their own belief is completely fixed that there are enough of men in Down and Antrim to conquer all Ireland again" (74). Here Banim would have been more comfortable with his literary hero.

As we have seen, Scott was influenced by Edgeworth in formulat- ing his ideas about how to write a novel and, more specifically, about

how to portray particular social classes in a particular setting at a particular time. Davie points out, moreover, that in *Castle Rackrent* Edgeworth preceded Scott in "building her fiction about a morally weak individual so that in his unsteady destiny should be mirrored the turning-point of two epochs of history." It was Scott, however, not Edgeworth, who established the novel which we now call the historical novel, and it is Scott's influence, not Edgeworth's, that is evident in the nineteenth-century Irish historical novel. Davie writes that "Scott of course is fully aware of [the] historical perspective and establishes it with masterly precision without once stating it explicitly. It is implicit in *Castle Rackrent*, but in an altogether more shadowy way." He argues that Edgeworth did not write historical novels because she lacked an organic sense of history. In *The English Historical Novel*, Avrom Fleishman argues that the historical novel sprang from an organic sense of history linked to nationalism.[5] "This is how our nation came to be as we know it," the historical novelist seeks to explain.

Edgeworth's later work did not live up to the promise of *Castle Rackrent*; Scott's reputation and achievement, by the time Banim began to write in the 1820s, far surpassed hers. For Banim and his successors, "His was a broader cloak for them to shelter under," as Davie notes, "than the authority of their own compatriot, Miss Edgeworth."[6] It is the shape of the historical novel as created by Scott and elucidated by modern criticism that we must understand in order to understand the Irish historical novel.

Scott was a progressive who believed in the vast superiority of the present in which he lived over the past about which he wrote, but this is a truth about him which was misunderstood, or lost, for decades, perhaps a century, after his time. The nineteenth century, by and large, saw Scott as a romancer, a nostalgic antiquarian, a glorifier of times past over time present. The most notorious statement of this position was Mark Twain's: that Scott's novels caused the American Civil War because they established a cult of adherence to old clan loyalties over present realities.[7] That Scott did not in fact favor the past, that he had the historian's desire to understand the past in order to see how the present came to be, was an insight achieved only in the twentieth century. Nineteenth-century Irish historical novelists tended to share the misunderstanding: they responded to Scott with inflated, romanticized, chivalric heroes who could do no wrong.

The nineteenth-century view of Scott as romancer and antiquarian, pure and simple, is somewhat understandable in view of the fact that he assumed, at particular points in time, both of these poses. He was obsessed with romances and with folklore from his earliest youth. Speaking of a childhood friend, Scott notes in his "General Preface to the Waverley Novels" that "we told, each in turn, interminable tales of knight-errantry and battles and enchantments" (1:xvi). Later, he sought out the Edinburgh circulating library and, engrossed, like Edward Waverley, he "read almost all the romances, old plays, and epic poetry in that formidable collection, and no doubt was unconsciously amassing materials for the task in which it has been my lot to be so much employed" (1:xviii). When subsequently turning to history, Scott read it at first with the eye of a romancer: "I began by degrees to seek in histories, memoirs, voyages and travels, and the like, events nearly as wonderful as those which were the work of imagination, with the additional advantage that they were at least in great measure true" (xviii).

Sent, like Waverley, to visit the Scottish border country, in order to gain the fresh air of his grandfather's farm as an advantage for his delicate health, the young Scott was fascinated by the border folklore he discovered there. In anecdotes, in tales told round the fire, in ballads sung by farmers and farm servants, he heard narratives of clan warfare, heroic deeds by historical characters, battles, slayings, and escapes. When as a young man Scott entered the literary scene, it was as a folklorist. His first significant publication was *Minstrelsy of the Scottish Border* (1802–1803), his famous collection of ballads, which still has a respected place in Scottish ballad history and the study of ballad manuscripts.[8] To compile that work Scott traveled the border countryside, collecting ballads and gaining a keen appreciation for the specific local significance of each ballad. He achieved a sense of topography and of the connection of place and time that he would carry into his novels. His historical imagination was a product not merely of the history books but of the historical lore he absorbed. He would recall that "my memory . . . seldom failed to preserve most tenaciously a favourite passage of poetry, a playhouse ditty, or, above all, a Border-raid ballad; but names, dates, and other technicalities of history, escaped me in a most melancholy degree."[9] Irish writers such as Banim and O'Grady were similarly influenced by Irish romances, ballads, and folklore.

Scott came to the study of history with the sense gained from the traditions absorbed in his childhood, believing that the past was very much preserved in the present, and that the present was a constant process of reacting to the past. The Scottish philosophers and historians under

whom he studied at Edinburgh reinforced this sense on a more formal, academic, philosophical plane.[10] From them he learned that the present was a development of the past, a synthesis of conflicting forces in the past, and an improvement of the past. Therefore, the past was to be understood in light of the present, and the present in light of the past; they were seen to be in a vital relation to each other.

Because of this perception, Scott was to reject the view contained in the old romances and in Gothic fiction that the past was of interest primarily because it was different from the present, that it was strange, that it was fanciful. In his "General Preface" Scott recalled that he wrote *Waverley* with two impulses: first, the inspiration of Edgeworth; second, his reaction to Joseph Strutt's medieval, antiquarian romance, *Queenhoo Hall*, whose posthumous publication he had aided. He thought he could do better and "was led to form the opinion that a romance founded on a Highland story and more modern events would have a better chance of popularity than a tale of chivalry" (1:xxiv). While remaining always under the influence of many of the conventions of Gothicism, Scott rejected its fundamental view of the past as something strange, lurid, and, above all, different.[11] He was interested in "those passions common to men in all stages of society" (1:4–5).

At the same time, however, he saw the connections between Gothicism and historicism; history, after all, had entered fiction partly through the Gothic novel, specifically Horace Walpole's *The Castle of Otranto* (1765).[12] Scott understood that fairies, ghosts, omens, magic, superstitions, and the like were part of Scottish history. In one of his anonymous self-reviews he wrote:

> The traditions and manners of the Scotch were so blended with superstitious practices and fears, that the author of these novels seems to have deemed it incumbent on him, to transfer many more such incidents to his novels, than seem either probable or natural to an English reader. It may be some apology that his story would have lost the national cast, which it was chiefly his object to preserve, had this been otherwise. There are few families of antiquity in Scotland, which do not possess some strange legends, told only under promise of secrecy, and with an air of mystery; in developing which, the influence of the powers of darkness is referred to.[13]

For Scott, Gothicism was part of being historical, rather than an avocation to be pursued for its own sake. Gothicism was part of Scottish history and was to be understood in terms of that history. In short, Scott's Gothicism was an organic Gothicism.

Wʜɪʟᴇ ᴇɴᴏʀᴍᴏᴜsʟʏ ᴘᴏᴘᴜʟᴀʀ among the reading public, Scott was largely misunderstood or ignored by critics in the nineteenth century, who seemed hard put to make sense of his attitude to history. There were, however, two notable exceptions to this critical failure: William Hazlitt and Samuel Taylor Coleridge. As often seems to be the case with these two, what they had to say was very astute, but our record of their opinions is much too brief. The radical Hazlitt abhorred Scott's politics but, in his reviews, praised Scott's industrious, sincere attempts to make sense of history.[14]

Coleridge went further: he seemed to understand Scott's fundamental approach to the historical process. The only evidence we have of this insight is one brief passage from a letter of 1820:

> Scott's great merit, and, at the same time, his *felicity,* and the true solution of the long-sustained *interest* novel after novel excited lie in the nature of the subject . . . that the contest between the loyalists and their opponents can never be *obsolete,* for it is the contest between the two great moving principles of social humanity; religious adherence to the past and the ancient, the desire and the admiration of permanence, on the one hand; and the passion for increase of knowledge, for truth, as the offspring of reason — in short, the mighty instincts of *progression* and *free agency,* on the other. In all subjects of deep and lasting interest, you will detect a struggle between two opposites, two polar forces, both of which are alike necessary to our human well-being, and necessary each to the continued existence of the other.[15]

Anticipating Georg Lukács, Coleridge shows here that he understands Scott's portrayal of history as a dialectical process, one of conflicts whose synthesis produces the present. In this insight, he appears to be almost alone among nineteenth-century critics; the rest tend to view Scott as a romantic escapist.

In the twentieth century an understanding was reached that Scott was not a romantic escapist but a historical realist, thanks largely to the work of two critics, Lukács and David Daiches. Lukács' chapter on Scott in his book *The Historical Novel* (1937), translated from German into English in 1962, and Daiches' essay "Scott's Achievement as a Novelist" both asserted Scott's status as a realistic, historical novelist. In a recent book on Scott, David Brown reaffirms the importance of Daiches and, especially, of Lukács: "These two essays (whose similarity of direction is remarkable, considering that they were composed quite independently) constituted a revolution against the accepted idea of a 'romantic' Scott. . . . Both men are united in their attempt to approach the Waverly Nov-

els in a new way, concentrating on Scott's achievement as an *historical novelist.*"[16]

Lukács and Daiches do this not just for Scott but for historical fiction at large, legitimizing the idea that it can be viewed critically and analytically, as well as enjoyed. Lukács' critique is relevant to Scott's Irish imitators and also (perhaps even more so) to later writers, not much influenced by Scott, whose politics are much closer to Lukács' Marxism. In understanding Liam O'Flaherty and James Plunkett, it is illuminating to return to Lukács.

Lukács' chapter on Scott, especially in view of its date of initial publication, is the single most germinal critical statement to have been made about Scott as historical novelist. The revolutionary nature of his critique is highlighted by a reading of Scott criticism before and since Lukács: before his essay critics misread Scott's method as historical novelist, while several critical statements about the matter since Lukács are largely elaborations of his views.[17]

Earlier scholars were ignorant of the progressive, pragmatic nature of Scott's attitude to the past. He had in fact written to his son, "Our ancestors lodged in caves and wigwams where we construct palaces for the rich and comfortable dwellings for the poor. And why is this but because our eye is enabled to look back upon the past to improve on our ancestors [*sic*] improvements and to avoid their passing events." Nor did they know that Abbotsford, while full of the historical relics which Scott collected, was also the first gas-lit home in Scotland, and that Scott, chairman of the first Gas Oil Company in Edinburgh, embraced a progressive vision of the Industrial Revolution and what it could do for Scotland[18] – a vision Irish writers could not share. Scott was fascinated with the interrelatedness of past and present. His Edinburgh was (and is) both an ancient and modern city, invaded within and without by the rural past: an ancient castle sits on a cliff in its midst, overlooking modern buildings; the green world of forests and mountains beyond its limits is always visible, even from its heart.

Lukács brought a coherent, critical way of understanding Scott's method as historical novelist. He applied to Scott the central argument of the great philosopher of history, Hegel, about history as progress. Hegel advanced the doctrine of progress through reason, asserting that things have come about rationally in history through thesis, antithesis, and synthesis – a dialectal process reconciling opposites. Hegel (1770–1831) and Scott (1771–1832) were close contemporaries, and, although he could not have read Hegel's *Lectures on the Philosophy of History* (published in 1837 although written several years earlier), it is fascinating to see how Scott

practices in his fiction what Hegel preached in his philosophy. Scott's hero corresponds, philosophically, abstractly, to Hegel's synthesis: he represents progress. Like Shakespeare's King Hal, he synthesizes thesis and antithesis, the winning side and the losing side, upper class and lower class, the past and the present.

Lukács came to Scott with Hegel's dialectic and the specific historical insight that the birth of the historical novel was linked to the growth of nationalism in the wake of the French Revolution: "The historical novel in its origin [and] development follows inevitably upon the great social transformations of modern times."[19] So was the Irish historical novel intimately linked to the growth of Irish nationalism.

As Lukács noted, earlier Gothic novels were essentially interested in history as a bizarre entertainment and featured only the trappings, the mere costumery, of history. In contrast, Scott was interested in "the specifically historical. . .derivation of the individuality of characters from the historical peculiarity of their age'"(19). Scott was deliberately and specifically historical from the outset of his fiction: he chose 'Tis Sixty Years Since as the subtitle for Waverley. In his introductory first chapter he discusses the historicity of this subtitle and argues that incorrect expectations would have arisen from "a tale of other Days" or "a romance from the German." "Would not the owl have shrieked and the cricket cried in my very title-page? . . . By fixing, then, the date of my story Sixty Years before this present 1st November, 1805, I would have my readers understand, that they will meet in the following pages neither a romance of chivalry nor a tale of modern manners," but a story to be concerned with "those passions common to men in all stages of society" (1: 4–5).

Scott was a moderate interested in careful progress, attempting "by fathoming historically the whole of English development to find a 'middle way' for himself between the warring extremes. He finds in English history the consolation that the most violent vicissitudes of class struggle have always finally calmed down into a glorious 'middle way'" (32). Lukács points out that in seeking the "middle way" between extremes, Scott goes to the big crises in history: championing peace and progress, he studies revolution and war. "Paradoxically, Scott's greatness is closely linked with his often narrow conservatism" (33). The Waverley novels portray history as a series of great crises, each resulting in progress—in contrast to the great crises in Irish history, in which the Irish novelist was often hard put to find any progress.

Scott's characteristic hero is a "passive" one—like us, a spectator to history, a visitor, an average person—serving as a lens for the reader.[20] He is a moderate in the midst, as Francis R. Hart later put it, of "opposing

fanaticisms,"[21] while the Irish hero more often moves beyond an initial moderation and passivity into partisanship. The hero's naiveté is valuable: it allows the novelist to educate his reader as well as his hero, so that when history really begins to happen, we're ready for it. When Waverley meets the Scottish clans, they are, at first, as unintelligible to him as they are to us. But he gradually learns their ways, and by the time Waverley goes to war with the clansmen, we, like Waverley, are prepared to understand them and, thus, the events of history. Scott's typical plot is a journey, one in which the hero travels from England to Scotland, from Lowlands to Highlands, from civilization to anarchy, from moderation to extremism — and back again. The journey and education of the hero are also the reader's. The Irish historical hero performs a similarly representative, didactic function, but he is used more often than not to sanction Irish nationalist partisanship, rather than moderation. Irish historical novelists began by imposing Scott's moderate hero on Irish history, but later novelists presented a more partisan, distinctively Irish hero.

Scott seeks to portray average people of the age. Rather than trace the development, the biography, of the great figures in history, Scott shows us the world in which they lived. The appearance of the "big names" of history in Scott's plot tends to be limited and late; these characters are not dominant. The "big name" comes to stand for, to embody, a whole movement. The rarity of his appearances serves to increase their significance: Rob Roy, for example, surprises us by his presence, revealing himself only in the most interesting poses. Even when a "big name," such as Claverhouse in *Old Mortality*, assumes an early and major role in the story, Scott uses him to represent a historical movement. Lukács wrote: "What matters . . . in the historical novel is not the re-telling of great historical events, but the poetic awakening of the people who figured in those events" (42). Scott represents history by synecdoche: the whole by the part. As he cannot show an entire age or a whole war, he uses particular events, a specific battle. He cannot show all the people, so he portrays particular, representative characters; he gives us average, believable people and specific, small conversations and actions. Irish historical novelists adopted the same strategy.

Scott's concern with "smaller relationships" takes him to the lower class: he is determined to portray not only both Highlander and Lowlander, but also both lordly and lowly, upper class, lower class, and middle class. He seeks to present a broad panorama of society. Like Shakespeare, he contrasts opposing kings and nobles with each other and, through subplots, with their servants. In *Old Morality*, for example, one of several purposes fulfilled by Cuddie Headrigg is that of a lower-class parallel to

the hero, Robert Morton. Cuddie talks differently, and being of the lower class, he gains the license to act differently: "the license both to kiss and to kill," as Alexander Welsh put it.[22] Scott's command of Scots dialect allows him to bring characters like Cuddie and Nicol Jarvie in *Rob Roy* wonderfully to life, and set them off markedly on the printed page from their standard-English-speaking equivalents, Robert Morton and Frank Osbaldistone.[23] At the same time, their speech and behavior reinforce the direction and development of their equivalents: they can speak more frankly and act more decisively than their more tentative friends and, thus, clarify things for them and for the reader. As Lukács noted, "Scott aims at portraying the totality of national life in its complex interaction between 'above' and 'below'; his vigorous popular character is expressed in the fact that 'below' is seen as the material basis and artistic explanation for what happens 'above'" (49).

Most crucially, Scott saw history from the perspective of the present and sought to understand it in terms of the present, not escape to it as a refuge from the present. He brought the "past to life as the prehistory of the present," Lukacs argued, "giving poetic life to those historical, social and human forces which, in the course of a long evolution, have made our present-day life what it is and as we experience it" (53). And so it is in the development of the Irish historical novel: the perspective of each novel on history is to be understood largely in terms of the period of time in which it was written.

Sᴄᴏᴛᴛ ʀᴇsᴘᴏɴᴅᴇᴅ to the Scottish background — to Scottish history and the romance of the Highlands — just as Irish novelists would have to make sense of Irish history and its mythos. Among more recent scholars, David Daiches, in particular, has added a valuable understanding of the importance of the Scottish experience to Scott's achievement and, specifically, to his attitude to history. Like Lukács, Daiches argued that Scott was no escapist, calling his best novels "antiromantic,"[24] and asserted that the Scottish novels are Scott's best and that Scott is better when dealing with the more recent past — the world of *Waverley, Old Mortality,* and *Rob Roy,* than with the remote past, the world of *Ivanhoe.* This is a view in which most critics have concurred ever since the 1820s. James T. Hillhouse, the chief student of Scott criticism, writes: "There has always been a sharp line drawn between the 'Scotch novels' and the 'romances' with practically universal agreement that the first group are far the more distinguished."[25]

Scott was better on his native ground, dealing with events about which he heard not only in the history books but also from the mouths of his countrymen, events that were still alive in Scottish tradition. Similarly, the Irish historical novel improved when it moved beyond romance to a realism informed by the actual events of Irish history.

Scott rejects the old romance of clan loyalty and warfare, but he celebrates, in fact, a new form of romance: the romance of property, "the myth," as Alexander Welsh puts it, "that property (real happiness) automatically devolves upon those who respect the existing arrangement of things."[26] Scott may have rejected the hero and the style of the old romances, but he follows them in his characteristic ending: the moderate hero is rewarded by marriage and property. Scott's knight may not slay the dragon, but he gets the girl, a heroine whose purity corresponds to his moderation, and a castle to take her to. So do nineteenth-century Irish historical heroes, while those of the twentieth century more often than not end without house or land (or life, sometimes).

In *The Anatomy of Criticism*, Northrop Frye writes, "The complete form of the romance is clearly the successful quest, and such a completed form has three main stages: the stage of the perilous journey and the preliminary minor adventures; the crucial struggle, usually some kind of battle in which either the hero or his foe, or both, must die; and the exaltation of the hero." Scott's hero is not exactly "exalted," but his quest is successful. Frye writes, "The hero of romance moves in a world in which the ordinary laws of nature are slightly suspended: prodigies of courage and endurance, unnatural to us, are natural to him."[27] Scott sought instead to adhere to, rather than suspend, "the ordinary laws of nature." He blurs the distinction between novel and romance. The distinction is similarly uncertain in the nineteenth-century Irish novel.

In his "Essay on Romance," Scott set forth his own definitions. The romance he defined as "a fictitious narrative in prose or verse; the interest of which turns upon marvelous and uncommon incidents"; the novel, as "a fictitious narrative, differing from the Romance, because the events are accommodated to the ordinary train of human events, and the modern state of society." Scott clearly sought to explore the "state of society" rather than to retreat to a mythical, idealized, "uncommon" world. Yet he generally referred to his own works as romances, even though their collective title was "the Waverley Novels." Welsh points out that "neither word was used with any consistency in Scott's time."[28]

What Scott wanted to do, it seems, was to accommodate romance to the novel. In the *Quarterly Review* in 1815, Scott referred to the novel as "the legitimate child of romance." He postulates the gradual develop-

ment of the novel out of romance: *The Progress of Romance,* as the title of Clara Reeve's 1785 book has it. The Maria Edgeworth he admired was congratulated by the *Quarterly Review* in 1812 for successfully "mediating between the extremes of novel and romance."[29] Scott sought in his own work to develop a historical realism out of the conventions of romance: he uses adventure, heroism, love, and war, as the old romances did, but he seeks to make them realistic, to abandon an ideal world for the real, historical world. This is a crucial transition, one most nineteenth-century Irish historical novels failed to make, even though they followed Scott's model.

As in romance, where the hero might slay the dragon in order to get the girl, Scott's novels link love to heroism. He personalizes history by showing how war separates the lover from the loved one, just as it can estrange brother from brother, so that history is something that happens within people's private lives, not merely on the battlefield or in the court. Historical polarities become personal problems; the dialectic of history is shown through the division of people, a strategy also adopted in the Irish historical novel. Only at the end of Scott's story, when peace is achieved, can lover be reunited with loved one. As in Shakespeare's history plays, the final marriage signals both private happiness and public peace.

O UT OF A READING of Scott's novels and Scott criticism, then, one emerges with a composite portrait of his historical novel. Drawing upon the facts of history as well as its folklore, the Scott novel seeks out the great historical crisis in order to understand how history works and what a particular historical era, or event, was like — above all, what it was like for the people who lived through it. The major characters are representative and fictional, with the great names of history withdrawn to the background. Scott sends out as hero a typical gentleman; a traveler to the historical world, he observes for us the opposing factions of history and tries to understand them. He meets a broad panorama of society — Highlander and Lowlander, Jacobite and Hanoverian, upper class and lower class — one or two important characters representing, in each case, the whole type. The different settings he travels to, as well as the different kinds of speech he hears, reinforce these societal contrasts. Two things happen to him: he gets involved in politics and he falls in love, but the love is frustrated by the politics. Finally, Scott's hero learns that the only way to survive history

is by steering a moderate course between opposed extremes. Through moderation, he survives war, wins a wife, and achieves prosperity.

Such moderation became impossible, however, for Irish historical novelists faced with a present that was nearly as nightmarish as the past. Irish history seemed to afford them no happy ending, as did Scottish history, with its glorious Union, for Scott. Scott saw the Scottish Union with England as bringing Scotland into the modern world, and he embraced it with nostalgia but determination. In contrast, Irish writers generally opposed the Irish Act of Union of 1800; even Standish O'Grady, who called himself a Tory and fancied himself Ireland's Scott, denounced the Union in the strongest terms. Yet nineteenth-century writers such as O'Grady persisted in ending their historical novels happily, imposing Scott's romance of property on Irish history. They seemed unable to face Irish history for what it was: an unresolved mess. Only in the twentieth century did Irish historical novelists depart from Scott and achieve a new vision of Irish history.

2

The Background: *The Mythos of Modern Irish History*

IKE WALTER SCOTT, the Irish historical novelist grew up with a national history, and a folklore surrounding that history, dominated by a political polarity: in this case, the Irish versus the English, in place of Highlander versus Lowlander, Scottish versus English, Tory versus Whig, and Covenanter versus Catholic. Unlike Scott, however, the Irish historical novelist could not see that history, that polarity, as resolved. This is where the Irish novelist departed from Scott; for that matter, so did many later Scottish novelists.[1] Scott embraced the Scottish Union with England, as he did the Industrial Revolution, believing that peace and progress had come to Scotland, that its place in the modern world was clear and its history resolved. Such a view was impossible for the Irish writer, especially the nineteenth-century historical novelist, who saw his country ravaged by famine and oppressed by English political domination. Therefore, in their novels the Irish writers explored the political and social polarities in Irish history in order to understand the polarities still at work in their own day, rather than to present, as Scott did, a peaceful synthesis, a glorious middle way that had resolved itself.

The typical hero of the Irish historical novel, instead of shifting from naive extremism to mature moderation like Scott's hero, moved more often than not from an initially naive, uncommitted stance to a deter-

17

mined commitment to the national cause. The evolution from naiveté to maturity is much the same; but the position in respect to moderation and partisanship is reversed. Instead of moving from one side to the middle, the Irish hero generally moves from the middle to the nationalist side. Instead of returning home from war, he tends to move away from home. In the Irish historical novel Scott's passive hero becomes a partisan hero.

In order to understand this partisan hero, we must first understand the mythos of modern Irish history—that is, the popular Irish view of Irish history familiar to Irish novelists. We must turn not only to the facts of modern Irish history but to the folklore surrounding it, to traditional tales and ballads. Richard Dorson, chief student of the folklore surrounding American history, wrote that one "cannot 'collect' or record the secular myth of a nation-state, for it exists in no one place or document, but permeates the culture; he must piece it together from a thousand scattered sources, and render it explicit." A folklorist trained originally in history, Dorson became the leading advocate of the value of folklore to an understanding of a people's view of history: "Oral tradition and popular folklore would certainly add to the sources available for the historian concerned with myth, symbol, and image."[2] The Irish folklorist Caoimhín Ó Danachair agrees with Dorson:

Nár mhinic, agus cuntas stairiúil ghá léamh againn, gur mhaith linn a fháil amach cad iad na tuarimí a bhí ag an bpobal coitianta des na daoine agus des na himeachtaí gur mhór lé rá iad anallód ins na cáipéisí staire agus ins na paipéirí stáit? . . . Is féidir an gabhail isteach sin in aigne daoine a bhí ann fadó do dhéanamh tré mheán an bhéaloideasa. . . . Is féidir linne a thuiscint cad é an meas a bhí ag an bpobal coitianta.[3] [Wasn't it often, having read a historical account, that we wanted to find out what the opinions of the common people were about the people and the events that were much spoken of long ago in the historical documents and in the state papers? . . . It is possible to enter the minds of people who were there long ago through the medium of folklore. . . . We can understand what the opinion of the common people was.]

Dorson points out that "folk memory selects and retains what it will of the past."[4] In Ireland that memory has been dominated by nationalism. During the nineteenth and early twentieth centuries to be an Irish writer was to be, at least in part, a nationalist. Joyce's epigram "History is a nightmare from which I am trying to awake" represents, in one way, a curious anomaly and, in another way, an ironic statement that proves the point: try as he might, the modern Irish writer has been unable to

escape Irish history—a history reverberating within a nationalist mythos, according to which not only the facts of history but its popular perception are crucial.

The Irish historical novelist has explored his history in order to understand it and to define a mature, contemporary nationalism according to which modern Irish history is seen as the story of the struggle to overcome British domination. The only Irish novelist I discuss who cannot be called a nationalist, Joseph Sheridan Le Fanu, eventually retreated altogether from history to Gothicism, rejecting politics. Herbert Butterfield's statement that to the historical novelist history is "a strange world to tell tales about" accurately applies to the Gothic Le Fanu. He moves from history to Gothicism rather than from Gothicism to history, as Scott did. He retreats from history rather than pursue it, and his retreat demonstrates the power of history in Ireland.

Dorson writes that "the national myth tells no connected story, although it contains biographies of culture heroes and their triumphs. But national myths resemble the tribal ones in unifying their possessors and providing them with common values, symbols, sanctions, and demigods." The sources for an understanding of the Irish nationalist mythos are many, for as Frank O'Connor notes in his literary history of Ireland, significantly subtitled A Backward Look, "among the Irish as among other subject races foreign rule has produced a certain stubbornness about the past."[5] The great popularity of the Irish historical novel is one indication of this "stubbornness."

The Irish novelists, like Scott, very often came to history through the ballads. Two of them, in fact, borrowed ballad titles as titles for their novels: John Banim (The Boyne Water) and William Buckley (Croppies Lie Down). Banim wrote a number of ballads himself. Irish political and historical ballads represent, as Georges-Denis Zimmermann points out, "a nearly collective expression of commonly held beliefs or prejudices and of popular aspirations, and we may regard them as a running commentary on Irish political life seen 'from below.' Historical events are converted into two-dimensional pictures, foreshortened and distorted by partisan spirit; but the very point of view is in itself interesting. The anonymous authors knew instinctively that, to be successful, a text had to be as close as possible to what was commonly accepted and expected."[6] Not all the ballad authors were anonymous: Thomas Moore, Thomas Davis, Banim, and many others attached their names to ballads. In relation to modern Irish history, the political ballads served simultaneously as cause and effect, as Zimmermann points out: "Expressing strong collective emotions, they could profoundly affect the climate of opinion. They were effective

in shaping a common memory of some events and in binding the Irish together." Such ballads were particularly prevalent just before, during, and after the major upheavals in modern Irish history, such as the Jacobite-Williamite war of 1689–91, the 1798 rising, and the campaign to repeal the Union in 1843. The editor of *The Nation* noted in 1843 that "we receive at least twenty songs every week, full of bitter complaints of the fallen condition of our country, or hopes of her speedy resurrection." "Every one of them," he added quite correctly, "we reckon of more value, as an evidence of the condition of the popular mind, than a dozen speeches or a score of petitions."[7]

Like these political ballads, Irish historical novels tend to focus on the high points, the major crises, of Irish nationalist history. Two of the novels I examine (John Banim's *The Boyne Water* and Le Fanu's *The Fortunes of Colonel Torlogh O'Brien*) are devoted to the Jacobite-Williamite war of 1689–91; five (Michael Banim's *The Croppy*, William Buckley's *Croppies Lie Down*, Francis MacManus' *Men Withering*, Eoghan Ó Tuairisc's *L'Attaque*, and Thomas Flanagan's *The Year of the French*) to 1798; two (Liam O'Flaherty's *Famine* and Walter Macken's *The Silent People*) to the Great Famine of 1845–49; and six (Ó Faoláin's *A Nest of Simple Folk*, O'Flaherty's *Insurrection*, Macken's *The Scorching Wind*, Iris Murdoch's *The Red and the Green*, Eilís Dillon's *Across the Bitter Sea* and *Blood Relations*), at least in part, to the events surrounding the Easter Rising of 1916. Three others (John Banim's *The Denounced* and Francis Mac-Manus' *Candle for the Proud* and *Stand and Give Challenge*) deal with the eighteenth-century Penal Age, while Walter Macken's *Seek the Fair Land* focuses on the Cromwellian invasion (c. 1650); James Plunkett's *Strumpet City*, on the 1913 lockout; and Liam O'Flaherty's *Land*, on the late-nineteenth-century land wars.[8] In considering these novels we must always keep in mind that twentieth-century Irish historical novelists had more and better historical sources available to them, as Irish historiography improved and deepened considerably in this century. This advantage is one explanation for the superiority of the twentieth-century Irish historical novel.

J. C. Beckett dates "the making of modern Ireland" from 1603 to 1923 — from the time of the unsuccessful attempt of Hugh O'Neill and Red Hugh O'Donnell, the Ulster chieftains, to defeat the English and maintain their traditional Gaelic way of life until the end of the Irish Civil War and the establishment of the Irish Free State.[9] These dates also encompass all of the history treated in the Irish historical novels discussed here, from the world of Standish O'Grady's *The Flight of the Eagle* to that of Macken's *The Scorching Wind* and Murdoch's *The Red and the*

Green. The dates 1603 to 1923 mark off what we may call modern Irish history, from the birth of modern Irish nationalism to its partial fulfillment in the Irish Free State.

Just as Scott's *Waverley* was written *Sixty Years Since,* in terms of the history they explore the Irish historical novelists look back about 130 years on the average, their retrospection ranging all the way from 30 to 310 years (see chart). Alfred Sheppard argued that the historical novel ideally ought to look back about a half century.[10] However, Scott's best historical novel, *Old Mortality,* traveled back in time more than a

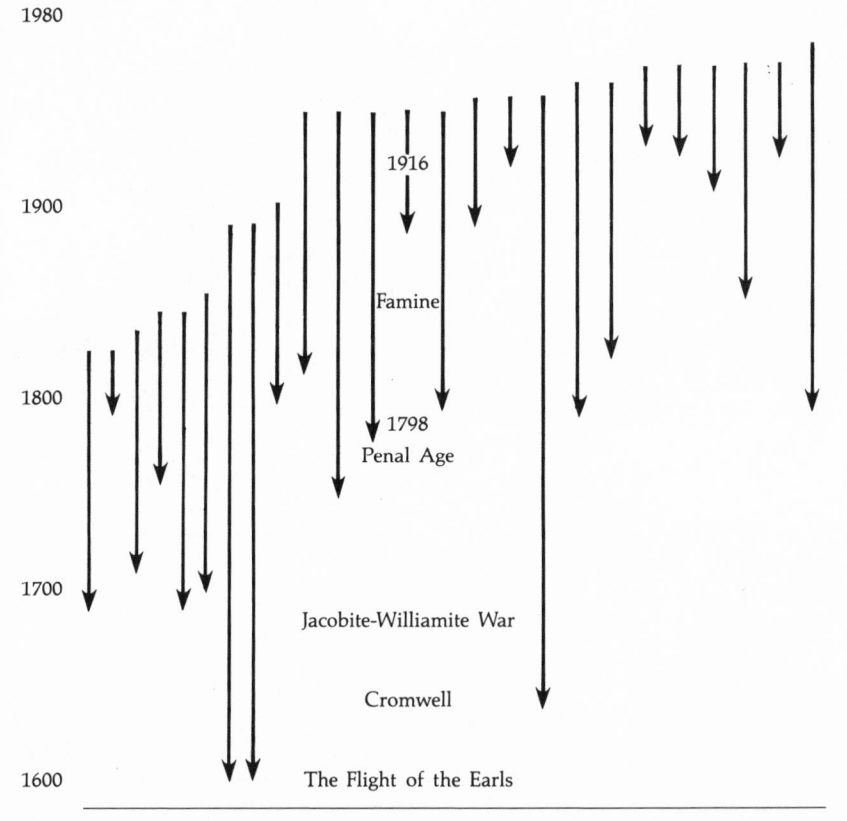

1980

1916

1900

Famine

1800

1798
Penal Age

1700

Jacobite-Williamite War

Cromwell

1600 The Flight of the Earls

1 2 3 4 5 6 7 8 9 10 11 12 13 14 15 16 17 18 19 20 21 22 23 24 25

(See accompanying book list on next page.)

Author and title	Date	Period dealt with	Years of retrospect
1 J. Banim, THE BOYNE WATER	1826	c. 1685–95	137
2 M. Banim, THE CROPPY	1828	1798	30
3 J. Banim, THE LAST BARON OF CRANA	1830	c. 1690–1720	140
4 J. Banim, THE CONFORMISTS	1830	c. 1750–60	80
(3&4, THE DENOUNCED)			
5 Le Fanu, TORLOGH O'BRIEN	1847	c. 1689–91	158
6 Carleton, REDMOND COUNT O'HANLON	1862	c. 1696–1700	192
7 O'Grady, ULRICK THE READY	1896	c. 1598–1602	298
8 O'Grady, THE FLIGHT OF THE EAGLE	1897	c. 1587–91	310
9 Buckley, CROPPIES LIE DOWN	1903	1798	105
10 Ó Faoláin, A NEST OF SIMPLE FOLK	1933	1854–1916	79
11 MacManus, CANDLE FOR THE PROUD	1934	c. 1740–50	194
12 MacManus, STAND AND GIVE CHALLENGE	1936	c. 1750–70	186
13 O'Flaherty, FAMINE	1937	c. 1845–49	92
14 MacManus, MEN WITHERING	1939	c. 1770–98	169
15 O'Flaherty, LAND	1946	c. 1880–85	64
16 O'Flaherty, INSURRECTION	1950	1916	34
17 Macken, SEEK THE FAIR LAND	1959	c. 1649–55	310
18 Ó Tuairisc, L'ATTAQUE	1962	1798	164
19 Macken, THE SILENT PEOPLE	1962	c. 1826–47	136
20 Macken, THE SCORCHING WIND	1964	c. 1916–22	48
21 Murdoch, THE RED AND THE GREEN	1965	1916	49
22 Plunkett, STRUMPET CITY	1969	1907–14	62
23 Dillon, ACROSS THE BITTER SEA	1973	1851–1916	122
24 Dillon, BLOOD RELATIONS	1977	c. 1916–24	61
25 Flanagan, THE YEAR OF THE FRENCH	1979	1798	201

century to events that were still very much alive in the Scottish imagination. Similarly, Irish novelists repeatedly returned, over a long period of time, to the 1798 rising, probably the single most celebrated rebellion in modern Irish history. The Irish historical novelist looked back to a high point during a previous generation in modern Irish history that was still alive in the popular imagination and that most kindled his own imagination.

BECKETT points out that "the Ireland of the 'protestant ascendancy,' out of which the Ireland of to-day has arisen, took form during the first four decades of the seventeenth century," from the defeat of O'Neill and O'Donnell during 1602–1603 and the Protestant plantation that followed it to the arrival of Cromwell in Ireland in 1649 (13). Until 1600 Ireland still existed in a state that had persisted from the Middle Ages: the authority of the royal English government extended nominally over all of the country but was effective only within "the Pale," a relatively small area surrounding the seat of government in Dublin. Most of the rest of Ireland was fragmented into fifty or sixty virtually independent regions, each ruled by a native chief, or rí (king), or by an Anglo-Irish noble. This was the era explored in Standish O'Grady's *The Flight of the Eagle.*

During the 1590s Red Hugh O'Donnell and Hugh O'Neill allied themselves in order to try to stop the anglicization of their Gaelic areas of Ulster. In 1595 O'Neill finally rose against the English, winning in 1598 the Battle of the Yellow Ford, at which point rebellion spread beyond the north, and O'Neill found himself at the head of a national movement that the English feared might subvert their dominance in Ireland. In 1601 four thousand Spanish troops landed at Kinsale in Cork but were quickly repelled by the English, introducing what would be, with the French in 1796 and the Germans in 1916, a recurring motif in modern Irish rebellions: the frustrated foreign landing. O'Grady recounted this episode in *Ulrick the Ready.*

After this defeat, Red Hugh O'Donnell fled to Spain, and Irish fortunes continued to decline until O'Neill's surrender early in 1603. O'Donnell and O'Neill would serve later Irish nationalists (and O'Grady) as symbols of gallant, if unsuccessful, rebellion. O'Donnell was celebrated in the famous ballad "O'Donnell Abú" ["Up O'Donnell"]:

> Rush to the standard of dauntless Red Hugh!
> Bonnought and Gallowglass
> Throng from each mountain-pass!
> On for old Ireland—O'Donnell abú! [11]

But to Gaelic Ireland, "the flight of the earls," their departure for the Continent in 1607, marked the end of the old order and soon came to be regarded as a national disaster, as an old Gaelic curse cited by Beckett shows: "Woe to the heart that meditated, woe to the mind that conceived, woe to the council that decided on, the project of their setting out on this voyage, without knowing whether they should ever return to their native principalities or patrimonies to the end of the world" (44).

English authorities took "the flight of the earls" as an admission of treason and proclaimed their lands confiscated and open to colonization and settlement, annexing counties Armagh, Cavan, Londonderry, Donegal, Fermanagh, and Tyrone. Thus, another very persistent motif in modern Irish history was introduced: the pattern of reprisal, according to which abortive Irish rebellions were met by much greater, longer-lasting, more extensive reactions on the part of the authorities. A short-lived rising led by Cahir O'Doherty in Derry in 1608 was followed by an expansion and acceleration of the Protestant plantation scheme in Ulster — just as the 1641 rising would be followed by the Cromwellian plantation throughout much of the rest of Ireland, the Jacobite-Williamite war of 1689–91 by the Penal Age, and the 1798 rising by the Act of Union of 1800.

Once the strongest and most thoroughly Gaelic part of Ireland, Ulster became in the eighteenth century the most extensively anglicized Irish province. The Scottish role in Ulster's plantation was considerable, and it was accelerated by the presence of a Scottish king, James I, on the English throne during the early seventeenth century. After 1615, plantation was pressed outside the north as well, through pseudolegal means. Finally, in 1641, the Leinsterman Rory O'More led bitter Ulster Catholics against the Protestant settlers, beginning a larger war that exposed Ireland to a more total English conquest. Catholic Irish rebellion, once again, was met by a greater Protestant backlash. To Protestants, O'More's rebellion was evidence of a preconceived Catholic plot to slaughter them. This feeling was so pervasive that almost ten years later Cromwell sought to justify the slaughter of the garrison of Drogheda as a divine judgment on Catholic wretches who had it coming to them.

Cromwell's arrival in Ireland in 1649 was the real turning point of the war. In eight months he broke native Irish resistance and opened the way for nearly total Protestant domination. Cromwell was not, as Irish folklore would have it, the devil; he was simply the most effective English military man ever to set foot in Ireland. He was probably no less moral than other English leaders of his day. George Fox's Quaker journal records a sympathetic conversation with him in which he seemed touched by Fox's sincerity and gentleness. What he was in his Irish campaign was successful and ruthless. His campaign began with the sacking of Drogheda on September 11, 1649, in which most of the garrison and many of the townspeople were exterminated. These events are narrated by Walter Macken in *Seek the Fair Land*.

The place that Cromwell and Drogheda still have in the popular Irish imagination is typified by Pete Hamill's foreword to Tommy Makem's and the Clancy Brothers' *Irish Songbook:* "Oliver Cromwell [was] a

seventeenth-century religious maniac who apparently thought that the Almighty had given him the right to murder. At the town of Drogheda, he slaughtered every man, woman and child in the town of three thousand."[12] Hamill's characterization is modest compared to the portrayal of Cromwell in Irish folklore. Next to Daniel O'Connell, no modern historical character appears more frequently in Irish oral tradition than Cromwell.[13] There are hundreds of references to him in the collection of the Irish Folklore Commission, all inspired by his eight months in Ireland ravaging the country, and all portraying him as a "folk villain." Seán Ó Súilleabháin notes that "the use of his name as a bogey-man hundreds of years later illustrates the terror which was associated with him: 'If a child was contrary or wouldn't go to bed when it was told, the father or mother would say: "Cromwell would come and bring you!"'"[14]

One of the most interesting features surrounding Irish history is that in the folklore Cromwell always loses and O'Connell always wins. Cromwell, the English historical victor, becomes a loser, and O'Connell, a loser during the 1840s if not during the 1820s and 1830s, becomes the always victorious Irish advocate. The reversal of their positions illustrates the power of wishful thinking in Irish folklore. The legendary accounts of Cromwell's death are remarkable. In truth he died in bed in London at the age of fifty-nine, but Irish oral tradition tells a different story. "He is generally said to have killed himself either by cutting his own throat or casting his body against a spear," according to Ó Súilleabháin. Like Saul, he throws himself on his own sword, sharing motive and method with the guilty Old Testament king. Ó Súilleabháin notes that "some accounts even say that he met his death in Ireland." Several versions explain that after its burial in Ireland, Cromwell's corpse was rejected by the Irish soil and the coffin was found back above ground each morning. It was then cast into the sea and drifted like a boat around the Irish coast, trying in vain to land somewhere, but was rejected everywhere; finally it sank to the bottom of the Irish Sea, which caused its waters to be particularly turbulent ever since.[15]

In these tales, the "curse of Cromwell" is reversed, applying not to Ireland but to Cromwell. His followers are similarly cursed in the folktales, an interesting and perhaps appropriate feature, since Cromwell's chief subordinates, such as Sir Charles Coote, were in fact often more vicious than Cromwell himself in the subjugation and administration of Ireland. Cromwell's demonic image is reflected in Macken's characterization of Coote in *Seek the Fair Land*. Joseph Damer, an Englishman who served in Cromwell's army and acquired an estate in Tipperary in 1662, becoming a banker and usurer, serves in Irish folklore as a miser figure much like

Midas. "As rich as Damer" is still a well-known saying in Ireland.[16] These features of Irish folklore exemplify the mythos of modern Irish history, according to which history is seen as a morality play opposing brutally vicious English Vice and noble, courageous, self-sacrificing Irish Virtue — polarities the Irish historical novelist grew up hearing about.

THE POST-CROMWELLIAN PLANTATION was the most complete one. It established the Protestant Ascendancy that was to control the life of Ireland through the nineteenth century. "To Hell or to Connaught" was the popular slogan after the 1641–52 war: "It was first announced that all 'transplantable persons' should remove themselves by 1 May 1654," Beckett writes, "and that they should be liable to death if found east of the the Shannon after that date" (107). The Protestant Ascendancy sought to exterminate the Roman Catholic clergy during the decades after Cromwell. Catholic priests were very often hunted down with a price on their heads. Religion was by now, as it would remain throughout modern Irish history, a convenient label used to isolate the opposed groups in Irish society, marking differences that were social and economic rather than simply religious.

Under the shadow of English rule and an increasingly powerful Protestant Ascendancy, the Irish saw little chance of open rebellion during the years after 1650. Instead, dissatisfied Irishmen operating as "tories" took out their frustrations in guerrilla activities, traveling the Irish countryside, often disguised, in sporadic, Robin Hood-like attempts to take back from the Protestant settlers what they felt to be rightly Ireland's. The most famous of these Irish Robin Hoods, Redmond O'Hanlon, has been popularly preserved in Irish folklore and served William Carleton as protagonist in his attempt at an Irish *Rob Roy*. Before finally being caught and shot in April 1681, O'Hanlon achieved a considerable renown. He has attracted the interest of many balladeers, the most recent of whom is the contemporary balladeer Tommy Makem:

> There was a man lived in the North, a hero brave and bold,
> Who robbed the wealthy landlords of their silver and their gold;
> He gave the money to the poor to pay their rent and fee,
> Count Redmond O'Hanlon, the gallant rapparee.

Both Makem and Carleton call O'Hanlon a "rapparee" (from Irish *rápaire* and French *rapière*), but this is anachronistic, as that term did not come into use until some of the former Irish soldiers in the Jacobite-Williamite

war of 1689–91 revived guerrilla activities during the late seventeenth and early eighteenth centuries. "I'm England's foe, I'm Ireland's friend, I'm an outlaw rapparee."[17]

Many earlier outlaw ballads like Makem's expressed popular discontent. The Irish Robin Hoods were perceived as romantic as well as nationalist heroes who, like the heroes of medieval English outlaw ballads, exercised a retributive justice.[18] Zimmermann writes:

> The "noble bandits" were dear to the people mainly for romantic reasons, as in other countries, but in Ireland they were more than just heroes of adventure stories or charming bad men. The social background of their exploits should not be underestimated. These outlaws who "robbed the rich and helped the poor," and defiantly refused to surrender and to "work for the government" were *also* heroic symbols of freedom, of resistance to a law which was called injustice by many. The Irish *tories* and *rapparees* of the seventeenth century, sheltering in the woods or mountains and waging a kind of guerrilla war upon the English who had taken their lands, were brigands of the worst sort according to the settlers and their government, but they were regarded with sympathy by the sons of those who had held the country previously. . . . In the second half of the eighteenth century and at the beginning of the nineteenth, cheap literature about them was sold at great profit. *A Genuine History of the Lives and Actions of the Most Notorious Irish Highwaymen*, first printed in the mid-eighteenth century, ran through many editions and was still one of the most popular books . . . in the 1820s, when it was usual, according to Crofton Croker, "to hear the adventures and escapes of highwaymen and outlaws recited by the lower orders with the greatest minuteness, and dwelt on with surprising fondness. It was said for instance of the gentleman-robber Redmond O'Hanlon that "he was always kind to his countrymen," his hatred being confined to the English. "He seldom robbed a poor man, but on the contrary was always generous to men in necessity or distress."[19]

In 1687, the Catholic King James II appointed the Catholic partisan Tyrconnel as chief minister in Ireland, which enraged Protestants, especially in the north. They recorded their reaction in the famous ballad "Lillibulero," written in a mocking, stereotypical imitation of Catholic "brother Teague's" Anglo-Irish dialect:

> Ho brother Teague dost hear de decree,
> Lillibulero bullen-a-la,
> Dat we shall have a new deputy,
> Lillibulero bullen-a-la.

The ballad graphically portrays Protestant paranoia and resentment:

> Ho by my soul it is a Talbot,
> Lillibulero bullen-a-la,
> And he will cut all de English throat,
> Lillibulero bullen-a-la,
> There was an old prophecy found in a bog,
> Lillibulero bullen-a-la,
> Dat our land would be ruled by an ass and a dog,
> Lillibulero bullen-a-la.
> So now dis old Prophecy's coming to pass,
> Lillibulero bullen-a-la,
> For James is de dog, and Tyrconnel's de ass,
> Lillibulero bullen-a-la.[20]

The Protestant Ascendancy believed that James meant to use Irish "papists" to destroy their domination. When he called Irish troops to his support in England in 1688, they were convinced of it. When the Protestant William of Orange landed in England in November of that year and proclaimed himself king, Protestant leaders in Ulster immediately declared their loyalty to him. In December, the town of Londonderry shut its gates against a new garrison from Tyrconnel, declaring, "No surrender!" Tyrconnel's troops, however, occupied all of Ulster except for Londonderry and Enniskillen.

On March 12, 1689, James arrived in Ireland and advanced on Londonderry, thus beginning the most celebrated siege in Irish history. Thousands starved, but this did not sway the Protestant commanders, Major Henry Baker and the clergyman George Walker (who reappeared in Banim's *The Boyne Water*). After nearly four months, relief from King William's ships finally got through, and the Jacobite army broke camp, beginning a disheartened retreat south. The sequel — Protestant victory at the Boyne and at Aughrim in July 1690, followed by the Treaty of Limerick in October — is, in the Protestant Unionist mythos, the most glorious chapter in modern Irish history. The Unionist legend, of course, is directly opposed to the nationalist one: heroes and villains are reversed. There were, incidentally, a few Protestant Unionist historical novels written during the late nineteenth century, but now they seem lost in obscurity in a genre whose major practitioners have been predominantly Catholic and nationalist.[21] Even the Protestant Unionist Le Fanu's version of the Jacobite-Williamite war, *Torlogh O'Brien*, was heavily colored, as we shall see, by the nationalism of Thomas Davis and *The Nation*.

The high point of the Ulster Protestant calendar to this day is the date of the Battle of the Boyne, when the forces of King Billy, the deliverer, reigned supreme. Huge parades and massive fife and drum bands still celebrate the victory annually in the north today. Beckett calls it "the decisive battle of modern Ireland."

> The Boyne marks the climax of a civil conflict that had grown steadily more explicit and more intense as the century progressed. The campaign was not over, but the result was no longer in doubt; and the result meant that in future the protestant minority would rule Ireland. . . . Until the impact of the French Revolution gave form and vigour to popular national feeling the "protestant ascendancy" was to rule unchallenged. (146)

THE EIGHTEENTH CENTURY reads like one long punishment of the Catholic majority by the Protestant minority for the Jacobite-Williamite war. In its initial form, the Treaty of Limerick expressed a conciliatory aim toward the defeated Catholics, but it was ratified by the Protestant Parliament only in mutilated form. Then began an anti-Catholic Penal Age so long that John Banim argued at the end of *The Boyne Water* in 1826 that the Treaty of Limerick had still not been kept.[22] Anti-Catholic measures during the Penal Age were social and economic as well as religious in their application. No Catholic was permitted, for example, to purchase land on a lease exceeding thirty-one years, or to own a horse worth more than five pounds. A Catholic landlord could not bequeath his land by will; it had to be divided equally among all of his sons, thus accelerating the extreme subdivision of holdings that was to afflict an overpopulated Ireland. If a Catholic landlord's oldest son converted, or "conformed," to the Protestant Church of Ireland, he was entitled to his father's property, with the father becoming a mere life-tenant. Thus, becoming a "conformist" was a great temptation and divided many Catholic landed families. This eighteenth-century phenomenon was explored by both John Banim and Francis MacManus, among the historical novelists.

Catholics were also required to pay tithes to the Church of Ireland. The tithes provided later agrarian rebels with a focus for their activities: Tithe Wars — organized, massive refusals to pay the tithes — were waged, especially in the 1820s. During the 1760s and 1770s, bands of guerrillas, commonly called "Whiteboys" and "Steelboys," roamed the countryside at night, throwing down fences and maiming cattle on Protes-

tant estates in protest against tithes, enclosures, and other agrarian in-
justices. An Antrim poet cited by Beckett wrote of the Steelboys during
the 1770s:

> Some of the tenants still remain that feel
> Their wrongs, and can resent with Hearts of Steel,
> Bravely resolved in mutual league unite
> To keep possession, and support their right. (178)

During the eighteenth century, the Gaelic poets, having lost their
patrons, moved away from the old courtly verse to more popular forms
which served to keep alive nationalist memories and hopes. Beneath the
shadow of the Protestant Ascendancy, there survived a "hidden Ireland,"
as Daniel Corkery would later call it, of Gaelic legend and folklore, a
people who, resenting the alien culture dominating their country, constituted a Gaelic underground that continued to influence Irish history. Among
the historical novelists, Francis MacManus made this "hidden Ireland" his
special province, and Thomas Flanagan tried to recapture it through his
characterization of Owen MacCarthy in *The Year of the French.*

Another eighteenth-century phenomenon occurred within the
Protestant minority: the appearance of Protestant Irish nationalism, beginning with Jonathan Swift's "Modest Proposal" and other angry jibes
at the ruling class during the 1720s, developing into the Protestant "Patriot
Parliament" of Grattan and Flood in the 1780s, and culminating in the
1798 rising. During this time significant portions of the Protestant intelligentsia and commercial class realized that they had independent interests and needs which called for a government that would be Irish, not
English. The resulting Patriot Parliament was allowed a short-lived period
of home rule.

At the same time, a stronger brand of nationalism was developing among those whose imaginations were kindled by the French Revolution and who wanted to go beyond federalism. The most significant figure among these nationalists was Wolfe Tone, the first in a series of Irish
rebels — including Robert Emmet, James Stephens, O'Donovan Rossa, Patrick Pearse, and James Connolly — who were perceived in the nationalist
mythos as self-sacrificing rebels ahead of their time. This series looked
back upon itself. Pearse, for example, was chiefly inspired by Tone and
gave his most famous speech at the funeral of Rossa, the Fenian, in 1913.
The nationalist legend saw all of these men as heroes in a single, ongoing
morality play, just as the ballad "Mackenna's Dream" portrays Brian Boru,

Sarsfield, King James, Father Murphy, and the 1798 rebels as soldiers in a single battle:

> They gave three cheers for liberty,
> As the enemy all routed flee;
> Methought I looked but could not see
> One foeman on the plain.[23]

Tone was also the first in a series of Protestant Irish patriots which included Robert Emmet, Charles Stewart Parnell, and many others. One of the more remarkable features of the movement that led to the 1798 rebellion, in fact, was that its vanguard was based among the radicals of Protestant Ulster, especially in Belfast, where a significant faction of the Presbyterian commercial class was particularly in tune with the idealism of the French Revolution and sought to band together with their Catholic brothers in order to seek Irish liberty. The location of the Republican vanguard in predominantly "loyalist" Ulster was an unusual phenomenon, and the cooperation of Presbyterian and Catholic in County Antrim was unique to that time. The Irish Volunteers, which became the military branch of Irish nationalism during the 1790s, was founded by the Protestant Parliament as a peace-keeping police force, and ironically enough, originally helped to defend Protestant landlords against Whiteboy activities.

Tone was an idealist who believed that all Ireland, once educated, would respond to the ideals of the French Revolution. He tried quite literally to bring the French Revolution to Ireland, spending much of the 1790s seeking to convince the French to land in Ireland and to help the Irish Volunteers win Irish freedom. Interestingly, the eighteenth-century Gaelic poets had prophesied the coming of the French:

> Tá 'n Franncach faobhrach 'sa loingeas gleasta,
> Le crannaibh géara ar muir le seal;
> Is é síor sgéala go bhfuil a dtriall go hÉire,
> A's go gcuirfid gaodhail bhoicht arís na gceart.
> (The Frenchman is eager and his fleet is dressed,
> With tapering masts on the sea for awhile,
> And the constant news is that they are voyaging to Ireland
> And they will restore the poor Gaels again to their rights.)[24]

The famous 1797 Anglo-Irish ballad "The Shan Van Vocht" borrowed the Gaelic figure of the *sean bhean bhoct*, the poor old woman who personifies nationalist Ireland, and linked her to the Great French Hope:

> The French are on the sea! says the Shan Van Vocht;
> The French are on the sea! says the Shan Van Vocht.
> The French are on the sea, they'll be here without delay,
> And the Orange will decay, says the Shan Van Vocht.[25]

The French did in fact come to Ireland in 1798, but they came too late. There were three separate risings that year, in Wexford, Antrim, and Mayo, each quite independent of the others in the recurrent Irish pattern of isolated rebellion. Among the historical novels, Michael Banim's *The Croppy*, William Buckley's *Croppies Lie Down*, and Francis MacManus' *Men Withering* focused on the Wexford rising, and Eoghan Ó Tuairisc's *L'Attaque* and Thomas Flanagan's *The Year of the French* on the one in Mayo; there were a number of other novels written about all three risings.[26]

The Wexford rising lasted from May 26 to June 21, 1798, and was, along with the rising in Mayo, the longest and single most successful Irish rebellion of modern times until the Anglo-Irish War of 1919–21. F. S. L. Lyons calls it "the most formidable uprising in modern Irish history."[27] It was also the most brutal, short of the Cromwellian war. Both the rebels and the government troops were fairly undisciplined forces, with the rebels bitter against their Protestant oppressors and the government troops fighting as if in enemy territory. Wexford in 1798 lacked, in truth, the self-sacrificing nobility of Easter 1916. But this was not the status that Wolfe Tone and 1798 were to assume in the nationalist legend. As Beckett notes, Tone, who was not on the scene in Wexford, "established, and later came almost to personify, a tradition of revolutionary violence that has never wholly died out of Irish politics. And in the light of this tradition the insurrection of 1798 is seen not as it was in deed but as Tone had hoped for it to be" (267).

The Wexford rising began with the rebels' victories in the towns of Wexford and Enniscorthy, was stymied by their defeat at New Ross, and ended with the capture of their stronghold at Vinegar Hill. The rebels had been commanded by Father John Murphy, "that hero," as one of the ballads put it, who "for your sake fought for liberty, / When violent pitch caps most lacerating / On your heads were placed in this country.[28] After their defeat, several of the rebel leaders, both Protestant and Catholic, were hung and burnt with black pitch in brutal executions intended by the government as intimidating examples for the populace.

The northern risings in June, led by Henry McCracken and Henry Munro, were predominantly Protestant and short-lived. By that time the vanguard of the United Irish movement had weakened, having withdrawn

their enthusiastic, heady support of the French Revolution, disenchanted by its imperialistic sequel.

Wolfe Tone had first brought a French expedition to the Irish coast off Bantry, County Cork, in December 1796. Bad weather and confusion had prevented a landing. But Tone persisted, and what would be the only successful foreign landing in modern Irish history occurred in August 1798, as General Humbert, the French Commander, led his troops off their ships into County Mayo. Thousands of somewhat startled and fairly untrained Irishmen joined them, and a rising commenced that lasted for a month. It was very different from the Wicklow rising, however, for Humbert maintained a tight discipline among his forces, which was met in kind by Generals Lake and Cornwallis on the English side. At first Humbert caught them by surprise, leading his troops from Killala inland, into the midst of County Mayo. It was only a matter of time, however, before Humbert would be outnumbered, surrounded, and defeated. He surrendered at Ballinamuck on September 8.

The Mayo rising was a "gentlemen's" war; Lake and Cornwallis took charge of Humbert peacefully. But the Irish rebels' moderation in this case made no difference to the government troops, who violently revenged themselves on the rebels. The yeomanry and militia had raced headlong before their French and Irish attackers in Castlebar, and they were determined to avenge this embarrassing defeat. In an interesting contrast, Eoghan Ó Tuairisc presents the Mayo rising from the Gaelic peasants' perspective in L'Attaque while Thomas Flanagan tells it almost entirely from the gentlemen's point of view in The Year of the French.

Another French expedition, with Tone aboard, was captured by the British off Donegal in October. Tone, condemned to the gallows after a speedy trial in Dublin, committed suicide in prison after being refused a request for death by firing squad instead of the gallows. He was, as Beckett notes, "the ablest and most vigorous" among the United Irish leaders. The issues he had worked for in the early 1790s, such as Catholic Emancipation and constitutional reform, continued to reverberate throughout the nineteenth century. His shift to open rebellion after 1794 was Patrick Pearse's chief inspiration before 1916.

Similarly, the name and the memory of "1798" dominated the nationalist imagination until 1916. Robert Emmet's attempt at rebellion in Dublin in 1803 was a mere whimper compared to the great big bang of 1798. The Young Ireland rising in 1848 and the Fenian rising in 1867 were equally short-lived. In 1798, Irish nationalism, in its truly modern guise, was born. More ballads were written about that year than any other year

in modern Irish history. "Who Fears to Speak of Ninety-Eight?" Thomas Davis asked.

Some of the songs expressed, for the first time, the concept of Christlike martyrdom in rebellion that later dominated Patrick Pearse's mind. "Rody MacCorly," for example:

> Since it's upon Good Friday, the day I am to die,
> The day Christ suffered for us all, Oh, why should I deny,
> His head was pierced, His crown was clad with thorns most severe,
> They nailed his body to a cross and pierced it with a spear.[29]

The "liberty tree" of which many of the 1798 ballads spoke was a symbol that seems to have been related to the ideas of Cross, Crucifixion, and Resurrection, like the identification of the tree of temptation in the Garden of Eden with Christ's cross in medieval Christian typology. In the nationalist vision, the 1798 rebels were hung from the "liberty tree" in order to save modern Ireland, an Ireland finally redeemed by the rebels of 1916.

THE NEXT SIGNIFICANT CHAPTER in the story of the Irish nationalist mythos is Daniel O'Connell's. He is the most popular modern Irish historical character in Irish folklore. The English response to 1798 was, as usual, backlash; the Act of Union, which eliminated partial Irish home rule in favor of London rule, was passed in 1800. The period from 1800 to 1820 was an empty one in Irish politics. O'Connell, the barrister and member of Parliament from Kerry, came on the scene during the 1820s as the great champion of Catholic Emancipation. Beckett records Lord Lytton's description of the scene at one of O'Connell's mass meetings:

> Once to my sight the giant thus was given:
> Welled by wide air, and roofed by boundless heaven,
> Beneath his feet the human ocean lay,
> And wave on wave flowed into space away. (325)

O'Connell was victorious in the 1820s. Catholic Emancipation was granted in 1829. But included was the stipulation that the voting franchise was to be increased from forty shillings to ten pounds; thus, Parliament took away with one hand what it had given with the other.

By the 1840s, O'Connell had weakened: he was older and his opponents were stronger. In the midst of all his fiery rhetoric, he was always the constitutional reformer, the patriot within the law, and he observed a ban on one of his mass meetings during his campaign in 1843 for repeal of the Union. From then on he never again enjoyed the dominance in Ireland that he held in the 1820s. In the face of increasing competition from Young Ireland, the nationalist movement begun by Thomas Davis in the 1840s, O'Connell's power declined.

Davis, founder of *The Nation*, was a very active journalist and balladeer, one of whose ambitions, cut short by his death in 1845, was to compile a "ballad history of Ireland": "We will endeavour to teach the people to sing the songs of their country that may keep alive in their minds the love of fatherland." Inspired by Scott, who made him "wish to heaven someone would attempt Irish historical fiction," Davis sought in his 1840s ballads to counter "the wail of a lost cause" in Moore's *Melodies* with "the virile and passionate hopes of a new generation." Davis' contemporary, the crusty Liberties singer Zozimus Moran, once claimed in court after his arrest the right to praise his native land like his fellow bards "Tommy" Moore, Walter Scott, Horace, and Homer, "on'y I haven't got me harp like them to accompany me aspirations."[30]

By the time he died in 1847, during the Famine, O'Connell – the "liberator," the "counsellor," the central figure in Irish politics – had become an object for ridicule to members of Young Ireland, who saw themselves as stronger nationalists. He was also the object for retrospective scorn from many later Irish revolutionaries. In Irish folklore, however, only the image of O'Connell as "counsellor," the witty lawyer who never loses, was preserved – not the figure of the old, weakened politician left behind by the times. As Caoimhín Ó Danachair observes:

> Is é an teideal a tugtar air imbéaloideas na Ghaeilge igconaí –"An Counsiléar." Tá an teideal *The Liberator* ann i Béarla, gan amhras, ach is cosúil gur as na páipéirí nuachta a tháinig sé. [In Irish folklore he was always given the title, "The Counsellor." There was the title *The Liberator* in English, without a doubt, but it appears that came out of the newspapers.]

This legendary Irish "counsellor" is independent of O'Connell's historical career as politician. Ó Danachair continues:

> I dtosach a shaoil phoiblí a tháinig Ó Conaill os comhair an phobail choitianta ina dhlíodóir trodach in aimsir Fuascailte na gCaitlíceach. . . .

Ach cén fáth gur thuill sé clú agus cáil mar dhlíodóir gan mórán trácht thar a shaol phoiblí mar fhear polaítíochta? . . . Arbh é coscairt an *Repeal Movement* agus teacht an Ghorta do chuir deireadh lena chlú mar polaiteoir, agus d'fhág a ainm in airde mar chounsiléar dlí . . . ? [At the beginning of his public life, O'Connell seemed to the common people to be a pugnacious advocate in the service of Catholic Emancipation. . . . But why did he earn that renown and reputation as advocate without much mention of his public life as a political man? . . . Was it the failure of the Repeal Movement and the coming of the Famine that put an end to his reputation as a politician, and left his name forever as counsellor . . . ?]

Ó Danachair implies that the answer to this final question is "yes."[31]

Again, the power of wishful thinking in Irish folklore is evident. The Irish nationalist imagination seeks to preserve a memory of O'Connell as successful and admirable, rather than as the unsuccessful repealer or as helpless in the face of the Famine. Walter Macken's characterization of O'Connell in *The Silent People* draws both upon the view of O'Connell as a failure during the Famine and on his image in folklore as the demigod of Catholic Emancipation. In many of the folktales about O'Connell, he is a Solomon or Portia figure who trips up his adversaries in the tangle of their own legalisms. The Irish seemed to enjoy stories about duels between lawyers. Sir Jonah Barrington noted that "in my time the number of killed and wounded amongst the bar was very considerable."[32] Concerning O'Connell, Ó Danachair notes that "seo scéal den tsórt san, scéal a bhí ana-choitianta an fuaid na hÉireann [Stories of this sort were very common all over Ireland]".[33] One of the stories explains how O'Connell tricked Parliament into allowing him to wear his hat there. In another, "Daniel O'Connell and the Trickster," he plays Portia to the trickster's Shylock.[34] As folklore character, O'Connell is always the clever lawyer who uses the law to win. He is a hero; Cromwell, a villain. In the nationalist mythos, the polarities of Irish versus English and nationalist versus Unionist are consistently preserved.

THE FAMINE of 1845–49 was Ireland's holocaust. It killed a million people and forced another million to emigrate. By the beginning of the twentieth century, the population was only about half of what it had been on the eve of the Famine. Virtually all of the victims were Catholic; most of them

were tenants of very small holdings, or farm laborers, and their families, and a large number of them were Irish speakers.

In the nationalist mythos, the Famine — for there were several famines in modern Irish history, but just one "Famine," or "Great Hunger" — would be perceived as the ultimate attack of foreign oppressors on poor Catholic Ireland. Pete Hamill's foreword to the Clancy collection of ballads typifies this view. He writes that during the eighteenth century, as a result of the Penal Laws:

> Farms became smaller and smaller, increasingly devoted to mere subsistence farming of potatoes, while the Anglo-Irish Protestant Ascendancy built great mansions on their stolen land and plush Georgian houses in Dublin. The result, of course, was the Great Famine of 1846–51. . . . The details were something else. Children walked the roads of Ireland, their bellies bursting with disease, their eyes hollow with starvation. Irish mothers were found with babies at their dry breasts, lying in fields, their mouths stained green from trying to eat enough grass to stay alive. . . . And through it all, the great landlords of Ireland went about business as usual: exporting the beef, pork, lamb and grain that might have saved the starving Irish. It was a mass atrocity that no Irishman has ever forgiven.[35]

Although Hamill's synopsis of modern Irish history is an oversimplification, it is true that while the immediate cause of the Famine was the repeated potato blight from 1845 to 1847, the extent of its damage was vastly multiplied by Irish rural overpopulation and overconsolidation, as well as by the peasantry's nearly complete dependence on the potato for their sustenance. While neither the English nor the Protestant Ascendancy in Ireland willed the Famine — no more than William Pitt, the English prime minister, deliberately incited the 1798 rebellion so as to ensure the passage of the Act of Union, as has often been argued — it seemed that way to the Irish nationalist, especially to the Irish nationalist looking back at these events later.

The Famine survived very strongly in Irish folklore. Writing in 1956, Roger McHugh in "The Famine in Irish Oral Tradition" noted that Famine experiences "in many places . . . are as real to the inhabitants today as are the events of last year. . . . The history of the Famine was indelibly printed upon the lives of our forefathers. . . . To them it was an accepted fact and might be recalled as a great and ruinous storm might be recalled." The oral tradition surrounding the Famine, McHugh notes, is "a tradition of an ominous season of mist, of storms of rain and wind

alternating with periods of vast and terrible stillness; of the names of fields where the blight first appeared and of men who first noticed the heavy smell of decay or saw the brown spots spreading on the leaves, the blackened stalks slowly leaning over, the potato-pits ominously sagging."[36] Irish folklore is rife with stories of people eating roots, grass, crows, and worse during the Famine and accounts of victims dying while trying to bury the corpses of their friends and families. These stories reinforce the moving account presented by the English historian Cecil Woodham-Smith in *The Great Hunger*. In *Famine*, Liam O'Flaherty would strikingly recapture the season of storms and blight as well as its disastrous sequel.

"While the immediate effect of the 'Great Hunger' was to impose an overwhelming burden of suffering upon an impoverished and defenceless people," F. S. L. Lyons notes, "it may well be that its most profound impact on Irish history lay in its ultimate psychological legacy. Expressed in its simplest terms, this legacy was given not only a new intensity, but also a new dimension."[37] After the Famine, there seemed to many Irishmen to be no alternative to nationalism. The Famine served to separate even further the two sides of what was now coming to be called "the Irish question." It made the Irish, as well as the increasing numbers of Irish-Americans, more bitter about the Union, while the ruling class, especially after the abortive 1848 rising led by John Mitchel and his fellow United Irishmen, became more contemptuous about the ability of the Irish to govern themselves. Ireland and England were, after the Famine, probably more estranged from each other than ever before. This estrangement is apparent in Fenian folklore of the late nineteenth century.

The Fenian, or Irish Republican, Brotherhood founded by James Stephens in 1858 was not a mass movement, but it had much tacit support among rural Irishmen. This support is reflected in the large body of Irish folklore about the common people hiding out and aiding the Fenians, one part of which has been studied by Seán Ó Súilleabháin. Stories about "the peelers'" searches for the Fenians are common, with the search commonly frustrated through clever means.[38] A larger-scale escape, that of Fenian leaders to America from Australia following their imprisonment there after the short-lived 1867 rising, was commonly celebrated in Fenian ballads:

> Now boys if you will listen to the story I'll relate,
> I'll tell you of the noble men who from the foe escaped.
> Tho' bound with Saxon fetters in the dark Australian jail,
> They struck a blow for freedom and for Yankee land set sail.[39]

What distinguished the Fenians from their seventeenth- and eighteenth-century outlaw forebears was that they had a clearly nationalist program to offer: the achievement of Ireland's complete separation from England through violent means. The Fenians also brought organization and discipline to the revolutionary nationalist movement. The IRB managed to survive right through 1916, when one of the leaders of the Easter Rising was the oldest IRB organizer, Tom Clarke. Among Irish historical novels, Fenianism is explored in Seán Ó Faoláin's *A Nest of Simple Folk*, and Eilís Dillon's *Across the Bitter Sea*.

Irish nationalism was broadened during the latter half of the nineteenth century by the merger of nationalist issues with social issues, specifically land issues. The movement for tenants' rights won a reforming Land Act from a sympathetic Gladstone in 1870, but the idea of court regulation of landlords, which proved to be ineffectual in practice, was not enough for the tenants: they wanted to *own* their farms. The Land League, the great movement founded by Michael Davitt and headed nominally by Charles Stewart Parnell, achieved fame and power through the imposition on "rackrenting" landlords of the "boycott," a word coined by the League after one such successful campaign against the Mayo land agent Captain Boycott in 1880. A pop-historical work by Philip Rooney later recounted this specific campaign. A better book, O'Flaherty's *Land*, explored some of the conflicts active during this general period.

The efforts of the Land League eventually resulted in an important reform: the Wyndham Land Act of 1903, which legislated a peasant proprietorship. Meanwhile, a second great voice of the Irish cause had died, as had O'Connell, before his dreams could be fulfilled. Having ridden the Irish Parliamentary Party and the Land League to fame during the 1880s, Charles Stewart Parnell had been acclaimed as the prime hope, "the chief" and "the uncrowned king," of popular Irish nationalism. When he died in 1891, following a divorce scandal and a humiliating political campaign in the midst of a divided Ireland in which his puritanical opponents "flung the lime in his eye," it seemed to Irish nationalists as if all the lights had gone out.

Eilís Dillon's fictional Parnellite in *Across the Bitter Sea*, James Fahy, is listless and unresponsive for months after Parnell's death. As Herbert Howarth shows in his study of the major writers of the Irish Renaissance, Parnell meant different things to different writers in several genres. The loss of "the uncrowned king" was lamented perhaps most memorably in the poetry of Yeats and the autobiographical fiction of Joyce.[40] Nationalist Ireland, it seemed, had lost the darling prince who had inspired Ireland

much as Bonny Prince Charley had earlier kindled the hopes of Scotland. The ballads, in fact, drew that comparison: "Instead of new songs it seems that the Parnellites preferred 'Charley is my Darling' and other old Jacobite praises of the Stuart pretender. All through his last campaign, Charles Stewart Parnell was hailed by 'We'll have no king but Charley.' 'O'Donnell Abú' became 'Parnell Abú'"[41]

The period from 1891 to 1910 following Parnell's death was bleak in Irish politics, much like the years from 1800 to 1820 after the crushing of the 1798 rebellion. In Parliament, Parnell's successors carried the flag of Irish home rule but with few concrete results. However, a second domestic social movement brought home to Irishmen in the cities, especially in Dublin, the message already carried to rural Irishmen by the Land League. The Irish labor movement, led by James Larkin and James Connolly among others, opened the eyes of the Irish working class to the fact that its best interests were served not so much by a campaign against England as by a determined effort to assert itself in the face of the economic ruling class at home.

The culmination of this movement was the Great Transport Strike in Dublin in 1913, when William Martin Murphy, leader of the Employers' Federation, locked out all his union employees for months. James Plunkett recreated this episode in *Strumpet City*. The Irish transport union lost the battle but won the war: the focus of all future attempts for decent wages and working conditions, in a world that even the ultraconservative Arnold Wright in *Disturbed Dublin* described as worse than the slums of Calcutta, would be the union movement. James Larkin went off to work in the American labor movement and returned later to immerse himself in the petty Irish union politics of the free state. As with O'Connell, Larkin is preserved in the popular memory not as the often unsuccessful factionalist of the 1930s but as the titan of 1907 to 1913. Meanwhile, James Connolly stayed home after 1913 to bring the interests of the Irish labor movement to bear on Irish nationalism, believing that socialism and nationalism, in the case of Ireland, were complementary. He became a key leader of the Easter Rising of 1916.

THE LAST GREAT CHAPTER in the story of Irish nationalism is the period from 1916 to 1923, with which so much of recent Irish historical fiction has dealt (particularly O'Flaherty's *Insurrection* and Murdoch's *The Red and the Green*) and which was so pivotal in the development of the pres-

ent state of Ireland. In the case of the Easter Rising of 1916, it is difficult to separate history and myth; several books have dwelt on the relationship between its events and the Irish literary imagination.[42] Three of its seven leaders—Patrick Pearse, Thomas MacDonough, and Joseph Plunkett—were published poets. The two most celebrated leaders of the rising were Pearse and Connolly: Pearse, the idealist, the dreamer, the advocate of an independent, Christian, Gaelic Ireland; Connolly, the practical military man and clear-headed political and social theoretician. By the time of the week-long rising, all of its leaders had come to share not only Pearse's realization that, in terms of military success, it was futile, but also his vision that they would be martyrs to Irish nationalism who would serve to wake up and to inspire a dormant contemporary Ireland.

They were right. Many Dubliners scorned the rebels during the Rising, but after the summary day-by-day executions of fifteen of its leaders, Ireland began to swing in their favor. Beckett notes that George Bernard Shaw warned the British that through the executions they were "canonizing their prisoners" (441). Later ballads celebrated the rebels:

> In Dublin town they fought and died
> With Pearse, McDermott and McBride.
> "Ourselves alone," their battle cry,
> And freedom sang to the Easter sky.
> They were the men with a vision, the men with a cause,
> The men who defied their oppressor's laws,
> The men who traded their chains for guns;
> Born into slav'ry, they were freedom's sons.[43]

After the Easter Rising, the ideal of "we ourselves" was carried by the Sinn Féin movement to an unprecedentedly receptive Ireland. In the general election of 1918 Sinn Féin representatives captured a strong majority of the Irish seats in Parliament and shunned Westminster by meeting in Dublin as Dáil Éireann in January 1919.

The sequel was the Anglo-Irish War of 1919–21, fought viciously between the Irish Republican Army, successor to the IRB and the British irregulars and "Black-and-Tans"—"two largely irresponsible military organizations," Beckett notes, "fighting in circumstances where the normal laws of war could hardly be said to apply, and the main object of each side was to break the morale of the other system of terror—an object that was pursued with increasing ferocity as the war went on." (448) This war was ended only at the cost of a treaty signed between Lloyd George, Michael Collins, and Arthur Griffith in December 1921. The treaty started yet

another war because it allowed the United Kingdom to retain the six counties of Northern Ireland, at the demand of northern Protestant leaders. The Irish Civil War of 1922–23 was remarkable, because for the first time in modern Irish history the conflict at work was no longer Irishman versus Englishman, but Catholic Irishman versus Catholic Irishman: the pro-treaty forces versus the anti-treaty forces. It was the most bitter, divisive period of Irish nationalist history. Families were separated in the civil conflict—a phenomenon explored in Walter Macken's *The Scorching Wind* and Eilís Dillon's *Blood Relations*. The figure of the informer became an object of particular hate. Not many ballads came out of this war, for the old English-Irish polarity was no longer there to be exposed. One of the few ballads of this period pathetically asks for unity:

> Now we are divided, I really don't know why,
> We've a glorious list of martyrs, who for Ireland's cause did die.
> So why not get together and join in unity,
> The North and South, the East and West, and soon we would be free.[44]

W HEN IRELAND EMERGED from the Civil War at the end of 1923, she emerged divided. The pro-treaty leaders, Collins and Griffith, were dead. Eamon De Valera, leader of the anti-treaty forces, was forced into a position of minority antagonist, having lost the election and the war. W. T. Cosgrave became the new head of state, seeking to enact the Irish Free State Constitution of 1922, which allowed the partition of Ireland but which also gained an unprecedented degree of Irish independence. Even though this settlement, in Beckett's words, "inaugurated for Ireland a longer period of general tranquillity than she had known since the first half of the eighteenth century," a great deal of bitterness remained (461). For many Irishmen, the old conflict of Irish versus English had still not been resolved, with Northern Ireland a sectarian state within the United Kingdom.

The period since 1923 has not yet become "history." Historical novelists have not attempted it; they have it still to live through, seeking the past in order to understand their own unresolved present. The year 1923, then, marks a watershed in modern Irish history, as well as in the nationalist mythos, with the old upper hand of the ruling class, for the most part, removed. The nationalist mythos, however, lived on. Irish writers continued to grow up with it, and Irish historical novelists continued to look backward to modern Irish history before 1923 in order to explore the polarities inherent in the Irish experience.

3
Beginnings: *The Banims*

INETEENTH-CENTURY IRISH LITERATURE, especially when contrasted with the great achievements of the Irish Literary Renaissance early in the twentieth century, presents itself to us as a kind of dark age. W. B. Yeats pledged his solidarity with "Davis, Mangan, Ferguson," but he was confident of his own superiority; their efforts pale next to his. Similarly, the nineteenth-century Irish novel seems feeble compared to the achievements of James Joyce, Samuel Beckett, and Flann O'Brien. Daniel Corkery would indict much of nineteenth-century Irish literature as "colonial literature" written by residents of an Irish colony for English publishers and a largely English readership. Unlike English writers, who benefited from long experience of the English literary tradition, Irish writers in the nineteenth century were struggling with a language fairly new to their country. They had no tradition of native literature in English to speak of, and they were hampered by fewer and less reliable historical sources than those enjoyed by twentieth-century writers. Yet their pioneering attempts must be understood if we are to appreciate fully the achievements of their successors.

Critical neglect and even scorn have helped to keep the nineteenth-century novel in the dark. While Joyce, Yeats, and their contemporaries have been published and republished, championed and scrutinized for decades, only recently has some attempt been made to reprint nineteenth-

century Irish novels. The nineteenth-century historical novel has remained in one of the darkest recesses of a generally dark age. Even Thomas Flannagan, author of *The Irish Novelists, 1800–1850,* refers to Irish historical fiction as having "fallen into a merciful oblivion." At the same time that he describes John Banim's *The Boyne Water* as "the best work of its kind since Scott," he implies that the rest is pure pulp: "If we were to judge it by its bulk alone, we would be tempted to say that nineteenth-century Irish fiction was devoted primarily to the production of historical novels, sumptuously bound in green and lavishly decorated with gilt."[1] Patrick Rafroidi writes that among nineteenth-century Irish historical novels:

> La qualité n'est pas à la mesure de la quantité, l'originalité non plus. Ce n'est qu'en de rares occasions que ces romans historiques arrivent à être autre chose sous-produits de Walter Scott.[2]

It seems forgotten that the Irish historical novel did in fact survive the nineteenth century. Twentieth-century novelists such as Francis MacManus, Liam O'Flaherty, and James Plunkett, writing as citizens of an Irish Republic and with the benefit of the experience and example of the Literary Revival, created historical novels that are not colonial, imitating Scott, but truly national, inspired by the example of Yeats, Synge, O'Casey, and their contemporaries. Looking at the Irish historical novel as a continuous national genre allows an understanding of how the nineteenth-century novelists, inspired and overshadowed by Scott, were groping toward a form that would bring the Irish historical experience to life and how their twentieth-century successors, observing the conventions of the genre but departing from strict imitation of Scott, for the most part achieved that form. The work of the Banim brothers foreshadows that development: at many points it is a close imitation of Scott, but occasionally it departs from his influence in order to portray a different, Irish experience, thereby moving toward an originality not fully achieved.

JOHN AND MICHAEL BANIM were the first Irish Catholic novelists. They were also the first to present a broad range of Irish characters true to Irish life. Mark Hawthorne points out that in this respect the Banims represent a historical link between two writers who have tended to overshadow them: Maria Edgeworth, "the Ascendancy lady who brought a little of Ireland

into the English novel," and William Carleton, "the Ulsterman who tried
to write of Ireland as he had known it for an audience that the Banims
in part helped to create."[3] The Banims' dilemma was that they wanted
to write from an Irish point of view in a country where the reading public
was small at the same time that they were trying to sell themselves to
English publishers and to a much larger and very different English audience. Their situation was tenuous because their Irish audience was limited
not only in size but in its degree of social, political, and literary self-
awareness, while English readers had been misled for generations by Irish
stereotypes in their own literature, from Shakespeare to Sheridan. Foreign
to both audiences was the idea that an Irish literary character could be
anything more than *Henry V*'s Macmorris, muttering, "What ish my nation?" Hence the explanatory, educational tone of much of the work of
the "peasant" novelists: John Banim's *The Anglo-Irish of the Nineteenth
Century* and Carleton's *Traits and Stories of the Irish Peasantry* sound
like textbook titles for an "Introduction to Ireland" course for English readers. Edgeworth's *Castle Rackrent* suggested that the passivity of the Irish
peasant was more apparent than real; Thady Quirk is an ironic explosion
of the old stereotype.

It was the historical fiction of the Banims, however, that first opened
up the broad panorama of Irish life to the literary world. It should be
noted, incidentally, that John Banim was not the first Irish historical novelist; that honor must go to James McHenry, author of *The Insurgent Chief*
(1824), about the northern risings of 1798, and *The Hearts of Steel* (1825),
about the Steelboys of the late eighteenth century. W. H. Maxwell in *O'Hara*
(1825), Eyre Evans Crowe in *The Northerns of 1798* (1829), and Matthew
Archdeacon in *Connaught: A Tale of 1798* (1830) also wrote of "the '98."[4]
Banim in *The Boyne Water* (1826), however, was the first Irish novelist
to attempt to understand Irish history by focusing on a major event in
an earlier generation within modern Irish history: the Jacobite-Williamite
war of 1689–91. *The Boyne Water* stood for more than a century as the
most widely acclaimed Irish historical novel — a remarkable achievement,
considering the dark age in which it was written. The Banims also traced
the eighteenth-century Irish national experience, in John's *The Denounced*
(1830) and Michael's *The Croppy* (1828), moving through the Penal Age
to 1798.

John (b. 1798), although younger than Michael (b. 1796), was the
dominant creative force of the two. After graduation from the prestigious
Kilkenny College, he ran off to London to seek his literary fortune. Michael stayed home to tend shop, eventually becoming the postmaster of
Kilkenny and living on to 1864. After a promising beginning, John con-

tracted a spinal disease, was bedridden during the 1830s, and died in 1842. Michael was more cautious about politics than his brother. For example, he expressed to John his fears about the English backlash with which *The Boyne Water* might be met; John went ahead with its publication anyway.

The two were collaborators; each sent his work to the other for editing and published under a shared pseudonym, "The O'Hara Family." John wrote the majority of the "Tales of the O'Hara Family," but *Crohoore of the Bill-Hook* (1825), *The Croppy* (1828), *The Ghost-Hunter and His Family* (1833), *The Mayor of Wind-Gap* (1835), and *The Town of the Cascades* (1864) were all clearly Michael's.[5] Flanagan is oddly alone in his assertion, offered without evidence, that John wrote all of the Banim novels, that Michael was merely a "collaborator" on *The Croppy*, and therefore that "it seems sensible to depart from the usual practice of referring to 'the Banim brothers.'"[6] John Banim's biographer, bibliographer, and other scholars all contradict Flanagan on this point, agreeing that Michael wrote *The Croppy*, as Michael's own preface makes clear.[7]

Perhaps Flanagan's confusion was due partly to the fact that the two brothers shared the same politics. The political position of the Banims has never been made sufficiently clear, even though it is, in fact, quite evident in their lives and work. They were O'Connellites. Their historical novels were written during Daniel O'Connell's great campaign for Catholic Emancipation. John Banim's belief in O'Connell and in Catholic Emancipation was strong enough that he rewrote *The Denounced* so as not to jeopardize the cause. The dark view of the most violent Wexford rebels of 1798 contained in Michael Banim's *The Croppy* was in line with O'Connell's own opinion. Richard Lalor Sheil, an O'Connellite leader, was for John an early mentor, friend, and collaborator on the play *Damon and Pythias*. Another great friend and fellow Irish literary soldier of fortune in London, Gerald Griffin, wrote to Banim after one of O'Connell's mass meetings, and John wrote back:

> You had a treat indeed in seeing the Clare heroes. They have wonderfully raised us in the moral scale, and as far as my feelings go, inspired me with admiration. Indeed the whole attitude of our dear country, is just now gratifying in the highest degree. I have lately been writing to it "Songs for Irish Catholics" (not yet done) which I hope may serve to connect my name with the present glorious struggle and (humbly indeed be it spoken) perhaps do some little good to our cause.[8]

One of these ballads was "The Shamrock and the Lily":

Sir Shamrock, sitting drinking,
  At close of day, at close of day,
Saw Orange Lily, thinking,
  Come by that way, come by that way,
With can in hand he hail'd him,
  And jovial din, and jovial din;
The Lily's drought ne'er fail'd him —
  So he stept in, so he stept in.

They drink and talk. Shamrock has the last word:

"Well — top your glass, Sir Lily,
  Our parting one, our parting one —
A bumper and a tilly,
  To past and gone, to past and gone —
And to the future day, lad,
  That yet may see, that yet may see,
Good humour and fair play, lad,
  'Twixt you and me, 'twixt you and me!"

The ending of this ballad is much like *The Boyne Water's*: Banim beseeches his listener or reader to put aside the old antagonisms of Catholic versus Protestant, Irish versus English, to transcend the past, and to achieve a bright future of a peaceful, unified Ireland. At the same time, he knows that the Catholic must be freed. Another of his ballads is addressed to a priest:

Am I the slave they say,
  Soggarth aroon,
Since you did show the way,
  Soggarth aroon,
Their slave no more to be
  While they would work with me
Ould Ireland's slavery,
  Soggarth aroon?[9]

The O'Connellite position that Catholic Emancipation and Irish freedom must be fought for, but through strictly constitutional, nonviolent means, thoroughly colors all of the Banims' work. The central idea

was that the English must be convinced, through a great educational campaign, to grant these rights to the Irish. Patrick Rafroidi writes that

> les romanciers "paysans," les frères Banim, Gerald Griffin, William Carleton avaient prêché la non-violence à leurs frères, tout en tentant d'expliquer aux Anglais et aux protestants irlandais la responsabilité qu'ils avaient dans le bruit et la fureur contemporains.[10]

The Banims sought not only to entertain but to educate an audience that they knew was mostly English.

John Banim adored Scott; his biographer Patrick Murray reported that "Sir Walter was his ideal of a national novelist."[11] The Banims became the first important Irish historical novelists by seeking to apply in their own work the historical and fictional coherence and form that they found in Scott's work. From Scott, whom he described in a letter to Michael as "the great master-hand of character," John Banim gained an appreciation for the individuality of characters and the wealth of material in rural peasant life. This was John's advice to Michael about characterization, as recorded by Murray:

> Of a dozen characters, each is himself alone. Look about you; bring to mind the persons you have known, call them up before you; select and copy them. Never give a person an action to do, who is not a legible individual. Make that a rule, and I think it ought to be a primary rule with novel writers. (139)

Like the young Scott, the young John Banim loved romances, as Murray observed: "His chiefest pleasure was to steal away from school, and lying under a hedge, or beneath the shelter of a haycock, to pore over some prized volume of 'romance or fairy fable'" (19). He wrote a romance himself at the age of six and took it to a printer to get it published, but was turned down. He finally succeeded seventeen years later, in 1821, when his poem *The Celt's Paradise* was published after Sir Walter Scott himself had praised the manuscript as full of "much beauty of language, with a considerable command of numbers and meters."[12]

That the Banims' chief influence was Scott is no news: critics have pointed that out since the earliest reviews. *The Literary Chronicle and Weekly Review* praised *The Boyne Water* in 1826 as the best thing since *Waverley*, while the *Edinburgh Review* referred to the Banim novels in 1831 as weak imitations of Scott. Father Brown noted in 1919 that *The*

Boyne Water was "closely modelled on Scott." Anna Steger's thesis *John Banim, ein Nachahmer Walter Scotts* (1935) carries the connection too far: she minutely traces novel-to-novel correspondences between Scott and Banim with no mention of the points at which Banim diverges from Scott.[13] In his chapter on Banim in *The Irish Novelists*, Flanagan notes that Banim's close imitation of Scott limited his own achievement. But Banim did struggle, however ineffectually, to break free of the Scottian model, especially with his partisan rather than "passive" hero, who reflects Banim's own commitment to Irish nationalism in contrast to Scott's conservative Unionism.

The Banims do occasionally depart from Scott. They mark the beginning of a tradition that would continue to use the Scottian model, yet increasingly depart from it. Up to a certain point, the Banims' strength comes from Scott: Scott's example suggested what sort of national novel could be achieved for Ireland. Beyond that point, however, the direction in the Irish historical novel that the Banims' work suggests is beyond Scott's influence. The Banims are best at the few points where they go beyond Scott; faltering and weak, where the Scottian model holds them back.

John Banim's *The Boyne Water* (1826) is the first and best of the Banims' historical novels. It is also their longest. John worked furiously upon it from July to December 1825, just after returning to London from three weeks in Ireland visiting Derry, the Boyne, and Kilkenny and having already spent months studying historical accounts of the Jacobite-Williamite war.[14] The novel tells the story of the Protestant brother and sister Robert and Esther Evelyn, who meet and fall in love with the Catholic Eva and Edmund M'Donnell. The two couples wage difficult courtships in the midst of the war. Robert Evelyn is the chief protagonist of the novel; as in John's *The Last Baron of Crana* and Michael's *The Croppy*, a Protestant hero is presented to the Banims' predominantly English readership. The aim is didactic: the Banims want to show their readers that their Protestant heroes' religious and political tolerance is a healthy alternative to bigotry and oppression. Like Robert Morton in *Old Mortality*, Evelyn moderates between opposing fanaticisms in the form of two sectarian extremists: the Protestant, Williamite Reverend-General Walker and the Catholic, Jacobite O'Haggerty. "The same farce, this Christian world over!" exclaims Evelyn.[15] Michael underlined John's didactic intent in the "Introductory Letter" prefacing the novel: "We have unhesitatingly restored to their shape and features all those we have found disguised according to the musty

fanaticism prevailing nearly two centuries ago" (xiv). John deliberately chose not only a Protestant hero for his novel but a title borrowed from the famous Protestant ballad presenting "King Billy"'s version of the Battle of the Boyne; he seeks to tell a new, different, in-depth version of the story of the Boyne, traversing the period from 1685 to 1695.

Robert Evelyn serves Banim thematically, as a voice of moderation between extremes, and structurally, as a convenient link between the different scenes of history as well as between the individual, imaginative world and the political, historical world. Through Evelyn's eyes we see both kings, James and William, as well as Generals Sarsfield and Hamilton. Evelyn's meeting with King James gives the king (and Banim) a chance to present a defense of his abdication of the throne. At this point James summarizes the usefulness of Evelyn as a political (and narrative) link: "Seldom has it chanced that we have been afforded the opportunity of demanding from an enemy, face to face, his reason for hostility" (438). Banim was concerned not to romanticize the characters from public history, writing to Michael that he did not want to make Sarsfield, for example, "a hero of romance"; instead, his fictional heroes and heroines, the Evelyns and M'Donnells, are presented that way. He notes at the opening of the novel that Robert and Esther had in their air "that certain, though indefinable something which proclaims the habits and feelings, if not the birth and lineage, of gentle maidens and gallant cavaliers" (1). These are the characters of romance — noble, flawless, and beautiful.

Banim sets up the double romance and marriage of Robert-Eva and Edmund-Esther in order to explore the political polarities of the time on a personal level. Their lives are invaded by military and social realities: their double wedding is interrupted by Walker, who announces that William has landed at Carrickfergus and takes Robert off to serve in his army. Banim had suggested the unusual nature of the friendship of the Protestant Evelyns and Catholic M'Donnells early in the novel by having them meet in the midst of a tornado. "Increased darkness attended it, and the tumbling and crash of loose rock, again found on its course, showed its unabated power" (41). Only in this otherworldly atmosphere do the Evelyns accept the hospitality of the M'Donnells; as in Scott, entrance to history is gained through the doors of Gothicism. At the same time, Robert's and Esther's warmth and tolerance are contrasted with the flaming bigotry of their aunt and Oliver Whittle, whose closed-mindedness is exposed pointedly to the reader. Banim obviously expects his reader to see through Whittle's narrow-minded disdain for the M'Donnells.

As in Scott, the Evelyns' journey to the M'Donnells takes them from "Lowland" to "Highland," from Belfast to Carrickfergus and Cushin-

doll, with Banim attempting to transfer Scott's topography to Ulster. The highest mountains in Ireland are actually in the south, in Munster, but Banim sends his hero north, like Waverley, to the Highlands of Antrim. The Scottian interaction of setting and atmosphere with character, plot, and theme is central to *The Boyne Water*. Banim follows his tornado with the introduction of the Gaelic otherworld in the person of Onagh:

> In turning upon the glen-road, the travellers were leaving to their right these caves, and a little behind them, when a voice was heard in that from which the light appeared, speaking loudly and dictatorially, but in a language unknown to the strangers of the party. Immediately after, the light increased in the mouth of the excavation; finally a woman approached from the entrance, with a piece of flaming wood in her hand, continuing to speak, and now evidently addressing the group. (49)

Onagh lays a curse upon them —"Starve!" — to which she later adds a prophecy about Esther, as she is jealous of Evelyn's love for her: "The bridal robe is nearly made. So is the shroud, though not so nearly" (161).

The presentation of Onagh, with all of her ranting and raving, assumes Gothic proportions in the novel. She forces Esther to repeat a spell, which conjures up the figure of Edmund, who is by now off fighting with the Jacobite forces, and then replaces it with a more frightening visage:

> "His face was pale, and his figure wasted. After he passed, there was another motion in the dark, as if he would cross the cavern again. When I again looked, my eyes met — instead of him — death, Eva, death!" (165)

Evelyn has a similarly Gothic vision, in the form of a dream, of his marriage to Eva:

> He dreamt that he was married to Eva; that he had entered the bridal chamber, and just pressed the bridal couch, when a skein was plunged into his breast. For a moment he felt the agonies of mortal pain, and lay, choked with suffering, unable to cry out: then the sound of a trumpet pierced his ears, and a figure, vaguely like his dead father, stood by his bedside, shaking his arm, and calling on him to rouse up. He awoke in terror, to see a person really standing over him, and holding a feeble lamp in one hand, while the other rested on his shoulder. He looked again, in some alarm, and recognized the pale, grave, and expressive features of Walker. (144)

Onagh's prophecy and Evelyn's dream accurately foretell the damage that history does to marriage in the novel: Walker separates the lovers; marriage is fractured by politics.

Onagh embodies the Gaelic/Gothic otherworld in *The Boyne Water*. Banim makes it clear that she and the other Gaels in the book speak in another language and from another culture. He continually notes that their dialogue "is translated from the Gaelic," until he finally grows impatient with the notation: "M'Donnell continued to speak in Irish, which, as usual, was rendered for the strangers, and this shall be our last notice of the fact" (70). It is not his "last notice." Banim's use of dialect is scrupulous but awkward.

The use of opposed dialects in *The Boyne Water*, standard English versus various varieties of Anglo-Irish speech and translations from the Gaelic, reinforces the social polarities in the novel, as does the contrast of standard English, English Scots dialect, and Gaelic translations in the Waverley novels. Banim's biographer fails to comment on the extent of his knowledge of Irish Gaelic, but Banim's meticulous attention to the footnoting of his "Gaelicisms" in *The Boyne Water* indicates that he must have had a working knowledge of the language, though a few of his translations are shaky enough to suggest that he was no native speaker.[16]

When the Evelyns travel north into the Gaelic otherworld, Banim sets up an outsider's point of view, one which he himself shared. The middle-class, English-speaking Banim speaks from a world dominated by genteel, English-speaking heroes and heroines. The peasant mercenaries Rory-na-Chopple and Galloping Hogan do not belong to this world. Characters such as these are reminiscent of many of Scott's vivid "fringe" characters. Moya Laherty and Carolan love Robert and Eva, respectively, but these Gaelic peasants cannot match their loved ones' status and their love is not reciprocated. When Moya finally makes her overture and Robert turns her down (369), Moya's rural, peasant Anglo-Irish speech is contrasted with Robert's educated, genteel standard English, setting the two of them off sharply from each other on the page and underscoring their different social status. The Anglo-Irish dialects presented by Banim exemplify the typical nineteenth-century pastiche, not much bettered (except perhaps in William Carleton's best works) until John Synge.

Mark Hawthorne argues that the Banims' novels are "balanced between the ancient oral tradition of the Gaelic culture and the realism of the English novel," noting that they were writing at a time when "folklore, not literature, was the moving force of the native tradition."[17] In *The Boyne Water*, Banim records from the mouth of Carolan, the famous blind harpist, the story of "conloach-mac-Cuchullin" (76–79) in which

Cúchulainn kills his own son in hand-to-hand combat, ignorant of his identity.[18] Lady Gregory's version of this story later inspired Yeats's Cúchulain plays. Banim uses the story, which embodies a common motif in European folklore, to foreshadow the "foreboding" subsequently felt by Evelyn and Edmund "that their relation to each other might be affected by the disruption of the times — by the disseverance of parties" (135). Later, not recognizing each other in uniform, Evelyn and Edmund nearly kill each other. We move from "They were together, and they loved; that is our syllogism!" (91) to "Now the spirit of exclusion, nay, of extermination, is busy again; we are once more marked out and proscribed" (168).

Thomas Flanagan writes that Banim "saw Scott's cavaliers as bearing a rough equivalence to the Norman Irish of the Pale, and his roundheads to the Ulster Presbyterians, and his highland chieftains to the 'old' Irish."[19] It turns out that the M'Donnells are actually Scots-Irish. In the history of the clan which he relates to Evelyn, Edmund states that they are descendants of a Scottish chieftain (67), although in the present conflict they insist that they are "'Irish . . . and, as poor Eva says, to the last drop of blood within us. If, indeed, our first derivation was from Scotland, the memory of it has passed away. This'—stamping his foot on the ground—'this is our native land'" (74). By setting his story predominantly in County Antrim in the extreme north of Ireland, only twenty miles at one point from the coast of Scotland, Banim enabled himself to draw not only upon his own knowledge of the speech and culture of the area but upon the model of Scottish speech and culture already laid down by Scott.

Both the English and Irish Gaelic dialects spoken in Northern Ireland were and are, in fact, closer in many ways to their Scottish equivalents than they are to the dialects of southern and western Ireland. The term *Gaelic*, whose use sometimes tends to confuse the fairly different Celtic languages of Ireland and Scotland, is actually accurate in this case, for the Gaelic phrases recorded in anglicized form in *The Boyne Water* are drawn from nineteenth-century Antrim Gaelic speech, a dialect as close in many ways to Scottish Gaelic as it is to the Gaelic of Connacht or Munster.[20] Flanagan's assessment of Banim as an imitator of Scott is somewhat misleading, for if it is true, as he writes, that "much of the machinery of *The Boyne Water* has been lifted bodily from *Waverley*"[21] and that Banim imitates Scott's use of language and presentation of culture, it is also clear that the imitation does not distort his Irish materials, for Banim and Scott were writing about two very similar cultures. Where Banim does go wrong, Scott has often preceded him with a similar error. For example, the names *Edmund* and *Eva* can hardly be said to be Gaelic and

were undoubtedly grafted onto the story in order to propitiate English readers. Similarly, many of Scott's names are only pseudo-Gaelic: the Mucklewraths and all the rest. Neither writer achieves linguistic precision. Both do manage to make a traditional culture accessible and understandable, conveying its flavor to a wider audience, while at the same time letting it retain its dignity and its distinctness.

Banim departs from Scott in his presentation of his hero: the formerly passive Evelyn moves toward partisanship. Searching for Eva, who serves the Jacobite cause, Evelyn spends as much time with the Jacobites as with his own Williamite army, traveling as a noncombatant with Sarsfield from Dublin to Limerick, where the final Williamite victory occurs. Evelyn recognizes the rightness of the Catholic cause. The Protestant hero is taught the Catholic point of view — just as Banim seeks to educate his readers. By the end of Banim's very long story, Esther, trapped by Walker in the siege of Derry, has died from sheer anxiety and from the starvation forecast by Onagh; Edmund is exiled to France; and Evelyn, reunited at last with Eva, remains in Ireland brooding over the vagaries of Irish politics. Evelyn may have exhibited earlier the anxieties of the passive hero and some of the indecision of a Waverley, but by the end he has become very clear about the course of Irish politics; he has become a partisan. Sarsfield, in signing the Treaty of Limerick, has tried to conclude an honorable peace which would preserve the dignity of the Catholic cause, but he is quickly betrayed by the English Parliament. With the Penal Age beginning, Evelyn writes to Edmund:

> In the great country of England, there must also arise a feeling to right the present wrong to which it has just lent itself. For, without her affirmation, the wrong could not have been committed. The descendants of the men who have sanctioned, and by that means caused the deliberate breach of their own treaty, made in the field, will awake to vindicate, as far as in them lies, the name of their ancestors. A son, jealous of his father's honor, pays his father's debts, even to a common creditor. Englishmen will yet pay their fathers' debt of faith to Ireland. The treaty of Limerick will yet be kept. (552–53)

Writing in 1826, in the middle of the fight for Catholic Emancipation, Banim provides a clear moral to his story. As an O'Connellite and a literary spokesman for English-speaking and bilingual Catholics as well as the rising class of Irish tradesmen, Banim sought to draw a clear connection between the Jacobite-Williamite war and the struggles of his own day in order to argue that the old sociopolitical polarities had still not

been resolved, that the Treaty of Limerick had not been kept, and that Catholic Emancipation would finally enforce it. "IT WAS NOT" (550) a happy country, he tells us. The present intrudes upon the past at several points in Banim's narrative, as when he comments upon how the Derry city gate changed in appearance after 1690 (311); cumulatively, the suggestion is that there is a definite connection between the past and the present. Banim's Jacobite Ireland is viewed from his own nineteenth-century O'Connellite perspective.

The Boyne Water does not grant the happy ending of a Scott novel; it is the only one of the Banim's historical novels that does not. This feature, along with its thoroughgoing faithfulness to local ways and to history and its sheer energy, marks its superiority to the nineteenth-century novels that followed it. The Evelyns and the M'Donnells begin as heroes and heroines of romance, but they end as realistic characters. Robert, Eva, and Edmund are survivors of a tragic chapter of Irish nationalist history. Esther does not even survive. Banim is weakest at the points where he allows his imitation of Scott to deprive himself of originality and where he permits his zealous desire to present a balanced view of history to obscure his own position. Robert Evelyn is palest where he reads like Edward Waverley traversing the Irish countryside and most interesting where he replaces wavering with commitment. Rather than return from Irish "Highland" to Irish "Lowland" as a moderate, Evelyn remains in Ireland, convinced of the rightness of the Catholic cause.

Banim, of course, saw his own position as a moderate if partisan one. As he wrote to Michael, "Englishmen of almost every party, who may honour our book with a perusal, are now prepared to recognize the truth of the historical portraits we sketch and allude to" (xi). Yet he weakens his own artistic and political statement by seeking always to sweeten the bitter pill of Irish nationalism for his English audience. Cautious in his nationalism, he is unable to throw off caution and to show Irish history as the nightmare that it was. He cannot fully transcend romance and reach tragedy; of course, neither could any other nineteenth-century Irish historical novelist.

JOHN BANIM's political commitment to Catholic Emancipation ennobled The Boyne Water, but his fear of jeopardizing the cause emasculated The Last Baron of Crana and The Conformists, two novels published in 1830 under a single title, The Denounced (whose adjective may be taken to

apply to the unfortunate Catholics of the Penal Age). John had completed a draft of *The Denounced* by the summer of 1829, but after the passage of Catholic Emancipation in that year, he carefully revised his tales before he allowed them to be published the next year. The historical context and Banim's reaction to it are very significant. *The Boyne Water* was written and published relatively early during the Catholic Emancipation campaign, when Daniel O'Connell was busy whipping up the fury of Irishmen and the sympathy of liberal Englishmen; Banim wrote *The Boyne Water* in this O'Connellite spirit. *The Denounced*, on the other hand, was written when Catholic Emancipation was in its most sensitive stage of negotiation before Parliament. Not wanting to endanger the act, Banim pulled his political punches. By the time he had finished the first draft of his book, the Emancipation Act had been passed, and Banim was concerned not to reopen any old wounds of the Protestant-Catholic, English-Irish battle.

In his preface, dedicated to "Sir Arthur, Duke of Wellington," he wrote:

A new apprehension troubled us. . . . It would not be difficult, we thought, in the changed aspect of affairs, to apply to the allusions spoken of as necessarily existing in our pages, such criticism as —"continuing prejudices," "opening wounds afresh," &c. We answer by anticipation, that if we believed these tales calculated to wound a single generous feeling, or to fix a single prejudice we would destroy them rather than publish them. To guard against any such chance, after the late great decision, we carefully and anxiously reviewed them, remodelled them,— in fact, rewrote them, (and therefore they come tardily before the public.) Supposing our endeavours not to have proved literally successful, let the will be taken for the deed, and let our good friend (imagined) only point out a passage hostile to peace among all men, and that passage shall be expunged.[22]

Writing in the first full flush of the Catholic Emancipation victory, too early still to realize that the realities of Catholic Emancipation would not equal its promise, Banim felt that liberty was won, that "the musty folios of penal enactment have become so much lumber."

If, however, our stories are to be read with any feeling except that of reading a story, such feeling, in the breast of The Lately-Made-Free, will surely amount to no more than gratitude to God and to Man for his own escape from the shackles worn by his forefathers; and in the breast of the reader who still honestly disapproves of the slave's enfranchise-

ment, perhaps a glance over the old rusty chain of legal disability, may help to banish even his regret that he has lived to see broken its last festering links. (vii–viii)

He seemed unaware that for the forty-shilling holder a ten-pound voting franchise did not banish political slavery at all and that Irishmen would continue to struggle with political and economic bondage for another century or more. By 1833, Murray records, John would write to Michael, "We have given perhaps too much of the dark side of the Irish character; let us, for the present, treat of the amiable; enough of it is around us" (279).

Banim's reaction to Catholic Emancipation was not the only debilitating factor in the composition of *The Denounced*, for he was sick and hard put for cash during this time. Murray writes that the book was

> put together hurriedly; while sickness was a frequent visitant, while the working mental power was available only at . . . desultory intervals, and while compulsive inactivity, and the inevitable heavy outlay consequent on illness, together with the constant change of residence, in search of the health that was not to return, were causing at the same time a necessity for funds, and an incapacity to create them (209).

Floored by a spinal disease, Banim was unable to carry out the kind of in-depth historical research with which he had prepared for *The Boyne Water;* visits to historical sites in Ireland were impossible.

Falling short of true historicity, Banim retreated to romance and melodrama. His use of local settings, dialects, and traditions greatly lessened. *The Last Baron of Crana* is set rather vaguely in the north of Ireland and around Limerick; *The Conformists*, in a single southern townland, perhaps Kilkenny, although this is never specified. The meticulous footnotes to Irish and Anglo-Irish speech that peppered *The Boyne Water* drop out of *The Last Baron* and *The Conformists* almost entirely. The happy endings of these novels, given the nightmarish Penal Age with which they are concerned, seem unconvincing—contrived merely to please author and reader. *The Boyne Water* manages to present a realism emerging even out of romantic trappings, as the heroes and heroines of romance learn realistic lessons about survival. In contrast, *The Last Baron* and *The Conformists* impose romantic resolutions upon the unpleasant scenario of eighteenth-century Irish history.

The Last Baron of Crana is a tale of chivalry. As in *The Boyne Water*, the hero is a Protestant, Miles Pendergast. Fighting in the Battle

of Aughrim in 1691, Pendergast promises his dying Catholic foe Redmond O'Burke that he will adopt his son, Patrick. *The Last Baron* is thus doomed to implausibility from the very beginning. Banim fails to achieve the integration of public history and personal fiction that distinguishes *The Boyne Water*. He follows Pendergast's promise to O'Burke with a somewhat intrusive account of the specifics of the Treaty of Limerick, self-consciously citing "*Smollett, Continuation of Hume*, chapter iii section 12" (1:29). Always the educator, Banim seems almost painfully defensive about his attempts at historicity:

> In these pages, as well as in others which the writers have submitted to their readers, an endeavour has been made to guard against prejudices of country and creed, while alluding to historical events necessarily bearing upon the task in hand. Upon former occasions, whenever the words of a neutral, or even an adverse historian could be found to convey, briefly, the information required, he has spoken to the reader — and oftener, perhaps, than some readers gave him or his transcribers credit for. (1: 120–21)

The Last Baron follows the story of Miles Pendergast and Patrick O'Burke from 1691 into the early years of the eighteenth century. Miles adopts young Patrick and takes him north, where they both suffer the harsh treatment of John Gernon, a vicious Protestant demagogue. Later they retreat to the Limerick estate of Philip Walshe, the Baron of Crana, where Patrick falls in love with Lady Dorcas. Miles, Patrick, and Lady Dorcas live cheerfully ever after upon a newly purchased estate. The plot is built upon melodramatic questions of identity: Is Gernon really who he seems to be? Is the mysterious Sir Randal Oge O'Hagan, the roaming rapparee, actually Roger Walshe, Philip's brother, the lost "Last Baron of Crana"? Who is the true father of the homeless Louise Danville, lately come from France? Is it Roger? Will all of these characters achieve happiness? The answer to all of these questions, of course, is "yes."

The best character in *The Last Baron* is none of these, but rather John Sharpe, Miles Pendergast's servant. Sharpe is a Protestant bigot, much like Oliver Whittle in *The Boyne Water*. His earthly views balance the almost mindless, implausible tolerance of the Protestant Pendergast, who gladly raises Patrick as a Catholic, risking his own life by bringing along the outlawed Father James to do the teaching. In contrast, Sharpe disdains "Papists," reporting that his horse, "George Walker" (named after the Protestant hero of Derry), refuses to transport them, and he carries on constant verbal combat with Rory Laherty, Patrick's Catholic servant. Banim

uses Sharpe and Laherty as a study in cultural contrast; as always, he takes pains to present Protestant and Catholic sectarianisms as polarized, mirror-image delusions. Rory "thought John Sharpe as great a blockhead as John Sharpe thought Rory Laherty."

> Nay, they hated and despised each other with equal force on both sides, although each made the egotistical mistake of imagining that it was impossible his companion could respond his sentiments; or, it should rather be said, such an idea never entered into the head of either. Their mutual oversight, as well as their mutual rancour, sprang from their ignorance. Had Rory thought less uncharitably, and more justly, of the heresy of Protestantism; and had John Sharpe known an iota of Rory's creed, they would have proved better friends: and again, had they previously observed the different manners in which subdued, though strongly-felt sentiments were indicated in their different communities — that is, had John had opportunities of studying the Roman Catholic people of the South, and Rory the Protestant people of the North (than whom scarce any two of the nations of the earth can differ more widely,) John's sententiousness and sober gruffness would not have seemed stupidity to his entertainer, nor Rory's garrulity and vivacious energy, something of the same kind to the entertained person; at the same time, that neither manner could have long hidden the mental reserves which both were now so successful in disguising. Such are the mistakes occasioned by not knowing the world. (1: 71-2)

Unlike Oliver Whittle, Sharpe does modify his views; he gets educated beyond simple bigotry. He defends Patrick against the brutal Gernon, becoming a hero in his own right: "Then hear what I tell you, Johnny Gernon — as sure as you, or any mon for ye, does this injustice, in the name o' Protestanteesm, so sure I, John Sharpe, will forswear ye a', root and branch, and go til the mass-house, itsel, with Master Patrick, the next sabbath at morn" (1: 235). While overcoming simple bigotry, Sharpe maintains his preferences. For example, when they return south, Rory is overjoyed to be able once again to speak Irish "as fluently as gushes a long pent-up river, to almost every person he met on the road," while Sharpe still thinks it "a manner of speech not becoming to pigs" (2: 3). Sharpe is a delightful exception to the generally black-and-white characterizations in *The Last Baron*, a romance that for the most part opposes pure evil (Gernon) and pure good (Pendergast, Patrick, Lady Dorcas).

The only other ambiguities of character come with the novel's outlaws. Roger, the rapparee, and Father James, the hunted priest, are presented as somewhat lurid in their outlawry. Father James is pathetic and

insane. Outlawed by the Penal Code, he conducts bizarre Gothic services in a cave. Roger, although a good Robin Hood, has lost his nobility by becoming a rapparee. Not quite the knight in shining armor that Carleton's Redmond O'Hanlon is, Banim's rapparee is introduced as a "notorious freebooter" (1: 186). He doesn't fit Banim's nonviolent O'Connellite code, even though he's on the right side.

The Conformists is better than The Last Baron of Crana. Here at last Banim's protagonist, Daniel D'Arcy, is a Catholic, and the social world of the novel is entirely Banim's own world: southern, Catholic, middle-class Ireland. The Conformists could have been a great novel rather than merely an interesting one. The subject is an important one, but Banim's treatment of it does not live up to its potential. Set during the 1750s, the novel explores conformism – Catholic conversion to Protestantism in order to escape the Penal Code and achieve prosperity – a phenomenon that divided many Catholic families during the Penal Age. There is a suggestion of Cain and Abel to the story of the brothers Daniel and Marks D'Arcy. Their father, Hugh D'Arcy, had unexpectedly inherited from his conformist uncle a modest fortune with which he had bought an estate in 1703. Dan, haunted by sin, impelled by acquisitiveness, and frustrated by the greater parental favor enjoyed by Marks, finally conforms and seeks to disown the rest of his family. He is the black sheep of the family and Marks is the fair-haired darling, yet the story is told from Dan's point of view. His gradually building resentment of his brother and inarticulate rage over his own position (defiantly plowing the fields of the Red House farm) are graphically portrayed in a way that looks forward to the motifs in Irish fiction of the white-haired boy and sibling rivalry. In his frustrated desire to do something with his hands, Dan is something like Farrington in Joyce's story "Counterparts." Unlike Farrington, however, and unlike Cain, Dan repents, at the last moment repudiating his conversion, which he has been talked into by the evil lawyer and conformist Micky Doolly. At the end Dan restores his family to their home.

Like The Last Baron, The Conformists jolts to a stop, in the happy ending of romance, a happy ending that deflates the novel. Micky Doolly gets hauled in by the magistrate, with evidence against him from his own wife. He ends up getting caught by a delicious technicality of his own invocation, like Shylock by Portia: evidence from a wife is inadmissible, but since they're not legally man and wife, as Mrs. Doolly never converted from Catholicism, her evidence is valid and their marriage invalid under the Penal Code. And since Micky "married" a Papist, he is, according to another statute, one himself, and thus disbarred. "And now, listen –

scoundrel! According to the letter of the law you would inflict, shall you be dealt with!" (3: 286). Saved from Doolly, Dan and Marks face each other:

> "But I can never forgive myself, Marks dear," he said. "I won't let you, Dan, my boy," replied Marks, "until you say something for me to Helen, in return for what I said to Dora, for you when she was so vexed with you, last night."
> THE END. (3: 292)

We are left with their double wedding about to occur, as at the end of the traditional romance.

The happy ending seems an empty escape in view of what the novel's most recent editor describes as "the grinding injustice of the times" (1: xli). Banim shows in *The Conformists* that he was well schooled about this injustice. We shall probably never know how much of this perception he edited out of the final, published version. The first question Marks asks when he returns home from school in Spain is about the absence of horses, which he was accustomed to riding in Spain but which Irish Catholics are prohibited by statute from owning if worth more than five pounds apiece. History, in the form of Dan's near conversion, nearly destroys the D'Arcy family, but generally history is incidental; the focus is on Dan's character and development. Most of the novel is a long flashback to the time before Marks's return from Spain, delineating the failure of Dan to match his brother's success in his studies and his degeneration, occurring mostly in the Gothic dark and the wrong company. Dan gets caught by his parents in a bog hole with Jinny Haggerty (worth noting since sex is a rarity, to say the least, in the Banims' works), leaves home to make his own way with his own hands on a farm, falls in love with Dora Donovan but feels unworthy of her, and is tempted to convert. Banim hints that he is aware of the escapist nature of some aspects of his story. After describing the sunset scene in which Dan and Dora declare their love, he notes, like author speaking to narrator, "'Romance.' Well, serious Sir. Attend to plainer facts" (3: 64). Thus is "Romance" undercut.

When public history does enter Dan's story, Banim seems apologetic about it:

> It is regretted that the complexion of the time of the story unavoidably forces into notice another allusion to penal enactment. This would be avoided, if possible; but so domesticated, we may say, was the statute-

book of former days, at the very fire-sides of the Irish people; so literally
was it the text from which they read every thing they were permitted
to do; and so fully and minutely did it command their feelings, their
passions, their hopes, and their prospects, that in rehearsing, as in the
present instance, the fortunes of persons living under its sway, fact and
nature must be departed from, if they be said to have taken one important step independent of it. (3: 33–34)

Rather than apologizing for this perception, Banim should have been constantly exploring it. Instead, we are lost once again in melodrama and
questions of identity: Who are the mysterious man in gray and the dark
woman who try to turn Dan and Dora from each other? Will Jinny and
Dinny Haggerty succeed in their plot against the lovers? Jinny loves Dan
but can't have him, like Moya Laherty in *The Boyne Water*; once again,
Banim portrays his peasants as unworthy of his middle-class protagonists.
The focus on Dan as dark protagonist in a dark age of Irish history is
effective and appropriate, but the end of the novel escapes that dark age
too easily. Like Patrick O'Burke and Miles Pendergast, Dan D'Arcy is finally
not "denounced" at all, even though the Penal Age threatened that fate.
Instead, Banim lets his heroes off the hook: they escape the nightmare
of Irish history and flee into the fairyland world of marriage, property,
and progress.

JOHN BANIM had written to Michael in August 1825, "I think I shall write
one of your volumes after all. A thing connected with R. Emmet's insurrection."[23] He never did. Instead, Murray records that Michael, describing
himself as "the stay-at-home member of the family," directed all of his "lei-
sure hours" during 1826 and 1827 "to the composition of a three-volume
novel . . . 'The Croppy'" (191). Writing of the events of 1798, which were
still virulently alive in the public mind, Michael, always the more cautious
of two cautious brothers, wanted to be as impartial as possible about his
subject, fearing a negative reaction from the reading public. After reading
Michael's manuscript, John reassured him in a letter cited by Murray: "Your
anticipations of failure, though they did not convince, put me on my guard
against deciding too partially, and precisely, as I felt, I now candidly as-
sure you, that I think you need not apprehend failure in this your trial"
(192). He was right: the British press reviewed *The Croppy* favorably following its publication in 1828. The reviewer for *The Scotsman* wrote: "This

novel will be much read. Its great topic—the policy of England towards Ireland—the question, what ought now to be done with the Irish Catholics? is uppermost at present in the public mind." In particular he commended Banim's treatment of English and Irish feelings, praising "the manner in which they are dealt with, involving the quiet and prosperity of an empire."[24]

The view of Wexford in 1798 that emerges from The Croppy — that the rising was planned with high idealism by United Irish leaders but degenerated into a bitter, bloody sectarian war that failed to live up to their ideals—is an O'Connellite one. Both Daniel O'Connell and the English Parliament would have agreed with Michael Banim's condemnation of the sectarian leaders. However, Banim takes care to show how Wexford Catholics were goaded by their rulers into violence. He does this quite directly and didactically, attaching both an introductory historical chapter and (in a later edition) a set of historical notes as an epilogue to the novel. In his introductory chapter he explains how the United Irishmen evolved and argues that Catholics rebelled in Wexford because they had no other option; they were pushed to it. He attempts to show that the ideal of an Ireland united across religious lines—high principled, inspired by the French Revolution, and based in the north—became in the south a religious war of Catholic against Protestant, motivated by sectarian hatred. To the Catholic peasant, he argues, "Protestant and Orangeman became, in his mind, synonymous words. And in this delusion he caught up his rude and formidable pike, when, without time afforded him to reflect, he was precipitated, by United Irish emissaries on the one hand, and by monstrous and wanton outrage on the other, into the mêlée of civil strife."[25] In his "Notes" he adds that "the baneful feeling created was contemplated, if not encouraged, as a game to result to the advantage of the state" (431).

Writing less than three decades after 1798 in Kilkenny, just across the border from Wexford, Michael Banim noted that he "could learn from those who spoke of the year 1798 from personal experience" (421). Even though Wexford in 1798 was much more immediate to Michael than Antrim in 1685 was to John, Michael prepared himself for The Croppy with extensive historical research, as John had done for The Boyne Water. One of the problems with The Croppy, in fact, is that its author seems unable to decide whether he is historian or novelist. History is fairly well integrated in The Boyne Water; it intrudes in The Croppy. The long historical chapter that opens the novel seems an imposition. Like Scott's "Introductory Chapter" in Waverley, Banim's first chapter is really more a preface. He recognized this problem himself, writing in his "Notes" to the novel:

The historical introductory chapter to the Croppy was much more dif-
fuse, when I sent the tale to my brother, than it is at present; too length-
ened, in fact, for the place it was to hold. Of this I was conscious myself,
and I requested Barnes O'Hara to use his pruning-knife at discretion.
With this request of mine he complied quite to my satisfaction. On re-
reading, I am inclined to think it is even yet too long. Some such introduction was, however necessary, and my conscience tells me, that the
chapter is historically accurate. (n.p.)

The true beginning of the novel, chapter 2, opens with a description of
Wexford at peace: "The summer sun was slanting his evening rays over
the picturesquely winding Slaney. . . ." (11). Immediately we meet Eliza
Hartley, "our heroine," "pensively" trying to decide whom she loves. Her
love story dominates the next several chapters of the novel. We do not
return to public history until chapter 6, at which point the violence of
the outside world intrudes into Eliza's consciousness and the reader's.

The reader is left somewhat confused about whether *The Croppy*
is history or romance because of Banim's inability to integrate the two.
Curiously enough, Banim seems clearer and more committed as historian
than as novelist. His historical introduction and epilogue do not advocate,
but they do explain, the rebel position, by noting its historical causes.
The novel itself presents no such defense. In his story Banim seems to
go out of his way to placate his English readers. All of his major "good"
characters — Eliza Hartley, her father, Sir Thomas Hartley, and Harry
Talbot — are Protestants. The ultimate, deus-ex-machina hero is Harry Talbot, leader of a government platoon that helps to crush the rebellion. Harry
marries Eliza after finally exposing to her the villainy of her other suitor,
Sir William Judkin, a United Irish leader. The triangle of noble father (Sir
Thomas), virtuous daughter (Eliza), and courageous, heroic suitor (Talbot) is one that recurs in the Irish historical novel, specifically in Le Fanu's
Torlogh O'Brien and Buckley's *Croppies Lie Down*.

The plot of *The Croppy* revolves around a Gothic web, a melodramatic labyrinth, of unlikely occurrences. In the last two of these, Talbot appears with Eliza's father, whom she had thought Talbot had executed as a United Irish leader, and Judkin is discovered, in a thoroughly
Gothic scene, dying over the coffin of his bastard child by Eliza's friend
Belinda. The moral positions of Talbot, Judkin, and Belinda are reversed.
Throughout most of the novel, Talbot seems both to Eliza and to the reader
to be the villain; he turns out to be the hero. Judkin seems to be the hero;
he is actually the villain. Belinda, initially presented as Eliza's trusted con-
fidante, is revealed as a macabre witch. These are Banim's attempts at ex-

citing, melodramatic, Scottian plot reversals. Unfortunately, the involutions that end *The Croppy* are unconvincing. Reader sympathies sought throughout the novel are gratuitously contradicted at the end. Furthermore, the main plot has essentially nothing to do with history. Love story and history do not achieve the unity that they do in *The Boyne Water.* Like *The Last Baron of Crana, The Croppy* is a romance imposed on history rather than integrated with it.

The most interesting characters in *The Croppy* are minor ones. Beneath the implausible romance that dominates the novel is a more realistic, more interesting underworld of characters and events. Shawn-a-Gow, the blacksmith, sees his innocent son killed before his eyes by government soldiers and busies himself forging pikes for the rebels. Equally interesting are Nanny the Knitter, the old woman who makes a profession of matchmaking for money, and Rattling Bill Nale, a spy who plays both sides for profit. Father Rourke, whose corpse on the gallows is the final image of the novel, whips up Catholic sectarian passions by quoting a supposed Protestant oath to bathe in Catholic blood, which is the same oath that Protestant leaders attribute to the Catholics. Characters such as these are brought to life, as in *The Boyne Water,* by the use of dialect and faithfulness to local tradition. Several of them are based upon history or personal experience: Shawn-a-Gow and Rattling Bill, upon people Banim knew about in Kilkenny; Sir Thomas Hartley, upon Bagenal Harvey, the United Irish leader who eschewed sectarian rebellion but was executed anyway; and Father Rourke, upon Father Philip Roche, the Catholic leader who was hung for his role in the rebellion.[26]

Banim is at his best when he shows how characters like these were affected by the realities of sectarian war. This message, however, is obscured by Banim's melodramatic main plot. Only at the end of *The Croppy* does he return to the realistic, didactic, nationalist intent with which he had begun his story:

> The storm of insurrection blew away: not so its effects. The people saw their error, and politicians hastened to grasp the advantages which that error placed under their hands. Blood continued to be shed some time after the total discomfiture of the peasant-force, but at last its flow was allowed to cease. In the pause of terror, with a show of conciliation and a promise of advantages which have not yet been conceded, the Legislative Union,— that measure for which disaffection had been permitted to break out into actual disloyalty, nay, had often been goaded to the field, — the Legislative Union between England and Ireland was accomplished. (419)

Analogously, it might be said that the Banims' achievement was a passing one, but not so their influence. Their attempt to present Irish history realistically often got lost in the shadow of romance which they thought was Scott's, but they were remembered as pioneers of the Irish historical novel. *The Boyne Water*, in particular, was admired and imitated. In *Torlogh O'Brien*, Sheridan Le Fanu modelled himself on John Banim as well as Scott. As we shall see, both Le Fanu and Carleton eulogized Banim. Later still, Yeats pointed to the link between the Banims and Carleton in his assertion that the Banims were Carleton's "equals in gloomy and tragic power" and that all three "saw the whole of everything they looked at . . . the brutal with the tender, the coarse with the refined."[27] The future direction of the Irish historical novel was one suggested, if not fully achieved, by John Banim and *The Boyne Water*: an adherence to many of the conventions introduced by Scott but at the same time a departure from Scott's passive hero and happy ending in favor of a partisan, Irish nationalist hero and a scenario that became increasingly *un*happy, eventually leading to darker, more realistic endings. These beginnings represent the Banims' legacy.

4
Retreat to History: *Sheridan Le Fanu and*
William Carleton

THE BANIMS' historical novels were followed between 1830 and 1865 by a series of attempts by a wide variety of Irish writers to emulate the example of Walter Scott and John Banim. The word that must dominate any attempt to describe these novels has already been met in Scott and Banim: *romance.* During the mid-nineteenth century, Irish historical novelists, participating in a cult of antiquarianism, chivalry, and heroism, focused on the periods in Irish history that seemed to hold out these ideals and thus lend themselves to the genre. Following a vision much more romantic than realistic, they tended to seek out remote rather than recent history, attempting to escape from their own dreary historical time to a seemingly nobler, more heroic age. Gerald Griffin, for example, returned to the coming of the Danes in *The Invasion* (1832), written in turgid, archaic language that presents a methodical examination of the time.[1]

Even those authors who wrote about more modern history seemed most interested in seeing it as exemplary of chivalry and heroism; each tended to focus on a dominant, chivalric hero. A brief chronological parade of these novels serves to underscore this emphasis on romantic heroism: Charlotte Elizabeth's *Derry: A Tale of the Revolution* (1839) tells the story of the Siege of Derry; Samuel Lover's *Treasure Trove; or, He Would Be a Gentleman* (1844) narrates the adventures of a member of the

eighteenth-century Irish Brigade in France and Scotland; Charles Lever's hero in *The O'Donoghue* (1845) is a Catholic noble during the time of the French expedition to Bantry in 1796; James French's *Clongibbon; or, The White Knight of the Forest* (1845) is a chivalric romance advancing a Catholic point of view on some of the pre-Cromwellian risings in the south; W. J. Daunt's *Hugh Talbot* (1846) presents the Protestant confiscations of the seventeenth century from a Catholic, O'Connellite perspective; Lever's *The Knight of Gwynne* (1847) exposes the Act of Union of 1800 as an English destruction of the Irish Parliament; Joseph Sheridan Le Fanu's *The Fortunes of Colonel Torlogh O'Brien* (1847) is set during the Jacobite-Williamite war; Lever's *Maurice Tiernay* (1852) recounts the adventures of a young Irish Jacobite exile in several foreign countries during the years following the Treaty of Limerick; the Reverend Charles B. Gibson's *The Last Earl of Desmond* (1854) tells of the flight of the earls; Selina Bunbury's *Sir Guy D'Esterre* (1858) presents English invasions of Ireland at around the same time; Mrs. James Sadlier's *The Confederate Chieftains* (1859) exposes the Cromwellian confiscations and plantations; William B. MacCabe's *Agnes Arnold* (1861) celebrates the 1798 rising in Wexford; and William Carleton's *Redmond Count O'Hanlon, the Irish Rapparee* (1862) exploits the Irish appetite for heroism in the mold of Robin Hood and Rob Roy.[2] If the foregoing sentence has conveyed by its deliberate long-windedness any of the sheer exhaustion of trying to read most of these novels, then it has succeeded in its other task, for it is true that many of them are, in Thomas Flanagan's phrase, best lost in "a merciful oblivion."[3] Irish novelists of the mid-nineteenth century seem hard put to understand Irish history or to fathom fully the making of a novel.

Writing during a period dominated by the catastrophic Great Famine of 1845–49, Irish historical novelists were often unsure of their readership, their own political allegiances, and, for that matter, the course of history. Many of them continued to write, like the Banims, for English publishers, but several began to align themselves with Dublin or New York instead. During this infant stage of the Dublin publishing business, the names of James M'Glashan and James Duffy repeatedly surface. Le Fanu's *Torlogh O'Brien* was published by M'Glashan (allied with Orr of London) and Carleton's *Redmond O'Hanlon* by Duffy (who was also republishing the Banims around this time). With Irish publishers behind them, writers such as these could begin to be more secure about the Irishness of their work; but at the same time, they seemed seriously in doubt about just what this "Irishness" entailed, especially given the as yet unformed, unclear nature of their readership. Le Fanu and Carleton, examined in this

chapter, exemplify the doubtful nature of the Irish historical novel during the mid-nineteenth century.

On the surface, these two writers and their novels seem to present a sharp contrast. By background, Le Fanu was a wealthy member of the Protestant Ascendancy, while Carleton was a poor Catholic peasant, although he converted to Protestantism. Le Fanu desired at first to become a barrister; Carleton, a priest. Le Fanu's principal historical novel, *Torlogh O'Brien*, was apprentice work, written well before later, greater works; Carleton's historical novel, *Redmond O'Hanlon*, was his last novel, published years after the books that had made him famous. Le Fanu is best known in Irish literary history as a Gothicist, a great teller of ghost stories; Carleton has been most celebrated for his vivid, realistic portrayals of Irish peasant life.[4] In this context, their historical novels are anomalous. They do not match their authors' other works, either in subject matter or in quality, nor are they as good as Banim's *The Boyne Water*. But their historical novels typify those of the period. Their forays into historical fiction are representative of a genre that was quite popular in its appeal, yet also quite limited in its achievement, in mid-nineteenth-century Ireland. Le Fanu and Carleton were among the best Irish novelists of the nineteenth century. Their best work lies elsewhere, outside the genre of the historical novel: for Le Fanu, it includes *The House by the Church-Yard* (1863) and *Uncle Silas* (1864); for Carleton, *Traits and Stories of the Irish Peasantry* (1830) and *The Black Prophet* (1847).

Beyond the contrasts they afford, Le Fanu and Carleton offer some striking similarities. Le Fanu rejected law to become a writer; Carleton rejected (or was rejected by) the priesthood and the schoolhouse, toward the same end. Although both were frequently frustrated by their native country, neither left Ireland. Both stayed, writing for Irish publishers and often, in fact, crossing paths. Each began his professional writing career as author of nonfictional diatribes in Dublin newspapers against Catholicism and repeal of the Union and in favor of Protestant supremacy, yet each subsequently softened or changed his position enough to do some writing for Young Ireland's *The Nation* and to write a historical novel that was pro-Catholic or at least tolerant of the Catholic cause. However, in total contrast to the Banims, Le Fanu and Carleton each maintained a lifelong distaste for Daniel O'Connell and his followers. Each lacked the historical thoroughness or even the historical curiosity of a Walter Scott or John Banim, although each imitated Scott and recorded his debt to Banim. And perhaps most importantly, each was finally unable to deal with the muddled, tragic events of the mid-nineteenth century in Ireland and turned

to historical fiction in a vain attempt to escape their dreary present in favor of a romanticized, chivalric, mythical past.

It is curious that the political career of Joseph Thomas Sheridan Le Fanu (1814–73) strongly resembles that of the hero of a Scott novel, especially Waverley, Scott's archetypical "imbecile" or passive hero. In this respect, Le Fanu's fiction mirrors his own life and Waverley's. Like Waverley, the young Le Fanu was an Ascendency type who fell in with romantic nationalists but then fell out again, permanently. Unlike Scott, however, Le Fanu did not perceive a "middle way." Politically, Scott was a true moderate, while Le Fanu was a waverer and finally a confused escapist, turning away from Irish history and politics toward ghosts and scenes of terror transplanted from his Irish experience onto foreign, English settings in his later novels. He resembles a Scott character more than he does Scott.

Le Fanu's own history begins well before his birth in 1814. He was obsessed by his ancestors, especially the playwright Thomas Sheridan, whose name "meant literary success and political nonconformity,"[5] and Charles Le Fanu de Cresseron, who had fought for King Billy at the Boyne (and who is the fictional narrator of some of his later, Gothic novels). Le Fanu's family descended from Huguenots who were persecuted in France after the revocation of the Edict of Nantes. His father was a Protestant clergyman in charge of a Church of Ireland parish in Abington, County Limerick, who was affected by the Tithe Wars of the 1830s in which many Catholics refused to pay the compulsory tribute to the established Protestant church. Le Fanu's biographer, W. J. McCormack, notes that "arrears of tithes due to the Dean came to £8 in 1829, £45 in 1830, and £118 in 1831, an alarming progression which reached in 1832 £778.11s.11½d., virtually the entire tithe income for the year. In common with other similarly distressed clerics he applied for an advance from the authorities, receiving £310 in 1832" (38). Nelson Browne adds that "with the beginning of the Tithe War everything was changed, and where formerly, like other Protestant clergy, the Dean had been received with smiles of welcome he was now greeted with howls of execration."[6]

Given such an ancestry and such a youthful experience, perhaps it was inevitable that Le Fanu grew up with a virulent distaste for the Catholic peasantry. McCormack writes that "the essence of society as Le Fanu grew to know it in his Abington years was the isolation of his people from 'the people'"(35). In 1836, McCormack records, he went off to Trin-

ity College, Dublin, racily writing home, "I intend speaking on every occasion at the Historical Society, of course in a favourably conservative strain, and it is no small consolation to me to think that while I am abusing the *Pisantry* in Dublin city, my brother may be shooting them in the country" (50). In 1840, sounding like one of Banim's sectarian extremists, he attacked O'Connell as "the sworn exterminator of Protestantism" (84). The young Le Fanu developed a taste for cutthroat journalism which he never completely left behind. He was involved with newspapers most of his life, first as a contributor to Isaac Butt's *Dublin University Magazine* and later as copartner in the *Dublin Evening Mail* and successor to Butt as proprietor and editor of the *Dublin University Magazine*. In the 1830s and 1840s the *University Magazine* was the chief intellectual organ of Protestant supremacy, with Butt as editor and Carleton (already established as a literary "lion," according to Le Fanu's own description [51]) as contributor. Le Fanu felt at home in this conservative circle.

Something of the poseur seems to have animated the young Le Fanu. Like George Moore, Le Fanu toyed with Irish nationalism at the same time that he criticized it. Another element in his inheritance was his mother's great admiration for Lord Edward Fitzgerald. She had even stolen his sword from the officer who captured Fitzgerald, keeping it with her for years. "So the romantic nationalism of the United Irishmen of 1798," Robert Lee Wolff notes, "was as much a part of Le Fanu's heritage as the conservative Protestants of the Ascendancy." Le Fanu contributed a ballad on Fitzgerald to the *Dublin University Magazine*, of all places, in 1839:

That day that traitors sould him and inimies bought him,
The day that the red gold and red blood was paid —
Then the green turned pale and thrembled like the dead leaves in Autumn,
And the heart an' hope iv Ireland in the could grave was laid.[7]

There runs throughout Le Fanu's thinking the impression that the nationalism of the past could be respectable and romantic, while the nationalism of his own day was a different, sordid, mundane affair.

Le Fanu continued his Protestant supremacist writings in the early 1840s, when he was realizing that he enjoyed writing more than practicing law, a career he abandoned almost before he had begun it. He became co-proprietor with Isaac Butt of

a militantly Protestant newspaper called *The Warder*, for which he also shared some editorial responsibility. He was active in the Metropolitan

Conservative Association, whose program was not very different from
that of the now nominally suppressed Orange Lodges. Le Fanu strongly
opposed Daniel O'Connell's campaign for Repeal of the Union of Ireland
with England, and for the Corporation Reform Bill, which would have
given Catholics a new voice in Irish municipalities. He attacked the Whig
government of Lord Melbourne for softness on these issues.[8]

He also became part-proprietor in 1840 of *The Statesman and Dublin Christian Record*, another vituperative anti-Catholic journal. However conservative these journals were, they did play an important part in the nascent
Dublin publishing business. Now, at least, writers such as Le Fanu and
Carleton were writing for Irish, not English, publishers.

Le Fanu's first novel, *The Cock and Anchor* (1845), had a Catholic protagonist. During the same year the Famine began, and so did Le
Fanu's brief liaison with Young Ireland and Thomas Davis' *The Nation*,
which Le Fanu saw as a Protestant nationalist alternative to O'Connell's
Catholic demagoguery. McCormack writes that in the spring of 1847 Le
Fanu, with both Davis and O'Connell dead, "promised his support to Mitchel
and Meagher" (102). In the same year he published *Torlogh O'Brien* under
the inspiration of Young Ireland. Gavan Duffy, to whom leadership of
Young Ireland fell after Davis' death in 1845, even helped him with some
of it. Davis had wanted to write a ballad history of Ireland and had implored, "I wish to heaven someone would attempt Irish historical fiction."[9]
But the 1848 rising caused Le Fanu to reject Young Ireland altogether. By
then he was terrified of Mitchel's "socialism" as well as by his republicanism, condemning him in the *Dublin University Magazine* a month before
the rising in the summer of 1848.[10] Thereafter, he sought busily to dissociate himself from Young Ireland — and, for that matter, from his own first
two novels, which he now saw as betrayals of his own caste.

The year 1848 thus marks a watershed for Le Fanu: he would never
again court Irish nationalism. W. J. McCormack notes that historical fictions "required an imaginative willingness to incorporate opposing ideolo-
gies into a single vision of the past, and after 1848 he did not reveal any
ability or desire to reconcile opposites" (212). Le Fanu retreated from politics following 1848. He briefly sought but then passed up a Tory nomina-
tion for the County Carlow seat in Parliament in 1852 and subsequently
had no more to do with public life. After his wife's death in 1858, Le Fanu
turned increasingly to Gothicism both in his fiction and in his life, surfacing to walk the streets only late at night in Dublin, where he became known
as the "invisible Prince" (197).

His next novel after *Torlogh O'Brien*, *The House by the Church-
Yard* (1863), was set in eighteenth-century Ireland, but it lacks the public,

political, and historical focus of his earlier work. McCormack argues that it "presents a narrative of the past explicitly as a retreat from the grimy present" (139). Thereafter, he avoided Irish settings altogether. Elizabeth Bowen has described *Uncle Silas* (1864) aptly as "an Irish story transposed to an English setting," and McCormack adds that "the exile locations of Le Fanu's fiction are not merely geographically remote, but are expressions of a deeper dislocation of the individual from society" (141, 142). Le Fanu's career is like Waverley's among the Jacobites: seduced by Young Ireland, the conservative Le Fanu "comes to his senses" and retreats.

The Cock and Anchor, A Chronicle of Old Dublin is too thin historically to be described truly as a historical novel, but its dominant features are worth noting briefly in preface to an analysis of *Torlogh O'Brien.* Set during the years following the Treaty of Limerick, it tells the story of the Catholic Edmond O'Connor's suit for the Protestant Mary Ashwoode, which is frustrated by the evil, bigoted machinations of her Ascendancy father and brother and finally ended by the lovelorn Mary's death in 1710, followed by Edmond's death in battle in 1712. Although *The Cock and Anchor* concerns the Protestant Ascendancy's suppression of Catholic ambition and frustration of love between Catholic and Protestant, its focus is almost entirely private and fictional, not public and historical. We meet historical personages such as Jonathan Swift and Lord Wharton, but only very briefly. The story of Edmond and Mary dominates, and there is no attempt, as in the Banims, to integrate the events of public history with the private, fictional plot.

In fact, Edmond O'Connor retreats from involvement in public history, even though he is clearly a victim of that history. He believes that history is solely in God's hands, and he is interested only in winning Mary's hand. When an Irish Catholic rebel speaks to him late in the novel about fighting for Catholic freedom, Edmond responds:

> Happy were I to see these things accomplished . . . but I hold their achievement, except by the intervention of Almighty Providence, impossible. Methinks we have in Ireland neither the spirits nor the power to do it. The people are heart-broken; and so far from coming to the field in this quarrel, they dare not even speak of it above their breath.[11]

Edmond twice falls into Jacobite hands and is twice rescued by the Jacobite Captain O'Hanlon. Like Carleton's O'Hanlon, Le Fanu's hero seems to have

been anachronistically inspired by Redmond O'Hanlon, who was in fact shot to death in 1681. Le Fanu's Captain O'Hanlon feels kindly toward Edmond because his father, Richard O'Connor, fought beside him in the Jacobite-Williamite war of 1689–91. Unlike his father, Edmond shrinks from combat. He is even more passive than Scott's passive hero. His encounters with the Jacobites are briefer and more accidental than Waverley's, and he retreats from them immediately. Robert Lee Wolff notes that "O'Connor, rather passive in love, is also passive in the cause."[12] His retreat from politics foreshadows Le Fanu's own retreat after 1848.

Contained already in *The Cock and Anchor* are many of the preoccupations that dominate *Torlogh O'Brien* and resurface in Le Fanu's later fiction, especially the obsession with nobility, heredity, and property (according to which Edmond cannot win Mary because he is of the wrong caste) and the fascination with Gothicism which overshadows the backgrounds of history. *Torlogh O'Brien* is full of terrifying torture scenes. Le Fanu drew his passive hero from Scott, but he was more interested in Scott's Gothicism than in his historicism. He felt that Gothicism had a dominant place in Scott's fiction, noting that it figured even in the novels of contemporary life, *The Antiquary* and *St. Ronan's Well*, the nonhistorical novels.[13] In his preface to *Uncle Silas* he celebrated "the legitimate school of tragic English romance, which has been ennobled, and in great measure founded by the genius of Sir Walter Scott." But, as Nelson Brown argues, "Le Fanu is a sensation-monger in a manner that Scott, in spite of the elements of Gothicism which his novels undoubtedly reveal, never would have emulated."[14] Scott, as we have seen, was inspired by Gothic novels to write his own historical novels. Conversely, Le Fanu shifted in his career from historical to Gothic fiction. In retreating to Gothicism, he abandoned history.

Le Fanu's decision to write a full-fledged historical novel was inspired not so much by Scott as by the example, more locally, of John Banim and the encouragement of Young Ireland. In 1845, the same year in which *The Cock and Anchor* was published, Le Fanu joined a committee to raise money for John Banim's widow. Organized by Gavan Duffy, the committee included Daniel O'Connell, William Carleton, Isaac Butt, Charles Lever, Thomas Davis, and Samuel Ferguson — a diverse gathering. As W. J. McCormack wryly notes, "Respect for Banim was probably the sole cause in which the committee could have been united" (94). Subsequently, Le Fanu, inspired very directly by *The Boyne Water* and encouraged by Duffy, wrote *The Fortunes of Colonel Torlogh O'Brien; A Tale of the Wars of King James* serially for James M'Glashan during 1846 and 1847. M'Glashan published it as a book in 1847, at the height of the Famine.[15]

Le Fanu records his debt to Banim when he reaches the Boyne in the novel: "The author of 'The Boyne Water' has, with a masterly hand, sketched the events of the momentous battle which gives its name to his work; we are not presumptuous enough to traverse the ground already explained by him."[16] Banim's influence is evident in Le Fanu's positive portrayal of both Tyrconnel and King James. Comparing *Torlogh O'Brien* with *The Boyne Water*, we see strong similarities: the historical events are the same; even the basic plot, according to which a Catholic-Protestant marriage is achieved in spite of the divisive forces of history, is the same.

The contrasts, however, are more interesting. George Walker, chief villain of *The Boyne Water*, is for Le Fanu "that holy man of Bible and bullet" (295). Peasants and rapparees, characterized with sympathy by Banim even though they cannot marry his middle-class heroes and heroines, are "savages" to LeFanu; he uses the word continuously, and his peasants speak a dialect considerably more removed from the realities of Irish speech than is the case in Banim. In contrast, Le Fanu's gentry heroes, Colonel Torlogh O'Brien and Sir Hugh Willoughby, are always "knights" and are characterized accordingly. The Willoughby estate is "Glindarragh Castle." This is the world of chivalric romance. The Protestant Le Fanu selects, in Torlogh, a Catholic protagonist, much as the Catholic Banim, seeking objectivity, chose a Protestant protagonist, Robert Evelyn. But Torlogh is a Jacobite who spends his time counterbalancing the violent excesses of his more ruthless Jacobite comrades and ends up marrying into the Protestant Ascendancy, while Robert Evelyn, as we have seen, moves in exactly the opposite direction, from Ascendancy neutrality to Catholic partisanship.

As in *The Cock and Anchor*, the basic plot of Le Fanu's second novel involves the Catholic hero's suit to win the hand of his Protestant beloved from her wealthy Ascendancy father. This time, though, the hero succeeds. Torlogh wins Grace Willoughby because Sir Hugh favors him and because Torlogh holds an ancestral deed to Glindarragh Castle. Their marriage is not only a moral, reconciling match, but an economic one as well. As in Michael Banim's *The Croppy*, we are met by a benevolent trinity of heroic suitor, noble father, and virtuous daughter. Le Fanu's escapist, romantic ending is typical of the mid-nineteenth-century Irish historical novel and anticipates Standish O'Grady's very similar endings. His version of Scott's middle way is a glorification of inheritance and property, a defensive view of history which seeks to justify Le Fanu's own Ascendancy position while tolerating an old Catholic brand of chivalry seen as far superior to the demagoguery of a contemporary like Daniel O'Connell. W. J. McCormack presents an interesting psychological and political

reading of the novel in light of Le Fanu's brief, uneasy liaison with Young
Ireland and subsequent rejection of it:

> The romantic narrative, of hero and heroine, from different camps fall-
> ing in love, enacts in fiction the Young Ireland programme, the recon-
> ciliation of Catholic and Protestant, Celt and Saxon, in the common name
> of Irishman. But where the more conventional saw Victorian female vul-
> nerability in the aboriginal, the female in Le Fanu's fiction is associated
> with corruption and confiscation — though innocent herself — and the male
> is dispossessed and relatively helpless. While this may take on psycho-
> logical importance in the light of his subsequent treatment of the sexes,
> politically the implication is of his pessimistic toleration of *The Nation's*
> policy. He accepted the outer shape of this historical fiction but rewrote
> its inner logic to accord with his own defensive view of history. (99–100)

Torlogh O'Brien grew partly out of two stories written earlier by
Le Fanu for the *Dublin University Magazine:* "The Fortunes of Sir Robert
Ardagh" and "An Adventure of Hardress Fitzgerald, a Royalist Captain,"
both of which celebrate upper-class military chivalry and include anti-
Papist footnotes that the novel omits.[17] Much blatant anti-Catholicism
remains in the pages of *Torlogh O'Brien.* A great deal of it is focused on
the novel's chief villain, Miles Garret, the evil, lower-class Jacobite who
vies with the more noble, upper-class Torlogh for Grace's hand and ownership of Glindarragh Castle. Torlogh is pure good and Miles pure evil. Since
they are both Catholic, the essential difference seems to be their contrasting positions in society. Torlogh is a cardboard knight, "stern, dark, and
silent" (127), full of "grave respect" (122); Miles, an "ugly, ungainly, and
repulsive" (122) peasant who speaks in an awful brogue and at one point
seems to Grace "if possible, more ugly, sinister, and repulsive than ever"
(141). Miles finally defects to King Billy and receives his "just deserts" at
the end, plunging over a "ghastly" cliff, "his skull . . . shattered like a gourd"
(342), his corpse found later by wandering children. Meanwhile, steering
clear of Jacobite extremists and finally liberating the captive Sir Hugh from
them, Torlogh wins Grace, "happy, thrice happy, in the true love of this
devoted and beautiful girl, with tumultuous greeting folds her to his heart,
and with the privilege of the betrothed, kisses her burning cheek — nay,
kisses her very lips" (339).

    In this ending Le Fanu seeks to merge, romantically, mythically,
the new Protestant Ascendancy and the old Gaelic aristocracy, through
the wedding of Grace and Torlogh with the blessing of Sir Hugh. There
is no message here, as in Banim, that the Treaty of Limerick must yet be

kept. Le Fanu implicitly affirms Protestant supremacy. Torlogh shares with Sir Hugh and Grace an upper-class inheritance. The wedding sustains Ascendancy. The upper class wins; the lower class loses. The aristocracy is restored, saved from the Jacobite scourge, and the Jacobites get what they have coming to them. "The waste which had been so recklessly committed upon the country, now reacted with fearful disaster upon the very army whose licentiousness had wrought it" (309). The rapparees are "savages" engaged in grisly tortures in which they "delight," as in an early scene: "The preparations all being completed, a wild, half naked boy, with one end of the halter between his teeth, climbed nimbly up the ladder and passed the cord over the topmost round; and as soon as both extremities of it rested upon the ground, the grinning urchin descended with a whoop of savage delight" (98). Like Miles Garret, the rapparees are doomed.

Le Fanu's position is not middle class like Banim's. It is that of the Protestant Ascendancy, defensive of wealth already won but being threatened by the rising Catholic middle class during the nineteenth century. W. J. McCormack quite rightly sees Le Fanu as a "transitional figure" (261). Le Fanu looks forward to the "shadowy heroes" of the 1890s explored by Wayne Hall: Anglo-Irish writers such as Yeats, Somerville and Ross, George Moore — and, among historical novelists, Standish O'Grady — who saw the ascendancy of their class undergoing erosion and glorified a mythical past in preference to their own dreary, threatening present.[18]

If Le Fanu prefigures some of the "shadowy heroes" of the Irish Renaissance, it should also be noted that its chief champion, W. B. Yeats, looked back to William Carleton (1794–1869) more than to any other nineteenth-century Irish fiction writer. Three titles by Carleton topped Yeats's 1895 list of "The Best Thirty Irish Books," along with two by John Banim and only one by Maria Edgeworth.[19] Yeats compiled an edition of *Stories from Carleton* (1889), celebrating in his introduction Carleton's "clay-cold melancholy" and hailing him as "a great Irish historian" and "the great novelist of Ireland by right of the most Celtic eyes that ever gazed from under the brows of a story-teller."[20]

It is true that Carleton wrote with a more intimate knowledge of the Irish Catholic peasantry, its language and traditions, than any other nineteenth-century Anglo-Irish novelist. However, Carleton the Catholic peasant converted to Protestantism as a young man, and entered the world of literature in 1828 — at exactly the same time that John Banim was clean-

ing up *The Denounced* to protect the cause of Catholic Emancipation — as an anti-Catholic polemicist. In 1826 Carleton had written a letter, since discovered among the papers of Sir Robert Peel, to his friend William Sisson, volunteering himself to Peel as one who could demonstrate a connection between terrorism and the Catholic Emancipation movement, thus subverting it; there is no evidence that Peel ever responded.[21] Wolff observes that publicly Carleton wrote: "The question of Emancipation is singularly mixed up with the immediate and personal interests of its most violent and outrageous supporters . . . a few lawyers and priests who make it the means . . . of raising themselves to popularity . . . whilst they are also stimulated by the prospect of unlimited ascendancy." They "insolently" blamed their own problems, Carleton claimed, on the English, working the people up by "images of imaginary oppression . . . Oh! let not the guardian of the British Constitution give these men power!" (21).

As Wolff concludes, "From the mid-1820s to the mid-1830s, the evidence shows, Carleton was himself a militant anti-Catholic, echoing the extreme Evangelical arguments of the time" (5). Carleton the Gaelic peasant agreed with Le Fanu the Ascendancy clergyman's son, preceding him, in fact, in the front lines of anti-Catholic journalism. This position was reflected during these years both in Carleton's nonfictional and fictional work, in his anti-Papist diatribes for Caesar Otway's militantly Protestant *Christian Examiner* as well as in his early stories about the Catholic peasantry, many of which remained mercifully unreprinted. And some of them underwent considerable revision, with the most anti-Catholic passages (which he later admitted that he "regretted") deleted in the collection *Traits and Stories of the Irish Peasantry.*

After writing for a number of Protestant supremacist journals, including Isaac Butt's *Dublin University Magazine*, Carleton, like Le Fanu, came under the influence of *The Nation* during the mid-1840s. He began to write fiction much more sympathetic toward the problems faced by the Catholic peasantry: *Valentine McClutchy* (1845), a Dickensian exposé of the abuses of land agents; *The Black Prophet* (1847), his best novel, a lament of the Great Famine which drew on his own youthful famine experiences during the 1820s and which was published the same year as *Torlogh O'Brien*; and *The Emigrants of Ahadarra* (1848), an attack on the causes of emigration. However, again like Le Fanu, Carleton reacted against Young Ireland following the 1848 rising, writing *The Tithe Proctor* (1849) as an attack on agrarian rebels and perversely exclaiming to Gavan Duffy in 1852, Wolff records, "may the curse of God alight doubly on Ireland and may all she has suffered be only like the entrance to paradise compared to what she may suffer" (118). By the time he wrote his single

historical novel, *Redmond Count O'Hanlon, the Irish Rapparee* (1862), Carleton was burnt out as a writer. Like Le Fanu, he sought to escape from his own dreary time to a more idyllic, romantic period of history.

If Le Fanu's political loyalties were divided, Carleton's were positively skewed. It is important to know that Carleton was a "spoiled priest," a type to which we shall return in Francis MacManus' fictional version of Donnacha Ruadh MacConmara, the eighteenth-century Gaelic poet. Like MacConmara, Carleton sought as a young man to become a priest but was rejected—a turning point recounted in Carleton's autobiography, where he abruptly describes himself standing outside the gates of Maynooth seminary, muttering, "What communication could a nameless wanderer like me expect with such an establishment?"[22] And, like MacConmara as well as John Banim's Dan D'Arcy, Carleton converted at least partly in order to court Protestant favors. He went to Dublin, with a copy of *Gil Blas* in his pocket, as Billy Carleton (anglicized from Ó Cearbhalláin or O'Carolan), the Gaelic peasant from Tyrone, but he became Mr. William Carleton, Protestant schoolmaster and well-respected anti-Papist journalist.

Like Le Fanu, Carleton was obsessed with financial and societal status and abhorred violence (although the fiction of both writers is full of it). As Wolff reminds us, Carleton wrote that "there is nothing more valuable in life than respectable connection" (17). Le Fanu, as we have seen, had been marked by the Tithe Wars. Carleton had caught it from the other side, experiencing a midnight attack on his family's home by Orange yeomanry and witnessing the black-tarred body of Paddy Devaun the Ribbonman hung in the center of his town. The sight made Carleton the young, nominal Ribbonman swear off violence and secret societies for good. Revolted by terrorism and rejected by the priesthood, he turned virulently against both.

In politics, Carleton was above all else a champion of his own cause, a chameleon figure who was always ready to shift with the wind in order to preserve himself. In the 1830s he prospered by walking beneath the militant Protestant banner; in the 1840s, by courting Young Ireland. Even though Daniel O'Connell generously hailed Carleton at one point as "the Scott of Ireland,"[23] Carleton maintained a lifelong hatred for O'Connell. For both Le Fanu and Carleton, part of Young Ireland's appeal was its Protestant leadership as well as its criticisms of O'Connell. Carleton began writing for *The Nation* in 1845 only after a disagreement with the editorship of the *Dublin University Magazine* had deprived him of that means of livelihood. He never joined Young Ireland. Gavan Duffy wrote later that "with all his splendid equipment of brains, he was incapable

of comprehending the principles and aspirations of Young Ireland."[24] Carleton saw *The Nation* as a useful ally in his latest cause: his attempt to inherit the late John Banim's government pension, which Robert Peel assured him could not be transferred, and was not. Eventually Carleton won his own pension. His degeneration as a writer during the 1850s and 1860s is to be explained not only by the effects of drink but also by the comparative security afforded by the pension.

In 1845 Carleton served with Le Fanu on the committee to help John Banim's widow. He had already contributed an article in 1843 to *The Nation* entitled "The Late John Banim," praising him as a "genius" and champion of religious freedom, nonviolence, and patriotism, but also noting that his work was marred by an overdependence on Walter Scott.[25] Apparently oblivious to his own position in 1828, Carleton argued in 1843 that "Ireland owes the exhibition of Banim's genius, together with the widespread sympathy which it created for her, to the mighty struggle for religious freedom in which she was then engaged." His anti-O'Connellism, however, shows: he seeks to dissociate the name of the O'Connellite Richard Lalor Sheil from Banim's, going so far as to suggest that "Mr. Sheil's share in the literary partnership was one more profitable to himself than honourable or labourious."

Carleton's tribute to Banim offers rather backhanded praise. "Generosity," writes Robert Lee Wolff, "seems to go against his grain" (91). Carleton notes that "Banim has written the best historical novels which this country has yet produced," adding that "Banim's works, published and read in England as they were, unquestionably produced a powerful influence over the English mind. . . . [He] did as much to vindicate our country from falsehood and calumny as any that ever bore a pen in her defense." Yet Carleton's contention that Banim would have done greater work had he "been deeply acquainted with the antiquarian and legendary lore of our country" and "fallen back upon grander events and more glorious names" is odd in light of his own rejection of antiquarianism, recorded in an unpublished sketch,[26] and his own inability to write compellingly of life in Ireland previous to his own lifetime. Benedict Kiely writes that Carleton "was in his high moments neither altruistic nor antiquary; he was himself one of the beggars, speaking and moving and laughing and weeping with an intimacy that began in the soul."[27] Carleton's assertion that Banim was overly dependent on Scott, for "there is something painful in beholding one original genius striving to tread in another's footsteps," is curious, because he himself was proud of a "fancied or real similarity between his own physiognomy and that of his master, and plainly hoped that Scott's mantle had fallen on his shoulders."[28]

Thanks to D. J. O'Donoghue, writing in 1905, we have some evidence of the origins of Carleton's own attempt at a historical novel, *Redmond Count O'Hanlon, the Irish Rapparee*. In the recent resurgence of critical interest in Carleton, this novel has been left in the shadow of his earlier, superior fiction.[29] Recounting Scott's trip to Ireland in 1825, O'Donoghue writes:

It is not known to many that he seriously contemplated the experiment of an Irish romance, and the present writer may claim the credit of making public for the first time the fact that Scott, having heard something of the famous Irish outlaw, Redmond O'Hanlon, asked an Irish lady of his acquaintance (Lady Olivia Sparrow), who was in a position to make the necessary inquiries, to obtain for him all the information procurable in County Down concerning the arch-rebel who gave the Duke of Ormonde and the English Government such trouble in the latter half of the seventeenth century. Unfortunately, the material available seems to have been too meagre for Scott's purpose; and Count Redmond O'Hanlon still awaits his historian. The details of his career are scanty, but a good deal more is known about him than Scott was able to discover. There are several contemporary tracts about this romantic figure, and County Down tradition still preserves his name in remembrance. When William Carleton, the Irish novelist, determined to make O'Hanlon's wild career the theme of a story, he found it just as difficult to unravel its mystery as Scott had found it thirty years before. It was in the course of his investigations that he learned that Scott—of whose writings he was an intense admirer, and of his facial resemblance to whom he was amazingly proud—had been an unprofitable gleaner before him. Carleton did eventually write a novel, called "Count Redmond O'Hanlon, the Irish Rapparee" [sic], but it does not really treat of the historical personage of that name, the hero being a creature of his own imagination.[30]

O'Donoghue's account suggests Carleton's fundamental problem in trying to write a historical novel: try as he might, and regardless of Yeats's opinion, Carleton was no historian. Or rather, he was an effective "historian" only of his own age, capturing nineteenth-century Irish peasant life compellingly in works such as *Traits and Stories of the Irish Peasantry* and *The Black Prophet*, in which he made admirable use of his intimate knowledge of peasant speech and tradition to present an unforgettable picture of the age that was remarkably realistic. But Carleton was out of his depth in the seventeenth century. He lacked Banim's historical instinct and accuracy. Irish historiography was fairly shaky throughout the nineteenth century, but the diligent Banim had largely overcome this dif-

ficulty. Carleton's apparent laziness as an historian, when added to the difficulty of obtaining reliable historical sources, simply made the problem worse.

The fundamental anachronism contained in *Redmond O'Hanlon* must be admitted immediately in a discussion of the novel: it is set in the period 1696–1700, but its hero in actual historical fact had been shot dead in 1681. Moreover,the word "rapparee" did not come into use until the 1690s. Carleton seems to have confused two O'Hanlons: Redmond, the infamous County Down highwayman, and one of his several rapparee relatives who, roaming the countryside after the Treaty of Limerick, carried on the family name. All of these O'Hanlons, after all, were alive more in Irish folklore than in historical tracts. Growing up in County Tyrone, beside County Down, Carleton would have come in contact with these various O'Hanlons in folklore. Benedict Kiely notes that the "O'Hanlons had ridden and robbed and lived gallantly in the mountains to the East of Carleton's country."

> In his youth Carleton had read "with more avidity than its literary merits warranted, a curious little chapbook, written by one J. Cosgrave, and sold no doubt extensively . . . at fairs and markets." It was called: "The Lives and Actions of the Most Notorious Irish Highwaymen, Tories, and Rapparees; from Redmond O'Hanlon to Cahier na Gappul." With this antiquarian detail at his hand, with a dozen folk-tales in his head, with the full authority of Thierry, Wordsworth and Sir Walter Scott, he still failed miserably to draw back out of the mists the great figure of Galloping O'Hanlon.[31]

Carleton's anachronistic treatment of O'Hanlon is remarkable, because O'Donoghue tells us that a "Mr. Crawford also sent Carleton a very curious and scarce tract, printed in Dublin in 1681, and entitled 'Count Hanlan's Downfall, or a True and Exact Account of the Killing of that Arch-Traytor and Tory, Redmond O'Hanlan, by Art O'Hanlan, one of his own party, on the 25th day of April, 1681, near the Eight Mile Bridge, in the County of Down'."[32] Historical novels, including Scott's, often depart slightly from fact to achieve an artistic purpose, but Carleton's anachronism seems blatant. He failed to do his historical homework, even though the facts were available to him. One senses from the novel that it was not history, in fact, that interested him, but romance: history as fairy tale. In this respect, *Redmond O'Hanlon* and the next novel which I shall discuss, Standish O'Grady's *The Flight of the Eagle*, represent polarized extremes in the slow development of the Irish historical novel: Carleton's

novel is all imagination and inaccurate history; O'Grady's, all history and little imagination.

In his argument in *Poor Scholar* that "if Walter Scott had made Rob Roy MacGregor the hero of a great story there was nothing in the wide world to prevent William Carleton making a hero of Redmond Count O'Hanlon,"[33] Benedict Kiely rightly notes the direct influence of *Rob Roy* upon *Redmond O'Hanlon*. But there is an essential difference between the two novels: while Bob Roy is a heroic artifact whom Scott's moderate hero must finally reject, Carleton's Redmond O'Hanlon is a simple hero of romance, dominant and victorious. With all of its shortcomings, *Redmond O'Hanlon* marks a significant shift in the Irish historical novel: the protagonist is openly, from the beginning, a partisan, a hero who carries the banner of Irish nationalism. This brand of hero was to dominate subsequent Irish historical novels.

Redmond O'Hanlon, like Torlogh O'Brien, is a chivalric knight, flawless, brave, and generous. As such, these two protagonists are representative of the hero of the mid-nineteenth-century Irish historical novel at large. However, instead of rejecting the peasantry like Torlogh, Redmond is their patron. The chief plot of the novel involves his intercessions on behalf of Con M'Mahon and Rose Callan, peasant lovers who, as always in the Irish historical novel, are separated by the forces of history. Rose's father, Brian Callan, completes the virtuous father-daughter-suitor triangle. The dirty villain this time, though, is not a Catholic peasant as in *Torlogh O'Brien*, but a Protestant military man, Cornet Lucas. Desiring Rose as wife and Patchy Baccach the rapparee as victim, Lucas kidnaps Rose and holds her captive, demanding Patchy as ransom. But Rose courageously holds out until Redmond frees her, the novel ending, after Lucas has been punished, with the joyous wedding of Rose and Con with Redmond in attendance as guest of honor. The typical formula of romance is thereby fulfilled.

Carleton glorifies not only O'Hanlon in particular, but the rapparees in general. The Ribbonmen of his own day, it seems, had been horrible creatures altogether, as he shows in *Rody the Rover: or, the Ribbonman* (1845), but now, having retreated to 1700, Carleton could safely celebrate the rapparee secret societies. His portrait is as positive as Le Fanu's was negative:

> The three great principles of their lawless existence were such as would reflect honour upon the most refined associations, and the most intellectual institutions of modern civilization. These were, first, sobriety; secondly, a resolution to avoid the shedding of human blood; and, thirdly,

a solemn promise never to insult or offer outrage to woman, but in every instance to protect her.[34]

These are knights—fearless, virtuous Robin Hoods. O'Hanlon himself is compared to Robin Hood (114–15) and to Hercules (162–63). The novel is dominated by his feats. Up against such a demigod, Cornet Lucas, representing Protestant oppression, never stands a chance. The Irish-English, Catholic-Protestant polarity is decided from the start rather than resolved during the course of the story. The most nonhistorical aspect of *Redmond O'Hanlon* is not the anachronism surrounding O'Hanlon, but the awarding of victory to Catholics at the beginning of a century in which it seems they never in fact won; the Penal Age was an era of Catholic defeat and degradation. Carleton's tale, like those about Cromwell throwing himself on his sword, evidences romantic, wishful thinking on his part as well as a nostalgia for his own picaresque, Catholic peasant youth. This kind of wishful thinking, which separates flawless heroes from hopeless villains, was all too common among mid-nineteenth-century Irish novelists.

In this sense, *Redmond O'Hanlon* must finally be described as anti-historical, even though its portrayal of polarities within Irish society and its use of Anglo-Irish dialect to reinforce these polarities place it squarely in the tradition of the Irish historical novel. Instead of explaining his own real world by seeking to understand these societal, historical polarities, as did Banim, Carleton, like Le Fanu, escapes to a historical but mythical world of his own making, retreating from the contemporary, political problems surrounding him, unable to resolve them. "I am not a Young Irelander," an elderly Carleton wrote to the *Evening Mail*, "nor, in a political sense at least, an old one. I am no Republican, no Jacobin, no Communist, but a plain, retiring literary man, who wishes to avoid politics."[35] Carleton, it turns out, was much more accurate in foreseeing the future than in interpreting the past. In 1863, the year after *Redmond O'Hanlon* appeared, Wolff finds Carleton predicting: "Banim and Griffin are gone, and I will soon follow them—*ultimus Romanorum*, and after that will come a lull, an obscurity of perhaps half a century, when a new condition of civil society and new phase of manners and habits among the people . . . may introduce new fields and new tastes for other writers" (127).

5
The Shift from
Romance to Realism: *Standish O'Grady*
and William Buckley

T HE LATE-NINETEENTH-CENTURY "lull" or "obscurity" predicted
by Carleton was true of Irish fiction: no work of high quality
was produced until Somerville and Ross and George Moore
made their presences felt in the 1890s. In the 1900s, poetry
and drama, especially the great works of W. B. Yeats and John Synge,
dominated the much-acclaimed Irish Literary Revival, or Renaissance. The
Literary Revival's first historian, Ernest Boyd, noted: "Anglo-Irish literature has been rich in poetry and drama, but the absence of good prose
fiction is noticeable. . . . Indeed, were it not for the essays of John Eglin-
ton, the occasional prose pieces of A.E., and Yeats's two volumes of stories,
one might say that the art of prose has been comparatively neglected."
More recently, Thomas Flanagan hyperbolized: "The great literary movement in Ireland at the turn of the century, the movement which produced
Yeats and Synge, Lady Gregory and Douglas Hyde, was rich in poetry
and drama, in essays and in critical theory, but it produced no novels."
What Flanagan means to suggest is that no *good* novels were produced
until James Joyce came on the scene in 1916, a point with which admirers
of Somerville and Ross's *The Real Charlotte* (1894) might well take issue.
At any rate, it is true that no Irish novelist of the Literary Revival matched
Yeats's poems or Synge's plays.[1]

If no great novel was produced during these years, more Irish nov-

els were published than ever before. And the history of the Irish historical novel is marked by an explosion in publication between 1890 and 1919, as a comparison of the numbers of historical novels published during each decade before 1920 indicates.[2]

1820s	6
1830s	5
1840s	6
1850s	4
1860s	5
1870s	7
1880s	12
1890s	23
1900s	31
1910s	17

Surfacing in the 1890s (by which time Fenianism had established itself as an ideology to be reckoned with) was the popular novel glorifying Irish military nationalism of past ages, with words such as "brigade," "Irish," and "Erin" particularly common among their titles. The Irish historical novel was persistent and prevalent during the Literary Revival which, it must be remembered, had its popular undercurrents as well as its Yeats, Synge, and Lady Gregory. Irish novelists of the Revival did not produce masterpieces, but they could at least see their books into print, and so they did, as never before. They constituted a vast league of unknowns who have remained unknowns. During the years between 1860 and 1919, 95 Irish historical novels by 71 different authors were published (even adhering to a narrow definition of the genre by which I exclude, for example, novels dealing with contemporaneous events, such as Charles Kickham's much-read *Knocknagow*). The names most recurrent among the authors of Irish historical novels during this period are not likely to inspire fond memories among even the most industrious literary historians: James Murphy wrote five historical novels; M. M'Donnell Bodkin, four; Miss L. Mac-Manus, four; D. P. Conyngham, three; Randal M'Donnell, three; L. L. O'Byrne, three. The growing legions of Irish-Americans in New York and Boston began their persistent contributions to the genre during the second half of the nineteenth century, with Mrs. James Sadlier, C. O'Leary, D. P. Conyngham, Anna Argyle, and others contributing historical novels.

During these years Irish historical novelists sought a more popular and, very often, a more youthful audience than had previously been reached. Writing on "Irish Historical Fiction" in 1916, Father Steven Brown stressed this very point:

There are sad lessons lurking for us in every corner of our history had we but manful courage to face them. Now, I would urge again that one of the best mediums for conveying this lesson, especially to the younger generations and to those whose studies cease with their boyhood, is historical fiction. . . . If there be any truth in these considerations why not see to it that among the works of fiction put into the hands of Irish boys and girls there shall be found some that will imprint in their imaginations what of Irish history is best worth remembering, and that will help to fix their affections upon the country whose children they are? How many even to-day are growing up among us well-educated in other respects, but knowing nothing about their country.[3]

Writing between the Famine and Fenian years and the Easter Rising of 1916, these new Irish historical novelists sought to teach a new generation of Irish nationalists the old lessons offered by Irish heroes of the past. Even today an Irish boy or girl can, for a modest sum, buy an abridged paperback edition of Thomas Fitzpatrick's anti-Cromwellian novel of 1898, The King of Claddagh, its cover graced by an illustration of a girl smiling at a knight in shining armor.[4]

It is neither my intention nor my desire to discuss the many historical novels published during the Irish Literary Renaissance. Most of them are pulp novels whose obscurity is, it is best said, appropriate. Instead, I wish to suggest the general direction of the genre through an examination of three novels by two Cork writers, one of whom will be remembered as the "Father of the Revival" and the other of whom is as obscure as the others: Standish O'Grady's Ulrick the Ready (1896) and The Flight of the Eagle (1897) and William Buckley's Croppies Lie Down (1903). O'Grady's work represents the last gasp of the nineteenth century imitation of Scott, while Buckley's is the first hint of a movement away from Scott in the twentieth century. Yet another paradox contained in this period is that Buckley's novel, a rare gem among the popular but paltry historical novels of the Literary Revival, is far superior to the romances of the "father of the revival" and more accurately points the direction that later Irish historical novels would follow: away from romance, towards realism. O'Grady was a more influential writer than the obscure Buckley, but Croppies Lie Down, the first twentieth-century novel considered in this study, is evidence of a major shift in the Irish historical novel at the turn of the century and foreshadows the genre's subsequent realistic mode. O'Grady and Buckley, rather than following the same pattern, illustrate the movement from nineteenth-century romance to twentieth-century realism.

IF STANDISH JAMES O'GRADY (1846–1928) was "Father of the Revival," a title conferred upon him by Ernest Boyd in *Ireland's Literary Renaissance*, it is at the same time apparent that his paternity was unplanned and discovered only relatively late in the game. The true moving force of the renaissance, W. B. Yeats, looking for a progenitor in the late 1890s, proclaimed that O'Grady's *History of Ireland* (1878) had "started us all."[5] Yeats's friend and O'Grady's admirer A.E., the poet George Russell, eulogized O'Grady after his death:

> When I read O'Grady I was as such a man who suddenly feels ancient memories rushing at him, and knows he was born in a royal house, that he had mixed with the mighty of heaven and earth and had the very noblest for his companions. . . . In O'Grady's writings the submerged river of national culture rose up again, a shining torrent, and I realised as I had bathed in that stream, that the greatest spiritual evil one nation could inflict on another was to cut off from it the story of the national soul.
> . . . I owe so much to Standish O'Grady that I would like to leave it on record that it was he who made me conscious and proud of my country, and recalled my mind, that might have wandered otherwise over too wide and vague a field of thought, to think of the earth under my feet and the children of our common mother.[6]

From 1878 to 1881, however, O'Grady had to finance publication of his *History of Ireland* himself, and Phillip Marcus, O'Grady's most perceptive critic and biographer, points out that the *History* remained largely unread after its publication (36). Even later, more popularly pointed books such as *The Coming of Cuculain* (1894) went quickly out of print after publication; O'Grady complained later that "the Cuculain story, in whole, has not been procurable for many years, though cordially praised by many representative literary men. A.E. in the Homestead [*sic*] last week praises it again most warmly, yet no one can get even a part of that tale."[7] Yet several of O'Grady's successors — Lady Gregory, Yeats, Eimar O'Duffy — picked up Cúchulainn as hero and refashioned him in their own images.

O'Grady had no idea of beginning a literary movement. He had neither Yeats's genius nor his organizing ability.[8] "Once begun, however, the movement did need," Marcus writes, "an 'ancestor,' and while still in mid-career O'Grady was elevated to that position" (79). Marcus notes that George Moore has a character in *Hail and Farewell* say of O'Grady, "He is very little read, but we all admire him. He is our past" (83). Yeats included most of O'Grady's books in his lists of the "Best Irish Books," becoming almost his patron. Of the dozen titles listed by Yeats under "Folk

Lore and Bardic Tales" and "History" in the *Daily Express* in 1895, five were O'Grady's: *History of Ireland — Heroic Period, The Coming of Culculain, Finn and His Companions, The Story of Ireland,* and *Red Hugh's Captivity.* In the *Bookman* that same year, Yeats allotted first place among "Contemporary Prose Writers" to O'Grady, arguing that his "multifarious knowledge of Gaelic legend and Gaelic history and a most Celtic temperament have put him in communion with the moods that have been over Irish purposes from the hour when, in the words put into the mouth of St. Dionysius, 'The Most High set the borders of the Nations according to the angels of God.'"[9]

O'Grady's romanticized version of ancient Ireland clearly appealed to the "Celtic Twilight" mood of Yeats and A.E. during the 1890s. In an 1895 review of O'Grady entitled "Battles Long Ago," Yeats expressed the view that his "Red Branch feasting with Cullan the smith, Cuchullin taming the weird horses, Cuchullin hunting down in his chariot the herd of enchanted deer, whose horns and hoofs are of iron, belong in nothing to our labouring noontide, but wholly to the shadowy morning twilight of time." Completely swallowing O'Grady's romanticized, chivalric view of the Ulster cycle, A.E. exclaimed, "Who could extol enough his Cuculain, that incarnation of Gaelic chivalry? . . . The figure of Cuculain which he discovered and refashioned for us is I think the greatest spiritual gift any Irishman for centuries has given to Ireland."[10]

Phillip Marcus points out that "much of the idealism attributed at this time to the ancient Irish was a misinterpretation arising from romanticized texts like those of O'Grady." Since O'Grady's day, scholarly translations of the great *Táin Bó Cuailnge* have made it clear that Cúchulainn was no simple, Tennysonian knight in shining armor, as O'Grady made him out to be. Benedict Kiely has written: "Standish O'Grady brought the heroes into Irish literature . . . heroes a little touched with the nineteenth century's and Standish O'Grady's ideas of what a hero should be."[11] But O'Grady's heroes were "touched" more than "a little": O'Grady freely added and deleted in order to maximize their Victorian chivalry.

In his versions of the old stories, Marcus notes, "prudishness and the desire to preserve an idealized vision of the subject-matter are blended with a strong vein of sentimentality" (25). In O'Grady, Cúchulainn's concubine, Ethne, for example, becomes merely " a very dear friend." Sex, as in the liaison between Fergus and Medb, is taboo. No bawdiness, such as Medb's epic urination, can be tolerated. O'Grady asserted that "a noble moral tone pervades the whole" of the early literature, which is clearly untrue. Irish saga may frequently offer a noble moral tone within its own context, but it also often violates Victorian ideas of morality. O'Grady

admitted many years later that he had found things in early Irish literature that he "simply could not write down and print and publish," features reflecting "the very loose morality of the age." O'Grady also added episodes of his own invention, such as the absurd depiction cited by Marcus of "Cu and Laeg walking through the city of Dublin and looking in the shop windows, where they saw a moving wooden model of a war chariot which Laeg, remembering the little child back home, bought as a present for him" (24, 25). Such a scene was not, unfortunately, intentionally comic, as was the satirist Eimar O'Duffy's reincarnation of Cúchulainn as a Ballsbridge tennis player in *King Goshawk and the Birds* (1926) or Joyce's mock-heroic descriptions of Bloom and the Citizen in the Cyclops chapter of *Ulysses* — both probably inspired in part by O'Grady's straight-faced pieties and language reminiscent of the nineteenth-century translation of Homer by Butcher and Lang.

O'Grady's romanticized view of ancient Ireland, one he would transpose to Elizabethan Ireland in *The Flight of the Eagle* and *Ulrick the Ready*, is to be understood primarily in terms of two crucial causes: his ignorance of the Irish language and his Ascendancy politics. Unlike his cousin Standish Hayes O'Grady, the Gaelic scholar, Standish James O'Grady was entirely dependent upon translations for his understanding of ancient Ireland. The version of it obtained from him by Yeats and A.E. was thus, at best, third-hand. Marcus argues that "it was not really faithful even to the spirit of his originals" (23). Yet he notes that A.E. felt that "whatever is Irish in me he kindled to life" (7), and the literary use of Irish legendary materials such as his was one of the dominant features of the Literary Revival. But the "Father of the Revival," like Yeats and A.E., knew no Irish and was apparently uninterested even in Anglo-Irish speech, limiting himself in his works to a conservative, conventional English idiom, the chief source of which was Carlyle.

Moreover, he was no Catholic nationalist, as his name and the titles of his literary works might lead one to expect, but a Protestant Tory. His background was much like Le Fanu's, or, for that matter, like many an Ascendancy youth in nineteenth-century Ireland: son of a Protestant clergyman and landowner in Castletown, County Cork, he studied for the clergy at Trinity College but instead was called to the bar in 1872. Like Le Fanu, O'Grady took an active part in Ascendancy journalism, urging Protestant landowners to assert their traditional rights and responsibilites in *The Crisis in Ireland* (1881) and *Toryism and the Tory Democracy* (1886), which were published in the midst of the great Irish Land War that led to the Wyndham Act of 1903 and the establishment of a

peasant proprietorship. Yeats described O'Grady's futile efforts to cajole the Ascendancy into responsibility as its "swan song." As Wayne Hall notes: "Like many writers of the Literary Revival, Yeats too followed O'Grady's lead in seeing Cuchulain as a model for the aristocrat fighting a doomed rearguard action against the changing social forces in modern Ireland."[12]

O'Grady's political writing was not, however, the strident, complacent anti-Catholic polemic of Le Fanu or the early Carleton. As Ascendancy threatened with extinction or at least diminishment could no longer afford to be complacent — nor was that O'Grady's natural inclination. However inaccurate he could be about ancient Ireland, he was always well intentioned about modern Ireland. He wanted the Ascendancy maintained, but he urged Irish landlords to move back onto their land, to treat their tenants well, and generally to take responsibility. He believed in the idea of Union, but he advocated in strong terms a Union in which Ireland would be an equal partner with England rather than a subservient colony. Hearkening back to the eighteenth-century Irish Parliament of Grattan and Flood and beyond that to the heroism of Cúchulainn and Red Hugh O'Donnell, he wanted an Ireland governed by an enlightened Irish landed aristocracy. In *Toryism and the Tory Democracy,* he scathingly attacked the English elimination of the Irish Parliament in the Act of Union, exclaiming: "We can beat our enemy, within the Constitution, and if, in his hate and fear, he would change the venue, preferring an extra-Constitutional verdict, we can beat him outside of the Constitution too." He hoped that an enlightened Toryism based on the principles of Lord Randolph Churchill would save the day; but, as Wayne Hall writes, "Lord Randolph was clearly not Cuchulain, nor did any other Messiah step forth from the aristocratic ranks."[13]

When by the turn of the century O'Grady saw that the Irish aristocracy had abdicated its responsibilities, permitting peasant proprietorship, and that equality within empire would not be easily granted by the English, he became more tolerant of the Catholic peasantry, on the one hand, and more impatient with English inactivity and misrule, on the other hand. Founding the *All-Ireland Review,* O'Grady emphasized common Irish interests in its pages, even going so far as to consider agrarian socialism. In his book *All Ireland* (1898), he urged an all-Ireland convention to assert Irish interests more strongly, noting that "the Imperial Parliament, in its dealings with Ireland, never yields to Justice, but always to Force." For this he has been called the "Fenian Unionist." Yeats related that O'Grady said at a party, "We have now a literary movement, it is not very important; it will be followed by a political movement, that will not be very

important; then must come a military movement, that will be important indeed," and urged that landlords drill the sons of their tenants and bid them "march to the conquest" of England.[14] A.E. argued that O'Grady's books "contributed the first spark of ignition" to the Easter Rising, a point of view since taken as the inspiration for William Irwin Thompson's *The Imagination of an Insurrection*.[15] A.E. linked O'Grady to the commander-in-chief of the Rising, testifying to "Pearse's love for the Cuculain whom O'Grady discovered or invented." In 1912 Pearse wrote, "What Ireland wants beyond all other modern countries, is a new birth of the heroic spirit," and, citing the *Táin* but sounding even more like O'Grady, he urged the boys of his school, St. Enda's, to "re-create and perpetuate in Ireland the knightly tradition of Cuchulain, 'better is short life with honour than long life with dishonour.'"[16]

To RECREATE the knightly tradition of Cúchulainn was exactly the aim of O'Grady's literary and historical work. Richard Fallis and Wayne Hall both find "imaginative recreation" to have been the core of O'Grady's artistic intent, and Phillip Marcus quite rightly emphasizes that the tension between history and imagination is the central conflict in his work. It is evident that O'Grady's evolution was always in the direction of attempts at more imagination; he repeatedly moves from history to romance. His trilogy on Cúchulainn — *The Coming of Cuculain* (1894), *In the Gates of the North* (1901), and *The Triumph and Passing of Cuculain* (1920) — is essentially an extended rewrite of *The History of Ireland* (1878–81) as romance, seeking to be more entertaining, more popular. Similarly, *Red Hugh's Captivity* (1889), a text replete with footnotes and scholarly digressions, was rewritten as the historical romance, *The Flight of the Eagle* (1897). He also shifted his sense of his readership, from a scholarly one to a more general and a more youthful one. *Finn and his Companions* (1892), Marcus notes, "was published in Fisher Unwin's 'Children's Library' series, and the youthful potential audience meant that any incidents involving sex or showing the main characters in an unfavorable light would have to be cut out" (43).

O'Grady's prefaces to his works reveal that his point of view on history was closer to Walter Scott's than was that of any other Irish historical novelist. Like Scott, he emphasized the necessarily tragic progression of society from feudalism to a superior modernism. The introduction to *Red Hugh's Captivity* states the case most clearly:

The history of Ireland during the sixteenth century is the history of a revolution, of the successive steps by which a radical and organic reconstitution of society was effected.

The Elizabethan conquest was, in my opinion, as inevitable as salutary, and the terrors and horrors which accompanied it, to a considerable extent, a necessary condition of its achievement. These petty kings and princes had to be broken once for all. In blood and flame and horror of great darkness it was fated that Ireland should pass from barbarism to civilisation, from the wild rule of "monocracies" to the reign of universal law. If it was England that presided over that death and new birth, the fact, I think was to Ireland's gain and not loss. It would certainly ill become an author, who is now enabled to address an audience so vast, to regret the events which have made that possible. . . . Whether our future be one of greater self-government, or of a closer and more vital union with England, we are and will remain part of the vast world-subdividing race that speaks the English tongue. . . . Between Ireland and her incorporation for ever with this mighty English-speaking race stood the Irish chiefs of the sixteenth century. The expanding genius of civilisation found such independent captains and princes, here as elsewhere over Europe, an intolerable bar to progress. Their extermination or subjugation was not only necessary but inevitable. And yet the men themselves have strong claims upon the sympathy of generous minds, more especially when their rebellions and their ruinous overthrow alike lie so far behind us in the quiet depths of the past . . . their wild lives not untouched with the mediaeval spirit of chivalry and romance.[17]

O'Grady had Scott's fascination with the old, doomed Gaelic way of life, emphasizing the connection between his work and Scott's and between Irish and Scottish materials:

Barbaric ages, too, have a certain charm of their own. The world taught by Sir Walter Scott feels this with regard to Scotland. Mediaeval Ireland also has that charm; it is there if only we have the wit to perceive it and to reveal it. Mediaeval Ireland closely resembled mediaeval Scotland, and the chiefs of Ulster were nearly related to those of west Scotland and the Highlands. Red Hugh himself was, on his mother's side, a scion of the house of Campbell and of the MacDonalds, lord of the Isles. Red Hugh was half Scotch; nay, as the reader will perceive in due time, there was in rebel Hugh a great deal more of his Scotch mother than of his Irish father. (*RHC*, 8)

In *The Flight of the Eagle* he echoes Scott's view of history as progressive, as a series of waves:

To the historian and his readers the fall of the O'Donnells is a nobler and more pathetic story than the rotting of the Burkes. And yet why particularize? Are they not all gone? Are not their successors gone or going?—*velut unda supervenit undam?* Do not all powers and dominions succeed each other as wave follows wave? Powers and dominions are only waves of that soundless deep called Man, which does not pass away.[18]

O'Grady was interested in the flight of the great earls—Hugh O'Neill and Red Hugh O'Donnell—because he saw their era of Irish history as the last great stand of the noble Irish aristocracy with which he identified. In his preface to *Ulrick the Ready* (1896), he exclaimed that this period "is the wild ending and the wild beginning of so much!"[19] In the preface to *Pacata Hibernia* (1896), he described the Battle of Kinsale of 1601 as "one of the grand turning-points in Anglo-Irish history. Indeed, it might well be reckoned amongst 'the Decisive Battles' of the world's history. Had its event fallen out differently all Ireland would have joined the Spaniards."[20] Instead, as with the French at Bantry in 1796, the Spanish were defeated, and the great earls fled with them to the Continent.

O'Grady published six books on Elizabethan Ireland over a thirteen-year period: *Red Hugh's Captivity* (1889), a narrative of the young Red Hugh O'Donnell's imprisonment by the forces of the crown from 1587 to 1591; *The Bog of Stars* (1893), a volume of stories; *Pacata Hibernia* (1896), an edition of Lord Carew's memoir of the events of 1600 to 1603; *Ulrick the Ready* (1896), a historical novel involving events surrounding the Battle of Kinsale; *The Flight of the Eagle* (1897), a revision of *Red Hugh's Captivity* which attempted a more imaginative style and form, increasing the emphasis on O'Donnell's escape, not merely his captivity; and *Hugh Roe O'Donnell* (1902), a short play, or series of dramatic sketches, about the same events. O'Donnell's brief but fiery career was closely tied to the fortunes of a nascent Irish nationalism. As a youth of fourteen in 1587, he was taken hostage along with several others so that his parents and the other Irish chieftains who had asserted their independence in the north would not join forces with the Spanish Armada against England. When Red Hugh and his friends finally escaped from Dublin Castle back to Donegal at the end of 1591, their newly won freedom was thus a great blow for the cause of the earls. "A biography of this youth—who was but twenty-eight when he died—is essential," O'Grady explained, "to a right understanding of that memorable struggle. . . . So it may be regarded as an explanatory introduction to the history of the Nine Years' War" (*RHC*, 16–17). The Nine Years' War ended with English victory at Kinsale in 1601,

and the subsequent flight of the earls. O'Donnell was later poisoned in Spain.

Although this chapter of Irish history was marked by the birth of what came to be understood as modern Irish nationalism, O'Grady did not view the Nine Years' War as a simple conflict of Irish against English. He felt that the great Irish lords were opposed not only by the English but by many of their own countrymen who, resenting their political power and control of the land, acquiesced to or even aided the English. In *The Flight of the Eagle* he claimed that "the Tir-Cullen peasantry would have hunted down Red Hugh with more alacrity than they would a deer. With him they were in no sort of feudal relation; with the Viceroy they were, to a certain extent" (*RHC*, 148). He empathized with the great earls as landlords caught in a bind similar to that of the doomed, degenerate landlords and land agents of his own day, yet possessed of a courage and nobility entirely lacking among his contemporaries: Red Hugh was another Cúchulainn, not a Captain Boycott. As his son, Hugh Art O'Grady, professor and member of another ascendancy in Pretoria, South Africa, explained: "His trained intellect easily discovered what is now a truism, that the Irish nation then rallied round the Tudors and made them kings of Ireland, and drove them and used them to overthrow the landlords of the day, the great Irish chieftains, who had become intensely unpopular for the sole reason that they were landlords, and that all Elizabethan wars were but 'of the crown plus the majority of the nation, versus the great lords.'"[21] So O'Grady's version of Red Hugh was colored not only by his romanticized view of an aristocratic Cúchulainn, but by his own political position.

An examination of *Red Hugh's Captivity, The Flight of the Eagle, Ulrick the Ready,* and *Hugh Roe O'Donnell* reveals an author involved in revising a single story about a single hero, beginning with a historical, scholarly text and transforming it into historical fiction and finally, drama. O'Grady was one of only two Irish historical novelists so thoroughly involved in a series of works in several genres about a single hero and a single period of history. The other was James Plunkett, who rewrote *Big Jim,* his 1955 radio play about James Larkin and the great Dublin strike of 1913, as a stage play and finally a novel, *Strumpet City* (1969). Interestingly, each author began with a documentary work dependent on hard facts and the dominance of the hero (*Red Hugh's Captivity, Big Jim*) and subsequently wrote a historical novel in which the hero was withdrawn to the background (*Ulrick the Ready, Strumpet City*), compensating for this retreat to fiction and withdrawal of the hero by also publishing historical narratives about the hero himself (O'Grady's *Pacata Hibernia* and

The Flight of the Eagle, Plunkett's essay "Jim Larkin").[22] The evolution of these works shows that both O'Grady and Plunkett came to the realization that the genre of the historical novel demanded that the historical hero, the "big name," be withdrawn to the background in order to avoid a confusion of biography and fiction and in order to give the stage to the creatures of the author's own historical yet fictional imagination.

The tension between history and imagination, between scholarship and fiction, was central in O'Grady's work and was never fully resolved in it. The prefaces and texts of *Red Hugh's Captivity* and *The Flight of the Eagle* indicate that O'Grady never completely decided whether he was writing a history book or a novel. Ernest Boyd called *Red Hugh's Captivity* (1889) his "first novel,"[23] but it is clear that the book is a history, not a novel. It is full of footnotes, and in the preface O'Grady insists that "the facts, well told, ought to surpass fiction, even in those respects in which fiction is most delightful." He added, "The historian relating only what is recorded may supply pictures of scenes and events, and portraits of historic figures, which in moving interest ought to bear comparison with the best imaginative work. We all prefer a pleasant fancy to a bitter fact; but when the facts are in themselves pleasant and are pleasantly told, fiction avowing itself to be fiction must go the second place." Sticking to the archives, to "the pages of contemporary historians, and the State papers which for this epoch are most abundant," O'Grady explained: "So perfect are the delineations yielded by contemporary historians and by the archives of the State, that it may be doubted whether Sir Walter Scott himself, having these before him, would do more than transmute their varied details and descriptions into one harmonious stream of continuous narrative." He could "hardly imagine a place left for the historical novelist," given how "prolific was the age in this respect" (*RHC, 14–15*).

O'Grady subsequently changed his mind about the superiority of history to fiction, after an experience recounted by Marcus: "Browsing one day in the library of the University Club he discovered that the club's copy of George Petrie's seminal archeological study of the round towers of Ireland was uncut; this experience, his son relates, 'opened his eyes to the mistake he had made. The public were not attracted by a sober treatise. Fiction and romance were their intellectual delicacies. Accordingly . . . he rewrote the Celtic legends in the guise of a novel'" (36). Under this inspiration, he rewrote the story of Cúchulainn, contained in his *History*, as a romantic trilogy. During the same period he also wrote his Elizabethan romances about O'Donnell, publishing *The Bog of Stars, The Flight of the Eagle,* and *Ulrick the Ready.*

The Flight of the Eagle (1897) is a thoroughgoing revision of *Red*

Hugh's Captivity in which O'Grady removed the footnotes to an appendix and sought to enliven the story stylistically as well as to popularize it by shifting the focus more to Red Hugh's heroic escape. Chapters in *Red Hugh's Captivity* not sufficiently focused upon Red Hugh, such as "Oxford Culture, and the End of It" and "Lord Burleigh's Interest in Irish Cattle," were deleted in favor of eleven additional chapters devoted to Hugh's escape from Dublin Castle and flight to Donegal. The plot is simple: Red Hugh is deceitfully taken captive and shipped off to London and then to Dublin Castle; his parents campaign for his release; on the second attempt Hugh and his cohorts successfully escape from the castle and flee to Donegal, aided by Turlogh O'Hagan and Feach MacHugh O'Byrne (the latter of whom is compared by O'Grady to Scott's Rob Roy and Vic Ian Wohr). The earlier book ended with a lament about Hugh's English captor, Viceroy Perrott—"Alas, poor Perrott!" (*RHC*, 277)—after a declaration that "this tale began with Perrott; let it end with him" (*RHC*, 276). In contrast, *The Flight of the Eagle* ends with a celebration of Red Hugh's freedom: "The caged eagle of the North is again in the North, and free" (*FE*, 307).

In one of the new chapters, the penultimate "Through the Mountain Gates of Ulster," which Yeats said continued to inspire him for a long time, he narrates the passing of Hugh beside the emblematic scenes of Cúchulainn's heroism: "The mountain was Cuculain's sign-post, when, a little boy driven forth by the war spirits, he secretly left his home and his dear mother, seeking Emain Macha" (*FE*, 287–88). At Slieve Gullion and Lough Liath, Red Hugh inherits all the ancient heroism of Gaelic Ulster as O'Grady saw it. O'Grady links Hugh to the "mythus," the long series of ancient Irish heroes and heroic deeds, in the phantasmagoric mold of "MacKenna's Dream," the ballad in which Brian Boru, Sarsfield, King James, and Father Murphy are all joined in battle, epitomizing the mythos of Irish history explored in Chapter 2. O'Grady's sacred topographical icons, Slieve Gullion and Lough Liath, create the "mythus."

> Here the sentinels of the Red Branch from their white watch-tower, Carn Fion, scanned afar the mearings of Ulster. Here Ossian's sire slew the enchanter Almain, son of Midna, who once every year, to the sound of unearthly music, consumed Tara with magic flames. On this mountain Cuculain seized the wild fairy steed, the Liatha Macha, new risen from the Grey Lake, ere steed and hero in their giant wrestlings and reelings encompassed Banba, and in the quaking night the nations trembled. Here, steeped in Lough Liath's waters, Finn's golden tresses took on the hue and glitter of radiant snow. . . . Names, deeds, grey legends, dire happenings and becomings without number, or the spiritual force and power of them, touched with awe the boy's heart as he gazed on the

haunted hill, so long familiar in his mind as a thought, as a name, now a great visible actuality looming before his eyes, crowned with cloud, crawled over by the travelling mists. Save with the mind's eye the boy could not see Lough Liath. . . . O melancholy lake, shaped like the moon! lake uplifted high in the arms of Slieve Gullion; boggy, desolate, thick-strewn with grey boulders on thy eastern shore and, on thy western, regarded askance by thy step-child the rosy heather, ruddy as with blood — aloof, observant of thy never-ending sorrow; unfathomable, druid lake: home of the white steed immortal: bath of the Caillia-Bullia, the people's dread; thy turbid waves aye breaking in pale foam upon the grey shore strewn with boulders and the wrecks of the work of men's hands; horror-haunted, enchanted lake; seat of dim ethnic mysteries, lost all or scat-tered to the winds; with thy made wells and walls and painted temples, and shining cairns, and subterrene corridors obscure — walked once by druids gold-helmeted and girded with the Sun; — scene of religious pomps, and thronging congregations hymning loud their forgotten gods obscene or fair; what mighty tales, what thoughts far-journeying, Protean, sprang once in light from thy wine-dark, mystic floor, Lough Liath! Sky-neighbouring lake vexed by all the winds! mournful, sibilant, teeming fount of thy vast phantasmal mythus, O Ultonia! (FE, 288, 289–90)

Stylistically, this passage, the impassioned high point of the book, resem-bles Thomas De Quincey's "Dream-Fugue" and other nineteenth-century English prose works much more than it does the Táin Bó Cuailnge, al-though a comparison of it with the overwrought prose style of the Stowe version of the Táin might suggest that O'Grady had some dim sympathy with Irish material after all, even though he could not read it in the original.

In the sketchy playlet Hugh Roe O'Donnell (1902), in which Red Hugh is finally allowed to speak for himself, an even closer identification between Hugh and Cúchulainn is made: "And that is Slieve Gullion, my benefactor — the spirit of Cuchullin broods over it this night — I feel stronger as the bracing air through the Gates of the North strikes my brow."[24] Both Cúchulainn and Red Hugh offered O'Grady — and the broader, more youthful readership he tried to reach with The Coming of Cuculain and The Flight of the Eagle — boyhood narratives exemplary of courage and nobility. From his opening description, Red Hugh is characterized in the mold of the boy's hero tale:

Of the three, one taller than the others stood in the middle. His compan-ions leaned towards him, talking Gaelic in low voices. He stood straight as a rod. His complexion was white and ruddy, brilliantly so; his eyes grey and bright, with a most keen outlook, expressing a tameless energy.

His long hair, a glowing auburn, rolled upon his shoulders. He was sixteen years of age, yet his countenance already bore signs of a mind beyond his years. Such was his bearing, that in any company a stranger would quickly observe him, and inquire with interest concerning a youth so remarkable for his beauty and proud air of self-possession and self-control.
This boy was the famous Red Hugh O'Donnell. (*FE*, 16–17)

Although O'Grady sought popularity and "readability" in passages such as these, and visionary imagination in a chapter such as "Through the Mountain Gates of Ulster," *The Flight of the Eagle* is still shackled by remnants of its scholarly first version, *Red Hugh's Captivity*. It retains continual, direct references to and quotations from O'Grady's historical sources, as outlined in his preface: "The authorities for the story are the 'Annuals of the Four Masters'; Philip O'Sullivan's charmingly Herodotean narrative, in Latin, entitled *Historia Hiberniae*; O'Clery's 'Bardic Life of Hugh Roe'; and the 'Calendar of State Papers, Ireland,' from 1587 forward. The colouring, the visualization and dramatization, are, however, derived from a wider circle of contemporary literature. I may add that the book contains almost nothing for which there is not direct or indirect historical justification" (*FE*, v-vi). This last assertion is, lamentably, too true: throughout the book O'Grady is unwilling or unable to fictionalize.
Most crucially, he does not write dialogue. The chief characters of *The Flight of the Eagle* almost never speak, and the novel, if it is a novel at all, fails because of this. Carleton, in *Redmond Count O'Hanlon*, had presented a tale that was all imagination and no history; here O'Grady, shackled by his historical sources, is guilty of a lack of novelistic invention. He states his dilemma in the opening words of his preface:

This tale, in spite of its title, is not a romance, but an actual historic episode, told with hardly a freer use of the historical imagination than is employed by the more popular and picturesque of our professed historians. There is, however, this difference between my method and theirs, viz. that while they write directly, I aim at a similar result indirectly through a certain dramatization. The same method has been adopted, I think very effectively, by Carlyle, at times, in his history of Frederick the Great. (*FE*, v)

But O'Grady's "dramatization" fails because his characters do not speak; and a narrator sounding like Carlyle only serves to distance his readers from his Irish materials. In a brief, oblique reference to O'Grady, Thomas

Flanagan complained of "a Red Hugh O'Donnell who talked like Sir Philip Sidney and comported himself like Walter Scott welcoming George IV to Edinburgh."[25] It would be more accurate to say that Red Hugh does not talk at all in *The Flight of the Eagle;* O'Grady's point of view on him is entirely exterior. The only point at which the narrator comes close to entering Red Hugh's consciousness is when Hugh escapes for the first time: "In his passage he struck against or passed between certain tarry lumps, about the size of cannon balls. They projected from poles horizontally above the gate. Perhaps his stick caught in these poles, and he had to turn it and his head sideways, to get through. What were these tarry lumps about the size of cannon balls? Heads! Perhaps his own will figure there in the morning with glassy eyeballs and long red hair flashing in the wind" (*FE*, 129). All too often, however, O'Grady merely tells us about an event rather than showing it to us, asking us to "imagine" a conversation rather than presenting it directly: "While Red Hugh is a captive, imagine Owen Ogue of the Battle-axes and the Dark-Daughter of the Isles ceaselessly warring and diplomatizing in order that the chieftainship of Tir-Connall might remain open, and that high place vacant, whensoever the boy should return to claim it" (*FE*, 64).

    Ulrick the Ready, or the Chieftains' Last Rally (1896) is more readable because in it O'Grady adopts the conventions of the historical novel as Scott exemplified them. He ignores his earlier claim that Scott, given sources like his Irish ones, would have shared his preference for fact over fiction. Yet apparently only a lack of sources convinced him to shift Red Hugh from the forefront to the background of the action. He notes in his "postscript" that "Tyrone and Hugh Roe, though they more through the story, are treated slightly. I fear to enlarge upon such characters without the assistance of the complete Calendar of State Papers" (*UR*, 282). Marcus notes that he added the disclaimer that "though the work is a romance, I know that the historical setting is in the main correct, and believe that the colouring and dramatization supply a true picture of the manners and men of the age. . . . It is not a story all in the air, but one rooted in fact" (56–57).

    The plot of *Ulrick the Ready* closely follows Scott's model and, even more closely, the plot of Le Fanu's *Torlogh O'Brien.* Like Torlogh, the noble Catholic, Gaelic Ulrick fights for the nationalist cause but ends up marrying into the Protestant Ascendancy, taking the "lily-white" hand of the Protestant Rachel Egerton, a heroine as pure and as innocuous as Le Fanu's Grace Willoughby. Ulrick is the steward of O'Sullivan Bere, a Gaelic noble from O'Grady's own area of County Cork. The other Gaels,

O'Grady explains to us, had it in for O'Sullivan, because he controlled the land; they sided with Hugh O'Neill when O'Sullivan fought him, and now they shift their allegiance to the crown when O'Sullivan throws in his lot with O'Neill, O'Donnell, and the Spanish. O'Sullivan is, like Red Hugh, the victimized aristocrat. As always, O'Grady's view of the past is thoroughly colored by his own position in the present. His explanation of Elizabethan Irish land management, for example, includes a veiled slap at the scheme of land nationalization advanced by his contemporary adversary, Michael Davitt:[26]

> Government by chieftains had its good side too. Order was strongly preserved by a man whose power and wealth, nay, whose existence depended on the maintenance of order. If the laws and customs lent themselves to tyranny, they were at least well understood, and were in harmony with the ideas and habits of primitive people. The lord of the soil was resident, and rents were consumed on the spot. Whatever advantages may accrue from the "nationalization of the land" accrued under the rule of the chieftain, for he was the State and owned the land, he as head and representative of the clan. The servile population had no share in the consumption of these rents, as they had no rights in the soil; but so far as the clan regnant was concerned, there was perfect land nationalization. (UR, 140)

In the midst of all of this, Ulrick, who is very much like one of Scott's "imbeciles," wages his suit for Rachel's hand, which for a time is frustrated by his poverty, like Edmond O'Connor in Le Fanu's The Cock and Anchor. When O'Sullivan is finally forced to flee to Spain, he rewards Ulrick's loyalty with a sum of money with which Ulrick is able to buy into the Ascendancy plantation of the north, winning, in thoroughly Scottian fashion, both a wife and an estate, emblematic of Union and the end of the war.

> Indeed, all over Ireland just now there was a vast amount of marrying and giving in marriage. The savage parties which so recently had been even slaying each other's children, showing pity neither to the bald head of the ancient nor the bald head of the babe, rushed now with alacrity, with pipings and trumpetings, into matrimonial alliances. For the century-lasting struggle was over and its great issues decided, and out of the bloody welter and the roaring surges, Aphrodyte arose new-born, shining like her own peerless star on the edge of night and morning. (UR, 276)

O'Grady appeals to Scott's precedent from the opening page of the novel, the first chapter's epigraph describing Ulrick in Scott's words: "'He rode all undaunted, / He rode all alone.' – (UR,3). What little peasant dialect there is in the novel is borrowed directly from Scott. Where Ulrick is described as "the purtiest *dhan-oosal* in the kingdom," O'Grady notes that "Scott always writes this word as *dhooney-wassal:* it means simply gentleman, *duine*-man, *uasal*-noble or gentle" (UR, 5). This is the O'Grady Donald Davie must have had in mind when he alluded to "Standish O'Grady . . . still pursuing the mirage of 'an Irish Scott.'"[27]

Although (or perhaps because) derivative of Scott, *Ulrick the Ready* is much more readable than *The Flight of the Eagle.* His characters generally still don't speak any dialect other than Carlyle's – for O'Grady disdained Anglo-Irish speech, describing Lady Gregory's experiments with it as "unfortunate"[28] – but at least they do speak. Deprived of extensive historical sources, O'Grady permits himself to fictionalize freely and to create a personal interest, however maudlin it may be, surrounding Ulrick. The novel fails to integrate love and war in a consistent fashion – Book I is mostly about war; Book II, mostly about love – but at least both are included, so that the reader's sympathies are sought both on a political, historical level and a personal, fictional level: "At the moment there were, in fact, two Ulricks under one hat; one immersed in visions and love's sweet sorrow, the other recording the words of the newsbringer" (UR, 232–33).

Mentioning the Spanish landing and the Battle of Kinsale in his preface, O'Grady notes: "The tale as it travels just touchs or glances at these historic and epoch-marking events, its essential purpose, if it have any, being only to exhibit life as it was then lived in Ireland, a work for which the materials abound even to profusion, if only the art to use them be not wanting. In other respects, too, this stormy century lends itself better than the rest to the work of the historical novelist" (UR, ii). He was determined to meet the demands of the genre by keeping the great figures and events of the era in the background, although occasionally he overdoes it. The Battle of Kinsale, for example, is covered in a single sentence: "Then at this juncture ensued the astonishing Battle of Kinsale, in which a mere handful of Royalist-Irish Connaughtmen, under the command of the young chief of the Burkes of Clan-Ricarde and a few English dragoons, utterly routed and put to flight an army of nigh ten times their number seasoned and long-victorious fighting men, and under the command of such famous soldiers as Hugh O'Neill and Red Hugh" (UR, 261). Ulrick meets the now full-grown Red Hugh only once; reinforced by quotations from "O'Donnell Abú," his appearance is brief and imposing, like Jim Larkin's in Plunkett's *Strumpet City.*

U LRICK THE READY was no better or no worse than many of the nineteenth-century Irish novels that aped Scott with mixed results. O'Grady is particulary notable not only because he was acclaimed as the "Father of the Renaissance," but because he focused so extensively upon Elizabethan Ireland and the flight of the earls. He was unable to deal effectively with later periods. In the Wake of King James, a romance set a century later, was described by Father Brown, who generally praised O'Grady, as "insipid" and "generally devoid of historical incidents."[29] Much more common during O'Grady's time — which was marked politically by Fenianism, the Land War, and a generally stronger brand of Irish nationalism — was the historical novel dealing with what seemed to be the great Irish nationalist thunderclap: 1798. Between 1869 and 1919, no fewer than thirty Irish historical novels on 1798 were published; the Jacobite-Williamite war, as the subject of thirteen novels during the same years, ran second in popularity.[30] Clearly, '98 and the Boyne had come to be viewed as the great battles of Irish nationalism, and the historical novel was nothing if not a celebration of nationalism.

The best novel on 1798 during the Literary Revival, and in fact the best Irish historical novel published on any subject during this period, was William Buckley's Croppies Lie Down: A Tale of Ireland in '98 (1903). This novel is both typical and outstanding among the historical novels of the Revival: typical in that it is just one of scores of such novels by little-known authors, but outstanding in its thoroughness and realism. It was the best Irish historical novel since The Boyne Water and pointed the future direction of the genre. Buckley seemed to sense, for the first time in the course of the Irish historical novel, that romance was not a prerequisite of good, readable historical fiction. He develops realistic characters, characters shaded by some measure of ambiguity and complexity, not comic-book, black-and-white, good-and-bad characters. In Croppies Lie Down, realism is born in the Irish historical novel, a realism that subsequently dominated the genre.

Very little is known about the life of William Buckley. Ernest Boyd praises Croppies Lie Down as "an isolated volume of . . . literary quality," a "powerful and well written study of the Irish rebellion of 1798," but he tells us nothing else about the book or its author. Comparing it to Michael Banim's The Croppy, Father Steven Brown notes that Croppies Lie Down is "equally realistic and even more conscientious in its fidelity to the facts of history." But even the incomparably industrious Father Brown can tell us little of Buckley's life: "Born in Cork, and educated there at St. Vincent's Seminary and the Queen's College. His first literary work appeared in MacMillan's Magazine. Resides in Dublin." The pious Father

Brown adds that Buckley's only other known book, *Cambia Carty and Other Stories* (1907), contains "close descriptions of lower and middle classes in modern Youghal. In places will be unpleasant reading for the people of Youghal. Pictures of Cork snobbery decidedly unfavourable to Cork people, and on the whole disagreeable and sordid."[31]

Modern scholarship unearths little additional information about Buckley. A search of the National Library of Ireland by its director revealed only a single paragraph about the man, in a 1913 article on Cork authors by John Gilbert, who noted that Buckley was "born at Sunday's Well" and "is an artist of ability" and "an art critic, and contributes articles to 'MacMillan's,' 'Temple Bar,' and the better class weeklies," as well as serving as "the critic of current literature for the 'Irish Times.'" Gilbert added that *Croppies Lie Down* "created a sensation," and he reviewed Buckley's other book more favorably than Father Brown: "He also wrote 'Cambia Carty,' a series of stories racy of the soil, and aglow with local colour."[32]

Not even the dates of Buckley's birth and death are known — but no matter. What matters is that he was the cream of a huge crop of nearly anonymous historical novelists of the Revival; somehow it seems fitting that the realistic Irish historical novel of the twentieth century should be so obscure in its inception.

The most realistic and novel aspect of *Croppies Lie Down* was that all of its main characters, caught in the midst of the disastrous Wexford rising of 1798, are frustrated in the course of the story, just as was the rising itself. Previously, Irish historical novels consistently presented heroes and heroines who somehow found happiness in the midst of political chaos, destruction, and degradation. Not so in *Croppies Lie Down*. Its very title suggests the despair of '98 — the real '98, the '98 which Michael Banim swept under the carpet in the ethereal happy ending of *The Croppy*. "Croppies Lie Down" was a well-known ballad:

> Down, down, croppies lie down.
> The rebels so bold — when they've none to oppose —
> To houses and hay-stacks are terrible foes;
> They murder poor parsons, and also their wives,
> But soldiers at once make them run for their lives;
> And wherever we march, thro' the country or town,
> In ditches or cellars, the croppies lie down.[33]

Buckley's novel certainly does not share the ballad's Ascendancy point of view, but it lives up to its violent, chaotic tone.

The plot of *Croppies Lie Down* adopts many of the conventions

of the romantic nineteenth-century Irish historical novel, yet it does so in order to frustrate them. In Irene Neville we meet again the pure Protestant heroine, but by the end of the novel she is neither pure nor alive. She gets married — not to the Catholic hero, Devereux, but to the evil government schemer, Gash, she has bought out the Neville estate. Mr. Neville is the noble father; instead of blessing the marriage of hero and heroine at the end of the novel, however, he is shot dead midway by rebel peasants while standing in a window of his own home, trying to speak to them in search of peace. In fact, more main characters are dead than alive by the end of the story: Mr. Neville, Irene, Devereux, Gash, and the good Kitty Creagh, who counterspies against the devilish government agent, Harrigan.

Croppies Lie Down opens much like Banim's The Croppy: with an idyllic description of the peaceful, pastoral river Slaney.

> The shimmering Slaney waters were radiant with many blended tints of sunset splendour as a cloudless day in May came to a fitting and most perfect close. The murmuring of bees in wayside gardens, the lowing of homeward-coming herds, and the faint, fitful bleating of distant flocks melted upon the ear into one harmony of sound which was but the expression of the peace that lay like a benediction on gilded plain and wood-crowned hill.
>
> So pastoral a landscape seemed to have the power of assimilating to itself the most discordant elements.[34]

A peaceful Wexford, however, is quickly cast into a chaos from which it never recovers in this novel. Irene is in love with Devereux, the romantic rebel who knows Wolfe Tone and has lived on the Continent as well as in Ireland. As a heroine, Irene is not the simpleton who dominated previous Irish historical novels. She is allowed by Buckley to experience complexities of feeling, such as a real person in her situation might have encountered: she loves Devereux, but she doesn't want to lose her position in society, so their romance must be a secret one. "She felt a thrill of satisfaction in the thought that she too belonged to this privileged class which could control the destinies of a nation" (28). At one point Irene is on the verge of throwing over Devereux because of his apparent poverty, until he shows up in full uniform and impresses her with his equally noble status.

After Devereux goes off to war, Irene is lonely, and allows the English Major Heathcote to woo her. Finally, after her father's death, believing that Devereux is also dead, Irene resigns herself to marriage with Gash, for the sole purpose of retaining a connection with the Neville family estate, of which Gash has gained ownership.

She cast her eyes over the glorious unfamiliar scene, the rolling woods, the shining water, the peaked mountains framing all, as if to appeal to some invisible presence of which they were the home. It was not the glance of a young girl bidding farewell to the rosy present in the glow of a golden future, it was the hopeless look of a woman who knows what life is and has learned the lesson its knowledge brings. The past had vanished from her as if it had never been, the future could bring no joy to equal that which was lost. She did not think once of any possible duty she might owe the man at her side, any obligation she was undertaking, her own sorrow, her own disillusionment swallowed up all else, nothing mattered — only Malplaquet should be saved if possible, for it had been her mother's. (467–68)

The novel is in part the story of a Big House laid low. Mr. Neville, short of money, had compromised himself with Gash and his cohorts; now Gash has obtained not only Neville's home, but his daughter. Irene tells Gash that her "heart owns the lordship of the dead" (465). Finally, Devereux reappears, angry that Irene has married another. Just as the lovers reach a sad reconciliation, Gash appears, duels Devereux, and accidentally kills Irene. Gash's tragedy is that he really loved her, but he is mired in an evil that exacts its own revenge: his suicide ends the novel.

Croppies Lie Down contains the same basic plot structure found in Le Fanu's *Torlogh O'Brien*, one typical of the nineteenth-century Irish historical novel at large: the Catholic hero (Devereux) vies with the government adversary (Heathcote) for the hand of the genteel Protestant heroine (Irene) and the approval of her noble father (Neville). But the conventional plot structure is confounded by a denouement in which all of these characters die, in lieu of the usual happy wedding of the Catholic hero and Protestant heroine. Furthermore, Heathcote, the government adversary, is not the ogre expected in the conventional story (Miles Garrett in *Torlogh O'Brien* and John Gernon in *The Last Baron of Crana*, for example). Heathcote is a government officer, but he is no bigoted fool. His assessment of the rebels and his anticipation of his own role in their demise are insightful and realistic: "'They will be goaded into doing something for which they are not prepared,' he murmured, 'they will be cut to pieces — I shall probably be one of the slayers'" (46). Indeed, Heathcote becomes the chief lens of the novel, through which the events of history are viewed. Instead of playing the role of the demonic villain as in the old romances, he is the novel's objective narrative focus. All the more credible because he is an English officer rather than an Irish rebel, Heathcote seems to speak for Buckley, as when he comments, "I recollect reading that an Englishman once said of those . . . Union projects —'Do not make

a union of us: we should unite with you only to rob you'" (140). Heathcote
is the moral king's soldier who sees how evil is the reality of '98 in Wexford. He has the nobility and impartiality of Banim's Robert Evelyn, but
none of his ability to act on his beliefs.

Bound up with Buckley's chaotic fictional world is the madness
and chaos of the rising, as viewed by Heathcote. Buckley does not glorify
war, as do most nineteenth-century Irish historical novelists. His is not
the world of romantic chivalry in combat, but instead that of real human
suffering: "On the road were seen many human forms, some in dull frieze,
some in gaudy scarlet, most of them motionless; a riderless charger with
severed bridle was quietly cropping the herbage along a fence side, and
a dying peasant was hoarsely repeating the Lord's Prayer in Irish, the bloody
bubbles breaking on his lips" (199–200). Buckley consistently describes
battle scenes in terms of "confusion," "turmoil," "chaos," "infernal din,"
and "indiscriminant firing." Heathcote, out of uniform and without his
papers, is beaten and nearly pitch-capped by his own side at the Hermit-
age, a dismal, degenerate government torture chamber. Nor does Buckley
neglect the atrocities committed by the rebel side, as for example when
Neville is shot dead by the Croppies in the window of his own home,
just as he is about to implore them to lay down their arms and talk to
him. Irene speaks for the author when she exclaims, "O God, what a thing
war is!" (360). There is no happy ending here, either personally or politically. In the midst of the rising and its brutal suppression, lovers are not
merely separated, as in earlier Irish historical novels, but killed. This is
the realistic message of the novel: this is the way it was.

In certain other respects, *Croppies Lie Down* is like a conventional
nineteenth-century novel. Buckley's dialogue, for example, follows the
typical Anglo-Irish speech presented in nineteenth-century fiction, full of
"bould," "yer haner," "take dat," and the like. There are the usual awkward-
nesses about explaining Irish habits to a partly foreign readership: "a ditch
as it is called in Ireland" (75). Yet the points where the novel adheres to
the conventions of its nineteenth-century predecessors serve to highlight
by contrast its unusually realistic departures in character and plot, thus
making Buckley's tragic denouement and his uncompromising exposé of
war seem all the more pronounced. *Croppies Lie Down* is a cumbersome,
often melodramatic novel, but it was the first attempt since *The Boyne
Water* to portray an Irish revolution as it really was, not merely the way
romantic authors such as Le Fanu, Carleton, and O'Grady wished it had
been. Buckley managed to move out of romance into realism. Subsequent
Irish historical novelists remained as unaware of Buckley's achievement
as his contemporaries had been, but their realistic visions were foreshad-

owed by his. Writing in the wake of a more prevalent realism and under the inspiration of greater literary models, Buckley's successors followed the realistic direction suggested by *Croppies Lie Down* and surpassed its achievement.

6

The Realistic Visions of
Seán Ó Faoláin and
Francis MacManus

THE EASTER RISING of 1916 was a great, echoing cataclysm in modern Irish history and literature. "A terrible beauty is born," proclaimed Yeats that year. Reflecting the attitudes of their countrymen, Irish writers and politicians are still reacting to the events of 1916 to 1923; indeed, Irish historical novelists have only recently treated the stormy period of the rising and the Anglo-Irish and Civil wars. In contrast to the popular explosion of the genre during the Literary Revival, far fewer Irish historical novels were published during the period immediately after 1916. Somehow it seems appropriate that copies of the first edition of Father Steven Brown's book *Ireland in Fiction*, including his exhaustive compendium of historical novels published before 1916, were destroyed when the printing office behind the General Post Office burst into flames during the Rising. When Father Brown published a revised edition of the book in 1919, he was able to list only one historical novel published since 1916: Louise J. Walsh's *The Next Time, a Story of Forty-Eight* (1919).[1] Francis Sheehy-Skeffington, whose socialism, pacifism, and feminism marked him out as an unusual, remarkable entity in Irish politics, published his novel on '98, *In Dark and Evil Days*, in 1916. In Easter Week that year, he was shot and buried in quicklime by a British officer in Dublin — even though he had spent the early part of Easter Week as a noncombatant, pathetically trying to dissuade looters from attacking the Dublin shops.

After 1916, more distant history seemed for a time irrelevant. Instead, several novelists busied themselves with *Bildungsromanen* tracing their own reactions to the Easter Rising. Eimar O'Duffy's *The Wasted Island* (1919), for example, was an attack on Patrick Pearse and his followers. Dermot Barry's *Tom Creagan* (1932) was set during the years before 1920 and imitated the quintessential Irish *Bildungsroman*, Joyce's *A Portrait of the Artist as a Young Man*, while the young protagonists of Louis d'Alton's *Death Is So Fair* (1938) and Michael McLaverty's *Call My Brother Back* (1939) responded to the events of 1916 to 1923.[2]

Until the 1930s, attempts by Irish novelists to return to history were few and feeble. Brinsley MacNamara's *The Clanking of Chains* (1920), for instance, was not really a novel at all, but rather a series of nationalist episodes or historical sketches ranging from Robert Emmet to Sinn Féin. And most of the novels still followed nineteenth-century models. Eimar O'Duffy's *The Lion and the Fox* (1922) and Joseph O'Neill's *Wind from the North* (1934) were couched in the romantic, remote mold of Standish O'Grady. O'Grady's influence on O'Duffy is reflected both in subject matter and style: *The Lion and the Fox* is a turgid account of the era of Hugh O'Neill in which O'Duffy adopts with a straight face the romantic approach to history, curiously enough, that he himself subsequently lampooned when he became a satirist in *King Goshawk and the Birds*. Robert Hogan has remarked that as a "swashbuckling historical novel," *The Lion and the Fox* was unlike anything else he wrote. In *Wind from the North*, Joseph O'Neill emulated O'Grady's romantic view of ancient Ireland, writing a first-person account, in the style of a memoir, about the coming of the Danes.[3]

Irish writers, like the Irish people as a whole, were slow in recovering from the divisive and disastrous Civil War of 1922–23. The new Irish nation-state suffered a violent birth and experienced slow growth. In *The Years of the Great Test, 1926–39*, Francis MacManus reminisced about the problems inherent in "The Literature of the Period":

> In the ten or fifteen years after the establishment of the Irish Free State, the unhealed wounds of the civil war seemed beyond even the slow medicine of time. Time was at work, however. The conflict of black and white idealisms, the inhuman war of the angels, was becoming blurred by the everyday business of living, by rebuilding, restoring farms, starting creameries and factories and making money. . . . There was reaction against the idealism that led to war and civil war. Denis Johnston's play, that dramatised delirium of Irish history, *The Old Lady Says No*, belongs to the new mood. What he was saying was that patriotism isn't enough and he said it with all the weirdness and baroque elaboration of a dream.[4]

The protagonist of Johnston's absurdist play — whose title he claimed were
the words written on the manuscript when it came back to him, rejected
by Lady Gregory at the Abbey Theatre — finds himself trapped in a Rath-
farnham Sunday afternoon tea with the statues of Cúchulainn, Robert
Emmet, and other Irish heroes, unable to escape.

In his discussion of "The Entrance of Realism" in *The Irish: a Character Study*, Seán Ó Faoláin, perceiving like MacManus a fundamental
shift of mood in Irish literature, outlined the rejection of romance in favor
of realism:

> In the most creative period of Anglo-Irish literature (from about 1890
> to about 1920) the writers saw Irish life, in the main, romantically. . . .
> Towards the end of the period a satirical note made itself felt, and in
> the plays of Sean O'Casey — all the natural wonder being removed, for
> they are set in the Dublin slums — we were left with an unassuaged real-
> ism. The novel, budding from the work of George Moore and James
> Joyce, and profoundly affected by the French and Russian realists, like-
> wise began to hold a far from indulgent mirror up to nature. When the
> revolutionary period of 1916–1922 ended miserably in a civil war, ro-
> mance died completely. Most Irish literature since 1922 has been of an
> uncompromising scepticism, one might even say ferocity. I will quote
> but one example, the novels of Liam O'Flaherty.[5]

By the 1930s W. B. Yeats, MacManus noted, "publicly bestowed
his benediction" upon Ó Faoláin and O'Flaherty at a banquet in a Dublin
hotel, "bequeathing them his mantle, and — I quote Joseph Hone's biography
—'stating to the stupefaction of his listeners' that 'the future of Irish literature was with the realistic novel.' The cause of the stupefaction," Mac-
Manus continued, "was that Yeats appeared to be handing over the glorious
laurels of the poet for the not quite so noble overcoat that realistic novelists wear. Yet, the ageing poet must have genuinely believed that the realistic novel . . . would in future dominate Irish literature. After all, Joyce's
Ulysses was then first being recognised as the novel of the age."[6] Of course,
Yeats himself had shifted in his poetry from romance to realism, proclaim-
ing in "A Coat" (1914) that he would discard his coat "Covered with
embroideries / Out of old mythologies," for "There's more enterprise / In
walking naked." He invented a new mythology, a new vision, of his own,
based on what he perceived as the realities of his own time, and although
there is a romantic tone to many of his later poems (the "Byzantium" poems,
for example), it is counterbalanced by a determination to present those
current realities, rather than the "old mythologies," in a new, "plain" speech.

Irish novelists during the first half of the twentieth century strove

for a new realism in their work, in much the same way that English, American, and European novelists had done a few decades earlier. While nineteenth-century Irish novelists had seldom transcended the dominant romantic mode — except perhaps in the best work of Maria Edgeworth, John Banim, William Carleton, and Somerville and Ross — the best Irish novelists of the twentieth century sought a new objectivity about the present and the past. Instead of the flawless, chivalric hero, these novelists developed more credible, representative protagonists. Like earlier English, American, and European realists, they made characterization the center of their novels, with a sharper focus upon the effect of action on character, and an increased tendency to explore the psychology of the protagonist. And their determination to be objective led to perhaps the most dramatic change from the nineteenth-century novel: the unhappy ending, reflecting the realization that a story truly told could end irresolutely or disastrously (in death, as Hemingway argued all real stories do), rather than in the escape to the happy, often quite implausible romance of marriage and inheritance all too common in the nineteenth-century Irish novel.

Seán Ó Faoláin (1900–) and Francis MacManus (1909–65), who wrote of the shift to realism in Irish literature, were responsible themselves during the 1930s for achieving a new realistic vision in the Irish historical novel: Ó Faoláin in *A Nest of Simple Folk* (1933) and MacManus in his trilogy, *Stand and Give Challenge* (1934), *Candle for the Proud* (1936), and *Men Withering* (1939). For young writers such as these — Ó Faoláin was thirty-three when his first novel was published; MacManus, twenty-five — Yeats, Joyce, Synge, and their contemporaries were much more direct and powerful influences than Scott, whose popularity and influence had greatly waned in Ireland as elsewhere. Father Brown lamented in 1915, "We have had no Scott — in which respect we are in the same case of as England [*sic*]." The title of a 1937 article in *The Irish Monthly* by Aodh de Blacam summed up the situation: "Who Now Reads Scott?" De Blacam complained that among young graduates there are "hardly any who have read Scott at all." Arguing that "all that was genius in him came from the Gael," de Blacam maintained the nineteenth-century view that Scott's materials were like Irish ones: "Did he not declare that County Cork alone had more matter for romance within its borders than all broad Scotland?" The puritanical de Blacam felt that a return in the schools to the romance of Scott would help to counterbalance the evil "vulgarities of the cinematograph culture, that chief enemy of all that we are striving to rebuild in Ireland to-day."[7]

Irish writers did not follow de Blacam's advice to return to Scott. Indeed, Irish historical novelists ever since O'Grady had been moving away from strict imitation of Scott. "At the end of the century," Donald Davie

has noted, "though Standish O'Grady was still pursuing the mirage of 'an Irish Scott' the influence that proved fruitful through George Moore's *The Untilled Field* was that of Turgenev."[8] Ó Faoláin's and MacManus' historical novels were written under the inspiration of specific Continental novels: Ó Faoláin was spurred on by Turgenev's *A Nest of Gentlefolk*, while Mac-Manus was inspired by the Norwegian Sigrid Undset's trilogy, *Kristin Lavransdatter*. They observed, and often extended, many of the conventions of the model Scott had established — the focus on fictional character-types rather than the "big names" of history, the presentation of a wide range of characters so as to achieve a panoramic picture of society, the use of contrasting dialects — but no longer did they imitate Scott. Explained Ó Faoláin:

> The Irish writer was a provincial while he imitated slavishly and tried to write beyond his talents; he ceased to be a provincial when he wrote of what he knew and could describe better than anybody else. . . . Plenty of people before Synge had written about Irish life — Lever, Lover, the Banims, Gerald Griffin, hosts of hardly-known poets and novelists. Only the exceptions, and the exception does not include any I have mentioned bar Lever, are readable to-day. The explanation becomes obvious immediately one opens their books. They never really got down to it. They are sometimes regionalists, exploiting Ireland as "a subject." . . . Each novelist is a kind of diluted Walter Scott, never really sure of the absolute interest of his material and, to make up for this imaginary lack, padding it up with some kind of contemporary (and so passing) social or political interest or literary fashion. . . . It was an entirely new thing for men to realise the full and complete dignity of the simplest life of the simplest people. Once they had acknowledged that then they were free to do anything they liked with it in literature — treat it naturalistically, fantastically, romantically, see it in any light they chose. They had conquered their material by accepting it.[9]

Ó Faoláin was inspired by Turgenev, and MacManus by Undset, but neither imitated these models in quite the way that the Banims, Le Fanu, Carleton, and O'Grady had all attached themselves to Scott. Ó Faoláin felt that the crucial distinguishing factors for his generation of writers were nationalism and the establishment of the Irish Free State:

> Without the national thing . . . an Irish writer was always in danger of becoming a provincial by becoming an imitator. He would not merely take models, that is to say Russian, or French, or German writers, and

> learn his trade from them, and be excited constantly by the work of other
> men as every writer is, and apply himself then to his own sort of life
> which he knew so well: he would if he remained an imitator try to be
> a man of another country and describe the life of another country, in
> which he must . . . fail. The national thing gave Irish writers the neces-
> sary resolution . . . to find in Ireland the stuff of their work. . . . The
> original Abbey Theatre would have been inconceivable without the na-
> tionalist movement.[10]

He recognized the possibilities opened up for the Irish writer by the events
of the first quarter of this century in Ireland. In *The Imagination of an
Insurrection*, William Irwin Thompson has traced the influences of the
Literary Revival upon the rebels of 1916, but the impact of Irish history
upon Irish literature was more powerful and more enduring. The establishment of the Irish nation-state provided Irish writers with a different kind
of audience; now Irish historical novelists returned to Irish history in order
to make sense of the new nation that had been achieved. They also had
the advantage of newer, more, and better sources for Irish history than
nineteenth-century Irish historical novelists had enjoyed.

To be sure, Ó Faoláin's loving descriptions of landscape and Mac-
Manus' occasional melodramatic plot involutions recall the nineteenth-
century Irish novel. However, the new departures found in their work
are far more striking. Both Ó Faoláin and MacManus were realists who
explored Irish history primarily in terms of character development. Their
protagonists are not knights in shining armor, but frustrated rebels who
eventually meet death, not victory. Both writers were considerably influenced by Daniel Corkery, the Cork realist; both were nationalists; both
were fluent in Irish. Their writing is more mature, their style more varied,
their characters more memorable — their novels, in short, far superior — to
those of their nineteenth-century predecessors. In their work the Irish historical novel comes of age.

Born in 1900, Seán Ó Faoláin grew up with the twentieth century and
with the new Irish nation. In many ways his early development reflects
the development of Ireland itself. Christened John Whelan, he grew up
in Cork, son of a constable in the Royal Irish Constabulary, Denis Whelan. Paul Doyle writes that the Whelan boys spent parts of summers with
their mother's sister on a farm in County Limerick where John was able

to "study the rural people and ponder local history." Limerick and Cork would provide the settings of *A Nest of Simple Folk*. Young John's series of reactions to the Easter Rising were representative of the Irish people as a whole: "Like his father," Doyle writes, "he was at first shocked" by it, "but, as the resistance continued and the rebel leaders were captured and shot, John Whelan's feelings began to change." He hero-worshipped his Gaelic teacher, Padraig Ó Domhnaill, a member of the Irish Volunteers; in the summer of 1918 he took his own Gaelic name. In September of that year Seán enrolled both in University College, Cork, and in the Irish Volunteers. He fought on the Republican side in the Civil War, serving as acting director of publicity for the cause in Dublin until January 1924, when he reentered U.C.C. Going on to Harvard University on a scholarship, he earned a master of arts degree in comparative philology and then made two important decisions: to get married and to become a writer. He married Eileen Gould in June 1928 in Boston and began writing short stories. His years at Harvard "gave him an opportunity to settle on a vocation as well as time to think out problems about Ireland and let the bitterness heal."[11]

Ó Faoláin's first volume of stories, *Midsummer Night Madness* (1932), dealt with the Anglo-Irish and Civil wars; it was acclaimed as a great success. Back in Ireland, he modified his political position, redefining it, Maurice Harmon notes, as "midway between the extreme Republican stand of those who wanted to continue the protest against the Treaty in arms and the constitutional policy of De Valera, who had moved into the Dail. He supported constitutional agitation in preference to further military activity because he wanted the country to have a period of peace in which to consolidate achievements and plan constructively for the future."[12] Now that Ó Faoláin, like Ireland itself, had begun to recover from the Civil War, he turned to the history of Ireland between the Famine and the Easter Rising in *A Nest of Simple Folk* (1933) in order to clarify how both he and his country had come to be. The 1930s were the years of history and politics in his writing: he also published biographies of De Valera (1933), Countess Markievicz (1934), Daniel O'Connell (1938), Hugh O'Neill (1942), and an edition of Wolfe Tone's autobiography (1937). In 1940 he became founding editor of *The Bell*, the chief voice of Irish literary conscience and an immense influence upon score of younger Irish writers, including James Plunkett and Eilís Dillon. "O Faolain and *The Bell*," as Vivian Mercier notes, "were one and the same."[13] By mid-century Ó Faoláin had established himself as the dean of Irish letters and, along with Frank O'Connor and Liam O'Flaherty, one of a trio of world-class Irish short-story writers.

A Nest of Simple Folk is not simply a historical novel, but a family chronicle as well. Ó Faoláin himself refers to it in his autobiography as "a bulky family chronicle."[14] The story extends from 1854 to 1916. At the point where it enters the twentieth century and approaches the Easter Rising, it is as if the novel ceases to be a historical novel in order to become a *Bildungsroman,* with young Denis Hussey (the chief protagonist Leo Donnell having been shifted to the background) serving as a focus for Ó Faoláin's own youthful experiences. Although it crosses generic lines, *A Nest of Simple Folk* is essential to an understanding of the twentieth-century Irish historical novel, for it was the first to focus so totally upon human psychology as a frame through which to view the events of modern Irish history. Moreover, the family-chronicle approach it introduced persisted in the Irish historical novel. Just as Ó Faoláin explored the world of his ancestors, James Plunkett wrote *Strumpet City* partly as an elegy to his father; and the family chronicle, a genre which has often overlapped with the historical novel, also provided the approach of Eilís Dillon in *Across the Bitter Sea* (1973) and *Blood Relations* (1977).

Ó Faoláin wrote in his autobiography that *A Nest of Simple Folk* "gave me so much satisfaction. It was an historical novel, or family chronicle, based on everything I had known, or directly observed in the countryside, of my mother's people, and the city life of my mother and father away back, some twenty years ago, in Cork City."[15] The novel is laced with autobiographical elements: like Ó Faoláin himself, young Denis Hussey has a falling out with his policeman father over the Easter Rising, influenced by his uncle, Leo Donnel, the old Fenian whose life story occupies most of the book. "An uncle of John's," Doyle notes, "had fled from the authorities after the Fenian Rebellion in 1867; John's father had often denounced the Fenians; and, of course, the lad had read about the Fenian movement" (18). In discussing the influence of Lennox Robinson's play *Patriots,* which featured a mysterious Fenian as protagonist, Ó Faoláin recalled being told about his Uncle Paudh who fled the country after 1867. Doyle writes that "when he wrote *A Nest of Simple Folk,* Ó Faoláin remarks that therein he found the Fenian of Robinson's play as well as his parents and his relations from Limerick" (44). The book is no documentary, however; like most other historical novelists, Ó Faoláin, beginning with a few known facts, freely fictionalizes. But he does so with a thesis constantly held in mind: Ireland, as it struggled with the increasing transition from town to city, with the oppressive influence of the Church, and with the continued dominance of the English and Anglo-Irish ruling class, inevitably had to rebel (or at least Ó Faoláin had to rebel) against all these forces. Ó Faoláin's loyalty to his thesis in the novel necessitates an episodic

plot and a protagonist who can, somewhat improbably, live out all the various rebellions required by his author.

A *Nest of Simple Folk* begins with the struggle of Leo O'Donnell's mother and with his dying father over the family inheritance, culminating in a deathbed scene in which Leo is willed the family's best plot of land, his older brother James getting the inferior homestead plot, causing him to hate Leo for life. Leo's mother and aunts then busily set about trying to "civilise" him; they rename him Leo Foxe-Donnel, deleting the Gaelic "O" and substituting their own Ascendancy surname. Ó Faoláin's choice of the name "O'Donnell" is significant: he notes that "Leo Donnel had a wonderful, fine, grand name entirely, a powerful name that was in Irish history and story."[16] When Leo rejects the civilized ways of the Foxes in favor of a life of dissolute rebellion, he becomes simply "Leo Donnel." He reacts against the civility and law and order imposed upon him, becoming a rebel. His rebellion is both political and personal: not only does he become a Fenian, spending several years in prison after 1867 and again in the 1890s and finally dying in the Easter Rising, but he rejects propriety and wealth, getting first a peasant girl and then his eventual wife, Julie Keene, pregnant, and gradually squandering his choice plot of land into the hands of his spiteful brother James. Leo and Julie live first in a Rathkeale (County Limerick) cabin, and then, after Leo's second prison term, in Cork, where Johnno, their "nephew" who is really their secret son, sets up Leo as proprietor of The Green Pike, a tobacco shop and front for bets and Fenian activities. It is there that young Denis Hussey, son of the policeman who secretly provided the information that put Leo in prison for the second time, comes under his influence.

The character of Leo Donnel was inspired not only by Ó Faoláin's mysterious Uncle Paudh, but by Tom Clarke, the old Fenian who, Doyle writes, "after spending fifteen and a half years in jail for Republican activities, eventually opened such a shop in Dublin which became a center of the rebel movement. Clarke later participated in the Easter Rising and was eventually executed" along with the other signers of the Proclamation of the Irish Republic (46). But Leo Donnel is no carbon copy of one man or two men, but rather a representative of a general type: the rebel. In *The Irish: A Character Study*, Ó Faoláin discusses this type: "The Rebel probably never cared. He was devoted to failure. He was a professional or vocational failure. . . . There was only one thing at which the Rebel wished to be a success and that was at rebelling. Death did not mean failure so long as the Spirit of Revolt lived."[25] Leo Donnel is a study in this kind of "failure" and "success." He is no saint; he is a very long way indeed from the chivalric heroes of the nineteenth-century Irish historical novel.

He is, like Stendhal's Julien Sorel, a social misfit. His title is repeatedly "a desperate character." This carrier of the noble name O'Donnell uses women, squanders money and land, and generally acts the fool, albeit the proud fool. He is no Wolfe Tone, no rebel who "sees beyond the immediate thing," as Ó Faoláin puts it in *The Irish*, "to the larger implications." He is the other kind of rebel, the first stage outlined by Ó Faoláin: the one who "rebels against an immediate injustice — peasant risings follow, peasant societies of revenge, workers' associations. He sees no further."[17] Listening to James Stephens, the founder of the Fenian movement, Leo decides to join the movement because it gives him a place to channel his natural rebelliousness and anger.

> Donnel forgot everything as he listened to the envenomed passion of this man, and stared at him through the heat-dimmed glass. He had always disliked the priests; now he could hate them. Those pubs of Irishtown had set in him, year after year, a seed of interest in his people and his country; at last it burst through him like a well. (153)

He is no political philosopher or Fenian visionary, but rather a man driven into rebellion:

> It was not love for them, but that little burly fury in the pub at Knockaderry that drove him to what he did. Aye! First it was his mother, forcing him to what he had no wish for, then it was his aunts, then came Frankie O'Donnell, with his smooth tongue, sending Stephens on his track; and then Stephens himself. (157–58)

Leo is a study in repression and rebellion: he is Stephen Dedalus with politics substituted for art, action substituted for intellect. Ó Faoláin would create a Joycean *Bildungsroman* in *Bird Alone* (1936). Here his initial inspiration was Turgenev, whose novel *A Nest of Gentlefolk* he admired. In his autobiography Ó Faoláin notes that his novel "was to be called, in a gesture of adoration toward Turgenev — whose work it no more resembled in treatment than in quality — *A Nest of Simple Folk*."[18] Turgenev was the favorite novelist of Daniel Corkery, Ó Faoláin's first mentor, who urged Frank O'Connor and him to study the Russian realists in order to see how to merge realism and lyricism in their writing. Doyle points out that Ó Faoláin has publicly "noted the influence on his work of Daniel Corkery and Turgenev. He asserted that Corkery stressed the value of constant rewriting and revision and forced him to concentrate on what he

wanted to say rather than on just how to say it" (136). An older Ó Faoláin
later gave similar advice to a young James Plunkett.
By Ó Faoláin's time, looking to the Russians was a common enthusiasm among Irish writers. In *An Untilled Field* (1904), George Moore
had modelled himself on *A Sportsman's Notebook*. Irish writers increasingly felt a kinship with the Russians who wrote about peasant life and
history. Writers such as Corkery, Ó Faoláin, and O'Connor wanted to do
the same thing for Irish history and Irish peasant life. By now Irish writers
realized that they could spark their imaginations by looking to the great
European writers, at the same time remaining vitally Irish. As Ó Faoláin
wrote, he would be inspired, but he would not imitate. In *A Nest of Simple Folk* he shares with Turgenev a realistic attention to the foibles of common people as well as a fondness for their ways, "always the same for
mile after mile through the whole length and breadth of Ireland," for "in
a little town like Rathkeale all the joy of life is in its changeless ritual"
(197, 187). But while Turgenev examined a tightly structured, highly class-
conscious society, focusing specifically upon the Russian intelligentsia, Ó
Faoláin was looking at "A Broken World," in the words of the title of his
best story. As Maurice Harmon points out:

> Turgenev, Tolstoy, Dostoevsky, and Chekhov handled all levels and classes
> of society in an inclusive and generous manner, but the Irishman had
> no corresponding variety of experience or inclusive sympathy. The Civil
> War and its aftermath had impaired or at least endangered their sym-
> pathy, but even more fundamental was the composition of Irish society.
> "In Ireland," Frank O'Connor sadly explained, "the moment a writer raises
> his eyes from the slums and the cabins, he finds nothing but a vicious
> and ignorant middle-class, and for aristocracy the remnants of an English
> garrison, alien in religion and education."[19]

Furthermore, Turgenev's *A Nest of Gentlefolk* was not a historical novel
at all; published in 1859, it centers on a love story occurring in 1842. In
short, Turgenev was for Ó Faoláin a general inspiration, not a specific
model. The only specific borrowing from Turgenev contained in *A Nest
of Simple Folk* is its title.
      Leo Donnel and Denis Hussey are characters who seem to live
lives of their own in the world of the novel, in sharp contrast to the knightly
mannequins who populated nineteenth-century Irish historical novels. The
great innovation in *A Nest of Simple Folk* is that the events of history
are heard of only as they relate to the lives of the characters. "History
has reverberated only in the distance," the narrator tells us, "and even then

but rarely and too far away to be heard, as when the Williamite grenades burst all through one terrible winter over Limerick city; it is a place into which news of the world's calamities has seeped by rumour and dying echo, and been felt in the end only for some small secondary cause" (4-5). But history is omnipresent in the novel — a history experienced by characters who develop and change, rather than history as an artificial parade out of the textbooks. Leo's grandfather Theo is Irish nationalist history personified: he has seen "Grattan's Irish Volunteers," "'ninety-eight," "the Union," "O'Connell," and "'forty-five" (23). "His bottomless memory, linked with these in their turn bottomless memories, reached back so far that in that one decaying brain one might see, though entangled beyond all hope of unravelling, the story (as well as the picture) of his country's decay" (28). Both James Stephens and Michael Davitt stay overnight in Leo's house, and Leo reveres Parnell, but in the world of the novel, it is Leo who matters: he thrusts himself into history, rather than history imposing itself on him, as so often seems to be the case in the nineteenth-century historical novel. Instead of merely serving as a thin lens on history in the novel, Leo *is* the novel. He fails, at length, and is much more believable and far more memorable in his failure than all the nineteenth-century heroes are in their successes.

Leo is not only a realistic character, but a symbol. His fortunes are linked with Ireland's. Where he is repressed, so is Ireland; when he rebels, so does Ireland. Thus, as in Scott, the personal and political, the fictional and historical realms are merged, but in a new and vital way. "As it was the winter of the year when he entered the jail, and the winter of his life, it was also the dead time of Ireland. Parnell was long since gone, and men squabbled for succession" (279). The novel is divided into three parts — "1854-1888, The Country," "1888-1898, The Town," and "1898-1916, The City" — tracing Leo's moves from Foxehall to Rathkeale to Cork as well as reflecting, as Doyle notes, "the ever-expanding shift in Ireland from the countryside to the towns and cities" (40).

Ó Faoláin was interested not only in the specific type — the rebel — but in the whole Irish tradition of rebellion and the conflict between rebellion and survival. He felt that "the rebel tradition" asserted itself "during the hundred years after Tone. It is that century in a nutshell. Tone died in 1798. O'Connell was at work from 1807. The next rebel movement, the Young Irelanders, began in 1842, and broke into armed revolt on his death. Ten years later Fenianism began under Stephens and O'Donovan Rossa, and there were attempted outbreaks in '65 and '67. . . . And so on."[20] Fenianism was a secret, underground movement. Ó Faoláin conveys its secrecy to the reader by keeping Leo's specific Fenian activities nearly as

invisible to the reader as they are to the police and most of the other characters in the novel. John Hussey, who informs on Leo, his own relative, is as devoted to worldly success and respectability as Leo is to failure and rebellion. The tension between these two opposed attitudes is central to the novel. While still writing *A Nest of Simple Folk*, Ó Faoláin, as Doyle records, discussed what he felt was its main theme:

> In America I had leisure to think back to my own people, the simple middle-class people of the towns whose lives are a slow tale of pathetic endeavor; that is a story worth telling—how a nation lives within itself a double life, each life in that duality thwarting the other, the instinct to strive violently, to erupt volcanically on the idealistic plane, the instinct, as deep and terrible of self-preservation. (43)

When Denis Hussey rejects his father's reactionary respectability at the end of the novel, in favor of Leo's rebellious stance, he reflects Ó Faoláin's own youthful rebellion, although the fictional Denis responds to the additional knowledge that his father informed on Leo. Doyle notes that Ó Faoláin remarks in his autobiography that he was early in life a natural rebel (38). In the 1920s he was a political rebel. In the 1930s rebellion became the theme of his books. In the 1940s, as editor of *The Bell*, Ó Faoláin was the chief voice of rebellion against Irish literary censorship and the "stuffed-shirt middle-class mentality," in Doyle's words (101). He was always the realist, determined to show Ireland as it was, not as others wished it had been.

Francis MacManus greatly admired *A Nest of Simple Folk*. He felt that "compassion" was its "dominant quality," calling it "a massive novel in human terms about the humus, the roots, of Irish patriotism as manifested by the Fenians, the Parnellites and the men of the Easter Rising. . . . This is the kind of historical burrowing which O'Connor never attempted."[21] Ó Faoláin's novel and MacManus' trilogy about eighteenth-century Ireland share many of the same strengths: accurate, effective use of Anglo-Irish speech; a "private" approach to history through character development; and the use of a realistic protagonist who struggles, changes, and finally dies, always reflecting the fortunes of the nation as a whole.

Like Ó Faoláin's *A Nest of Simple Folk*, MacManus' historical trilogy was apprentice work: *Stand and Give Challenge* (1934) was his first

novel. And like Ó Faoláin, he was significantly influenced by Daniel Corkery, especially by his two nonfiction books, The Hidden Ireland: A Study
of Gaelic Munster in the Eighteenth Century (1925), which sparked Mac-
Manus's own fictional exploration of that world, and Synge and Anglo-
Irish Literature (1931), in which Corkery championed Synge as the first
great Irish lyrical realist and urged Irish writers to be open-minded in their
inspiration but defiantly Irish in their artistic statement. Vivian Mercier
subsequently examined "Realism in Anglo-Irish Fiction" in an unpublished
Trinity College, Dublin, dissertation (1943) as a school of writing descended
from Synge and transported through Corkery, as Doyle observes (118);
Ó Faoláin, MacManus, Frank O'Connor, and Liam O'Flaherty could all be
included in this "school." However, unlike O'Flaherty, who was much influenced by naturalism, Ó Faoláin and MacManus both rejected it as too
constrictive; MacManus felt that Zola's "cult of naturalism" was a "straight-
jacket."[22] Ó Faoláin and MacManus were realists, pure and simple.

Beyond their similarities, which are striking, Ó Faoláin and Mac-
Manus were separated by some crucial differences. As Denis Cotter has
noted:

> MacManus' oeuvre is best viewed, like Paul Claudel's, as the fruit of
> a mind which accepted willingly and liberatingly the dogmas of ortho-
> dox Catholic scholasticism. In this religious acceptance, as in his benign
> acceptance of the Irish race and language (as witness his U.S. travel book,
> Seal Ag Ródaíocht/ On the Road for a Time of 1955), MacManus is
> the diametric opposite of James Joyce and is also estranged from his acer-
> bic contemporaries—O'Flaherty, O'Faolain, and O'Connor. An absence
> of overt sexual detail, dictated only by artistic preference, ensured that,
> unlike those contemporaries, none of his work was banned by the Irish
> Censorship Board.[23]

Sean McMahon adds: "Outside Ireland he never achieved the fame of
O'Connor or O'Faolain but his best work stands comparison with theirs."[24]
Ó Faoláin's work, like that of many of his contemporaries, was banned
repeatedly in the 1930s and 1940s, a period during which the infant Irish
nation-state was determined to maintain the myth that the one true Irishman was a sexless, devout, Gaelic-speaking peasant. When the real Irish
peasant was presented to them—for example, in Eric Cross's The Tailor
and Ansty (1942)—the censors bitterly rejected this reality, insisting on
the myth.[25] In this context, being banned became during this time almost
a point of pride among some of the better Irish writers. After all, the best
—Synge, Joyce, O'Casey—had already been banned and booed by "the

stuffed-shirt middle-class mentality." When Ó Faoláin's play *She Had to Do Something* bombed at The Abbey Theatre in 1937, Doyle reports that he wryly commented, "I am very pleased to say, it was soundly booed. One likes to be in the tradition" (38).

MacManus was much more at ease with the Irish Catholic nationalist establishment. He was a Christian Brothers teacher for many years, teaching, among others, James Plunkett.[26] Cotter traces his career:

> He was educated at the local Christian Brothers school, at St. Patrick's Teacher Training College in Dublin, and at University College Dublin. He taught for eighteen years in the Synge Street Christian Brothers school in Dublin before joining Radio Éireann in 1947 as general features editor. . . . He was a moving force in introducing the Thomas Davis lecture series on Radio Éireann. His genial and helpful disposition endeared him to many writers. . . . MacManus wrote eleven novels and two interesting biographies, *Boccaccio* (1947) and *St. Columban* (1963).[27]

Cotter and McMahon both argue that "absence of overt sexual detail" in MacManus' fiction was strictly a matter of "artistic preference," but it is clear that his "preference" was more than simply "artistic." When criticizing the "eroticism" found in his favorite writer, Sigrid Undset, MacManus noted, "The points I make are aesthetic as well as moral." Elsewhere he condemned D. H. Lawrence because "by sex he interpreted the world, and by the dark gods of the blood he promised a redemption. I could multiply these examples from Joyce, Proust, or from the dreary horde who harry the world with eroticism."[28] The only sex scene in MacManus' trilogy is metaphorical rather than explicit:

> He knew vaguely, as his arms closed on her and she yielded to him, that it was not the friendship of another person, for which he had thirsted, that he was receiving, but an enveloping outrush of her spirit in which he would burn as a wick in oil. Together amongst the trees they became a secret lamp.[29]

Catholicism was the core of MacManus's artistic and moral credo. His is not the Joycean "non serviam," but *serviam*. In an article entitled "The Background of the Catholic Novel," he set forth Realism and Catholicism as the roots of his work, with one leading inevitably to the other: "The highest compliment that you can pay to a novel . . . is that it is true to life. . . . The novel can be true to life only when the author's concep-

tions conform with reality. . . . Behind and infusing all this seeming tumult and turmoil, the apparent aimlessness and quivering pain, there is
spiritual reality, the background of Being whereby things are thrown into
significant relief. There is God, and life mirrors Him." He rejected the
"straight-jacket" of Zola's naturalism because he "perceived but observed
little more, that men sin. It is true that mankind leans towards evil by
reason of the Fall, but that truth must be regarded in the great network
of truths woven about the Incarnation and Redemption. Zola, however,
stressed the degeneracy of men without counterbalancing that stress."[30]

MacManus' fiction is unashamedly Catholic. But it is not propa-
ganda. MacManus can sound the propagandist in his essays, but in his
fiction he always sought, like Joyce this time, to serve Art, not Church.
Catholicism colors but does not dictate his fiction. He felt that Catholicism could "place a novelist on a centre-point of understanding" but that
it "may not help a novelist to write technically well." In "The Artist for
Nobody's Sake," he rejects the artist as moral propagandist: "His actions
in relation to the work to be made can be neither moral nor immoral.
His actions are not concerned with his last end and getting into heaven.
They are concerned simply and solely with making something well. If
he fails, he is not an immoral wretch. If he succeed, [sic] he is not a saint.
He is either a good or a bad artist." MacManus' Catholicism was like his
nationalism: generous and conscientious. Describing MacManus' "patriotism," Sean McMahon notes that it was "not arrogant 'my-country-right-
or-wrong' patriotism but the kind which, while portraying the warts —
smugness, narrowness, parochial xenophobia — could embrace the qualities
behind — gentleness, hospitality, concern for others." Assessing MacManus's
trilogy, Benedict Kiely writes: "Steady and continuous contemplation of
a degraded people is the best possible discipline for the emotions. One
result of that discipline, as far as an Irish writer is concerned, is that it
becomes possible to accept Ireland without being sentimental about Ireland," adding a bit more contentiously that "there is less softness of feeling
in the acceptance displayed by Francis MacManus than in the rejection
made classical by James Joyce and so subtly analysed, and sensed like a
burning in the bowels, in Seán Ó Faoláin's Come Back to Erin."[31]

Though MacManus generously admired Ó Faoláin's A Nest of
Simple Folk, he was inspired to write his trilogy about the Gaelic poet
and schoolteacher Donnacha Ruadh MacConmara by two other books:
Sigrid Undset's trilogy Kristin Lavransdatter (1920–22) and Daniel Corkery's The Hidden Ireland (1925). The latter gave him his material and the
former provided him with his method. Interestingly, another Irish writer
had already turned to Undset, who "during the third and fourth decades

of the twentieth century . . . was acclaimed as one of the greatest realistic writers of the time." Joseph O'Neill, author of *Wind from the North* (1934), about the coming of the Danes, noted: "I am indebted to Mrs. Sigrid Undset for carefully reading the manuscript and advising me on points of historical detail and on other matters."[32] That same year MacManus published the first part of his trilogy, *Stand and Give Challenge*, and contributed an article to *The Irish Monthly* in which he recorded his own debt to Undset.

> If Ireland is ever to possess an historical novelist who will adequately express the life of her people, that novelist must at least be of the power and calibre of Sigrid Undset, the Norwegian. Her historical writings have an immediacy for our country that is twofold; she writes of a past age that is closely akin to Gaelic Ireland in religion and somewhat in customs; and she offers an example, with reservations, of what might be done by our native writers in respect of method and achievement.[33]

Given the strikingly similar adherence of both writers to realism and Catholicism, however, MacManus' attachment to Undset seems to have been a case of discovery and agreement rather than direct imitation; that is, Undset's fictional exploration of medieval Norway gave MacManus the courage to do what he was already disposed to do with eighteenth-century Ireland, rather than serving as a model to be devotedly imitated, as Scott was by the nineteenth-century writers. Carl Bayerschmidt's assessment of Undset's achievement could serve as well for a description of Mac-Manus': "She described the outer world in all truth exactly as she saw it without romantic artificiality. She also probed deeply into the inner lives of her characters and sought to understand their thoughts and actions in relationship to the society in which they lived." Undset reinforced in MacManus a brand of Catholic realism that he had already been advocating, one which included, as Bayerschmidt notes, the rejection of "all political doctrines and collective movements that repudiate Christianity as the greatest obstacle to the realization of their programs. In Communism, Fascism, and Nazism, Undset, who converted to Catholicism in 1924, recognized forces which would deny man the freedom of his soul and his intrinsic worth in the world of the spirit."[34] This was exactly the argument MacManus made in a series of articles in *The Irish Monthly* during the 1930s.[35]

Undset's most significant influence on MacManus was her utter devotion to the development of her characters. MacManus too would seek characters who would be "catholic" in another sense: "Granting him the

ability and providing that he keeps his art in harmony with the truth, the creator of character who possesses the normal and complete viewpoint will not make unreal persons." Bayerschmidt argues that while Undset's "historical fiction is characterized by a solidity of knowledge which is in sharp contrast to the reconstructed history and pageantry of Sir Walter Scott's novels written in the early decades of the nineteenth century when such source material was not yet available," she was much more interested in "the inner lives of her characters."[36]

MacManus' trilogy, like Undset's, is unified by its focus upon a single protagonist: Donnacha Ruadh MacConmara, one of the many Gaelic poets about whom MacManus learned in Daniel Corkery's *The Hidden Ireland*. In similarity to Carleton's Redmond O'Hanlon and O'Grady's Red Hugh O'Donnell, MacConmara was a real historical personage, but as with these other characters "we catch only haphazard glimpses," as Corkery notes, "of that long life." Like O'Hanlon and O'Donnell, MacConmara was relatively obscure, almost semilegendary. The difference is that Mac-Manus avoids the extremes represented by Carleton's disregard of fact and O'Grady's enslavement to it, creating a MacConmara who is historically grounded yet a full-fledged fictional character in his own right. Corkery provided only the bare bones, merely suggesting the course MacManus' imagination would take:

> His life, when we . . . catch glimpses of it, with long darknesses between them — the roving "spoiled priest," the schoolmaster finding shelter here in farmers' houses, the pensive voyager, the grinning parish-clerk; then the old man, a blind beggar about the roads, according to one account; and, last of all, a stooped and venerable figure, eighty years of age, raising his voice above the corpse of his friend — thus haphazardly spied on, his life seems tragi-comedy from end to end. He was wild and reckless, reckless both of this world and the next; but then, over against this idea of him, one recalls his *Bán Chnoic Éireann Óigh'* . . . so poignant in feeling, so deep in colour, so simple, yet withal so rich.

Corkery also mentions MacConmara's abandonment of studies for the priesthood in Rome, his time in Hamburg and Newfoundland, his years of increasing poverty in Ireland, and an episode in which "he, a Catholic, applies for and obtains the parish-clerkship of the Protestant Church of Rossmire [sic]. 'Abjuration of the errors of Rome was a condition *sine qua non* for the post, and with the condition Donnacha determined to comply.'" Corkery adds that Donnacha, "it is likely, spent only [a] short term in the new faith," and claims that he "laughed, it is clear, at the foolery."[37]

But MacManus' Donnacha, when he conforms, does not laugh at all. Feeling trapped by circumstances, he mourns the sin into which he has been forced:

> Never again will I sweat my back of its fat,
> Digging and ploughing from end to end of the year—
> My creed I'll change, be an Englishman in a cocked hat,
> For it's he who drinks and eats and knows good cheer;
> With him, and why not? I'd as lief now sit or stand
> (Little I care for Louis the King or his seed),
> And draw the wine from morning till night with free hand;
> There's a life for you no Irishman lives indeed!
> . . . But a dismal plight it is, for a man like me
> To follow falseness, yea, in my own despite. (CP, 65, 66)

In his trilogy MacManus develops the various Donnachas sketched by Corkery, adding a number of allusive features to his protagonist. In his own way, he follows Joyce's "mythical method." There are three major archetypal frames developed: Donnacha is progressively Odysseus, Job, and Lear. MacManus' allusions, however, are direct and earnest, not subtle and ironic, as in Joyce. There seem to be three Donnachas, one for each book. In *Stand and Give Challenge* he is the courageous, arrogant young rebel, compared most frequently to Odysseus, or often thinking about Odysseus himself; he is, after all, a classically trained schoolteacher. The Odysseus motif continues in *Candle for the Proud*, but more often Donnacha is Job, the poor, oppressed, long-suffering sinner. In *Men Withering* he becomes Lear, the old man, the raging, tragic seer, feeling shirked by his offspring and forgotten by the world. The setting shifts, too, but always within County Waterford: first Donnacha returns from the Continent to be a schoolteacher in Slieve Gua; then he lives with his daughter in Kilmacthomas and serves as Reverend Grimshaw's sexton; finally, having reconverted, he joins his son in Knockanee before spending his last days at his daughter's. The Donnacha who emerges from the whole trilogy is, like Ó Faoláin's Leo Donnel, the rebel as failure, but a rebel who recognizes his shortcomings, repents his sins, and dies in peace. Like Banim's conformist, Dan D'Arcy, Donnacha recants his opportunistic Protestantism. Corkery had noted his *Duain na hAithrighe (Song of Repentance)*, finally suggesting that the author of *Eachtra Ghiolla an Amaráin (The Adventures of a Luckless Fellow)* in the end "may not have been so luckless a fellow after all!"[38]

Like *A Nest of Simple Folk* and *Kristin Lavransdatter*, MacManus'

trilogy was a family chronicle as well as a historical novel. He had to create a family for MacConmara from scratch, since Corkery had not provided one; and so his wife Máire and his children Máire Óg and Donnacha Óg revolve around him, Máire's death ending *Stand and Give Challenge*, her last words providing its title, and his children joining him in poverty during the rest of the story. Máire dies of the "wasting-sickness" and Máire Óg suffers from it too; starvation is a constant threat to all. Donnacha is driven to conform by Máire Óg's sickness and the example of several conformist friends.

While much of the power of the trilogy derives from the focus on the private plight of its characters, MacManus' Donnacha Ruadh Mac-Conmara, like Leo Donnel, is at the same time a personification of Ireland and its people. He is eighteenth-century Gaelic, peasant Ireland personified, the Penal Age made personal. We follow his life from the grisly days of the Penal Age through the nightmare of 1798. When Donnacha dies, the eighteenth century dies; the trilogy ends with his wake.

MacManus' "Foreword" to *Stand and Give Challenge* reads:

> This book may send shivers of pedantic disapproval up and down the spines of historians and biographers. It is not an essay in history of which I have been very sparing; still less an essay in biography of which we possess but rags and tatters; and again still less in Gaelic literary criticism. It is an attempt to present the lives of a few people, as I have conceived them, of the hidden Ireland. You or I, had we been alive and Irish and troubled with song, might have been such a person as the chief character who lived when a dark nightmare was on this nation. [39]

As in *A Nest of Simple Folk*, history is deliberately made to reverberate in the distance, realistically presented as it affects MacManus's characters. The Penal Age was like slow death until the cataclysm of '98. Even then MacManus does not take the easy way out by shifting the scene to Wexford; instead, "Like muttering from sleepers, news came out of the east" to County Waterford, "battles, towns taken and lost, villages burned to the ground, men hanged, shot and beaten to death: fragments of stories that could not be pieced together into a single tale." [40] In the best book of the trilogy, Donnacha is a man "withering" just as Ireland is made up of *Men Withering*. The two are identified, as MacManus shifts from one to the other in lyrical language that shows how far Irish fiction had come stylistically since the nineteenth century:

The dread of mortality, the terror of the inevitable shrouding of the body, fanned him icily, till shrinking like a cat from the cold outer-world to the warmth before the fire, he wished desperately in his half-sleep for everlasting shelter against the inappeasable winds of death. He could feel them, those ceaseless winds, flowing about him, crumbling him as a desiccate lump of earth is crumbled in a heavy rainfall, pulverising him back into the dust from which he had come; and so they had been flowing, year after year, minute by minute, while the flesh bloomed healthily and then shrank to a wrinkled casing and the hair fell from the shining pate, and the bones became almost as jointless as boughs; and he, with every desire withered except the desire to live, groped and reached forward along his earthly course with an apprehensive stick. As he sank now into his half-animal sleep, his fingers twitching on the blanket, he carried with him the thought of his own decay as though it were the destiny of the people among whom he lived. He was going. So were they. (*MW*, 18–19)

Donnacha's crime is to be a Catholic schoolteacher, a felony in the eighteenth century. He loses his job, for a time he loses his faith, and he is always in danger of losing his life. "It did not pay to be a master whom the soldiers had almost arrested, and a Jacobite and a Papist at the same time" (*SGC*, 126). Donnacha is one of the type of rebellious, despairing Gaelic poet-hedgemasters met again in Walter Macken's *Seek the Fair Land* and Thomas Flanagan's *The Year of the French*. Early in the trilogy Donnacha is a "flame," a "spark"; in view of MacManus' Catholicism, his use of fire and candles seems to be a spiritual metaphor. Later Donnacha is "withered," "wasting," a tattered old coat upon a stick.

He was prostrate like a tree, sapless, unrooted, withering, fit for the fire. Then, without stirring, lying as if he was frozen in that merciless frost, he began to think on himself and why he lay there as if he were an outcast, and in that thinking he began to see himself as a tiny creature, a speck of dust in the sunlight, a point of light in the night sky, a creeping thing in the tangle of the hay, yet not so lost and small but that God's unwavering eyes never left him in an eternal stare of love. He struck at his own pride and cursed it. (*CP*, 113)

The heroism of the trilogy is a Catholic heroism, but MacManus is no anti-Protestant polemicist. Evil Protestant landlords and bailiffs people his pages, but we also meet, in the Reverend Peter Grimshaw and Dundee, the landlord, another recurrent character-type in Irish historical fic-

tion: the well-meaning liberal Protestant caught in the middle, such as Banim's Robert Evelyn and Miles Pendergast, Le Fanu's Hugh Willoughby, Buckley's Major Heathcote, Plunkett's Yearling, and numerous others in the genre. Grimshaw gives Donnacha a job and takes care of his ailing daughter. Dundee admires Donnacha's spunk and rewards him for it.

In their historical novels MacManus and Ó Faoláin are always conscious of the reverberations, the continuum, of history—not only from the past to the present, but within the past itself. Their approach to history is expansive: MacManus covers a century and Ó Faoláin more than half that. As MacManus noted of Undset, "Her novels must be spacious, because they are family histories. . . . There is a host of people, a whole social life of which this one particular family is an organic part."[41] Wrapped up in the eighteenth century, MacManus is always looking back in his trilogy to the Boyne and forward to 1798. Much like grandfather Theo in *A Nest of Simple Folk*, Donnacha's own teacher, Micheál Ó Coffey, serves as a well of memory:

> Since the smoke-blindness veiled his eyes and age shivered in his limbs, he seemed to have turned into himself, where he held silent communion with things past. Sorrowful things they were. People said that he thought of the events he saw in Limerick, his birthplace, when the young blades went marching down with drums beating and fluttering flags to join the French ships after the Treaty; or of the priest he discovered one night hanging halfdead from a cross-roads gibbet. (*SGC*, 30)

Meanwhile, Donnacha suffers forebodings of '98: "I'll tell you what'll happen. The first move you make, if the French set foot in Ireland, will be the cause of destruction and burning and hanging and murder" (*MW*, 53). The government soldiers, *provocateurs* of '98, terrorize the countryside; they beat up old Donnacha. "Later, they returned. Grumbling about their quarters they were then; cursing, ripe for brawling" (*MW*, 23).

From Ó Faoláin and MacManus one remembers specific characters, their peculiarities, their words, and their actions: Leo Donnel grappling with young Julie Keene in the dark of an alley and raging against his mother on the Rathkeale road; Donnacha MacConmara facing up to Heavybottom Horsham the bailiff but later slinking "around the bushes and into the lane, his feet dragging heavily on the grass . . . like a badger

nosing out from a damp hole in the earth when the sun goes down" (*CP,* 64). History is seen through their eyes. Whatever their shortcomings, Ó Faoláin and MacManus achieved in their historical novels realistic visions which succeed in showing what it might have been like to "have been such a person as the chief character who lived when a dark nightmare was on this nation."

7
Liam O'Flaherty's Natural History

I N CONTRAST to the outburst of historical novels during the Literary Revival at the beginning of the twentieth century, very few noteworthy historical novels were published in Ireland toward mid-century, after Seán Ó Faoláin's and Francis MacManus' contributions to the genre. More common were political novels about the "Troubles" of the 1920s, such as Jim Phelan's *And Blackthorns* (1944), about episodes during the 1920s "when the fanatic peasantry defended their views with bombs, machine-guns, rifles, revolvers, shot-guns, old swords, and Blackthorns."[1] Mired in the present—in an Ireland that was still recovering from the Troubles, struggling through the infancy of nationhood, and maintaining a shaky neutrality during World War II—Irish novelists seemed unable to seek consolation or clarity in history. Philip Rooney returned to the romantic world of Redmond O'Hanlon in *North Road* (1940) and dramatized the late-nineteenth-century Land War in *Captain Boycott* (1946), but these books, especially *Captain Boycott*, were popular prose documentaries more than they were novels.

Not until the 1960s, by which time the events of 1918–23 finally seemed distant enough to be treated as "history," did the historical novel reestablish its great popularity in Ireland. There was, however, one important exception to the general avoidance of the historical novel among the best Irish writers around mid-century: Liam O'Flaherty, who returned

to the Great Famine of 1845–49, the Land War of 1879–80, and the Easter Rising of 1916, respectively, in his novels *Famine* (1937), *Land* (1946), and *Insurrection* (1950). These were O'Flaherty's last three novels. He turned to history after dramatizing the revolutionary events of the 1920s, some of which he experienced himself, in his political novels *The Informer* (1925), *The Assassin* (1928), and *The Martyr* (1933). Moving from contemporary political fiction to historical fiction, O'Flaherty shifted not only from the present to the past, but also from the personal to the societal: from a focus upon isolated protagonists who undergo identity crises, much like that of Dostoevski's Raskolnikov, to a presentation of a panorama of characters in historical society, where they are judged by their response to a historical crisis.

His historical characters respond passionately to history. They are partisans, not passive, moderate heroes like Scott's. O'Flaherty traces the development of their partisanship; they move away from moderation rather than towards it. Indeed, we shall see that the turbulent O'Flaherty was a sharp contrast to the genteel Scott (whose works he was forced to memorize in school) in his life as well as in his novels. Yet his historical novels adopt and transform many of the conventions introduced by Scott, even though Scott did not directly influence him. Like Scott, moreover, O'Flaherty utilizes folklore in his novels, but for different political ends. He was interested primarily in capturing the passionate and primitive elements in history, an interest largely explained by his own life. In his fiction, literary naturalism enters the Irish historical novel, and in his best novel, *Famine*, O'Flaherty's tragic view of Irish history creates a work that is one of the most memorable in the genre.

Much of the long and turbulent life of Liam O'Flaherty (1896–) seems lost in a fog. He has had no Richard Ellmann, largely because his extreme silence, exile, and cunning would frustrate even so industrious a biographer as Ellmann. As Paul Doyle notes, "O'Flaherty has been deliberately mysterious, vague, and contradictory about many aspects of his life and career."[2] Having written off academic scholarship a long time ago, O'Flaherty maintains a standing refusal to answer scholarly queries. But this stance has not quieted scholarly interest in his work: five books on O'Flaherty have been published within the last dozen years.[3] Little is known about O'Flaherty's life since World War II, which he spent in Connecticut, the Caribbean, and South America, occasionally surfacing to defend Irish

neutrality. Since *Land* (1950), *Dúil* (1953), a collection of stories in Irish, and *The Short Stories of Liam O'Flaherty* (1956), he has all but ceased writing or publishing. He began, but did not finish or publish, a novel in Irish, *Coirp agus Anim (Body and Soul).*[4] Concerning his life since 1956, Doyle simply notes that "he has been living in retirement and has spent much of his time traveling."[5]

Considerably more is known about O'Flaherty's earlier, more productive years. Between 1923 and 1935 he published nineteen books, two of which were autobiographies: *Two Years* (1930) and *Shame the Devil* (1934), which he wrote, he said, to steal the thunder of any later would-be biographer who might want to attempt his life. Like Sean O'Casey's autobiographies, *Shame the Devil* and *Two Years* must be taken with a grain of salt; they are books in which O'Flaherty as much mythologizes as explains himself. For example, he insists that he spent his early years studying for the priesthood only in order to get a free educational ride and that he never intended to become a priest. Given some of O'Flaherty's other self-interested machinations, this may have been true, but at the same time there seems to have been something of the spoiled priest about him, like William Carleton or MacManus' Donnacha Ruadh. The parallels between O'Flaherty and Carleton are striking: both were Gaelic-speaking, peasant novelists, spoiled priests who sought literary success, championed themselves and achieved popular acclaim but, never forgetting the early days of poverty, often wrote far below their potential in search of fast money.

Piecing together scholarly sources and O'Flaherty's autobiographies, one gains a reasonably coherent account of his early career. He was born August 28, 1896, to Margaret and Michael O'Flaherty in Gort na gCapall, near Kilmurphy, on Inis Mór in the Aran Islands. "Several details of the O'Flaherty family life," James O'Brien notes, "appear in his brother Tom's book, *Aranmen All* (1934). The family was large, and several of the children died in infancy and early childhood. The father was a Fenian and a Land Leaguer who apparently forgot at times his obligations to his large family. An incurable rebel, the older O'Flaherty harassed the land-grabbers on Aran and was the first *Sinn Feiner* on the island." O'Flaherty's mother was, among other things, a seanchaí, a teller of *seanchas,* of local lore. In *Shame the Devil* he recalled: "Even when there was no food in the house, she would gather us about her at the empty hearth and weave fantastic stories about giants and fairies, or more often the comic adventures of our neighbours." O'Flaherty inherited both his father's rebelliousness and his mother's storytelling abilities. In *Shame the Devil* he tells how the "angel of revolt" entered him at the age of nine

and he told his mother a fierce fictional tale about how a neighbor had murdered his wife, describing it so graphically that she rushed out to investigate.[6]

A youthful O'Flaherty left Inis Mór to study for the priesthood at Rockwell College in Cashel, County Tipperary (1908–13), and at Blackrock College, County Dublin (1913–14). Later, as a young writer, O'Flaherty would be inspired by O'Casey and Joyce, Dostoevski and Zola, but at Rockwell College he had to commit to memory four British literary classics, two of which, according to Patrick Sheeran, were Scott's *The Lady of the Lake* and *The Talisman* (59). But this exercise did not leave a lasting mark: like other twentieth-century Irish historical novelists, O'Flaherty did not imitate Scott. His historical novels adopt for his own ends, as we shall see, many of the conventions of the genre begun by Scott, but his work is best understood in light of his own politics and his own life.

At Blackrock College, the young O'Flaherty organized a student corps of Republican Volunteers. After a brief and desultory stay in 1914 at University College, Dublin, on scholarship, O'Flaherty left there — not for the priesthood nor for the Volunteers, but instead for the Irish Guards, serving in France and Belgium in 1917 when he was blasted by a shell explosion. He emerged from the hospital and from the Irish Guards in 1918 still in a semi-shocked state. The Easter Rising of 1916, about which he would later write, affected him not at all at the time. When he returned to it in *Insurrection* (1950), it was history to him, even though he was twenty years old when it happened. Concerning his decision to enlist in the Irish Guards, Doyle notes that there were "three explanations — disillusionment with the Irish Republican movement, a desire for excitement, and a fear that he might not retain his scholarship." He emerged from the service in 1918 to accept a bachelor of arts degree at U.C.D. "on the basis of special provisions for those who served in the war."[7]

Then began the "two years" (1918–20) during which O'Flaherty bummed around the world. After shipping to South America, he heard of Sinn Féin's declaration of an Irish republic in late 1918 and returned to Liverpool in excitement. But, as Sheeran relates, "Arriving in Liverpool, the events across the water seemed dull and commonplace, and O'Flaherty signed on a ship bound for the Mediterranean. These facts are at variance with the popular image of O'Flaherty as a Republican soldier and writer, a sort of Dan Breen of the imagination. The Rebellion of 1916 had made no impression on him and in 1918 'more important matters occupied my attention.' While guerrilla warfare ravaged the country, O'Flaherty, now a deck-hand, spun fantastic stories to the ship's captain to get out of work" (72). At Smyrna, O'Flaherty got himself mixed up in an obscure deal over

contraband arms. "This provided the money for a Gargantuan debauch, at the end of which he had delirium tremens. . . . When the ship left Smyrna, it sailed through a dangerous storm, and, after a stop at Gibraltar, sailed on to Montreal."[8] In Canada he hoboed, worked as a lumberjack, and dabbled among the Industrial Workers of the World. He moved on to visit his siblings in Boston, where he became involved in Irish-American radicalism—and then to the Bowery in New York.

He returned to Inis Mór in 1921 an "ill man, without money, disillusioned," as he recalled in his autobiography. In early 1922 he joined the Republicans in Dublin, where he and a small army of unemployed men seized the Rotunda and raised a red flag. Driven out after four days, he fled to Cork and then on to London. Concerning the Rotunda episode, O'Flaherty wrote in *Shame the Devil:*

> Ever since then, I have remained, in the eyes of the vast majority of Irish men and women, a public menace to faith, morals and property, a Communist, an atheist, a scoundrel of the worst type. . . . Crave forgiveness? Clip the wings of my fancies, in order to win the favour of the mob? To have property and be esteemed? Better to be devoured by the darkness than to be haunted by dolts into an inferior light.[9]

The Rotunda episode reinforced O'Flaherty's already rebellious nature. He would be a rebel in everything he did: as a Communist, as an Irish nationalist, and as a writer, which he chose to become in 1922. Communism and nationalism were convictions that would color all of O'Flaherty's writing. Yet he could never totally give himself to "the cause" —neither to Irish Republicanism nor to international socialism. He fled from the Civil War, in which Seán Ó Faoláin fought, and lived in London between 1922 and 1924 writing fiction, with the encouragement of his literary mentor, Edward Garnett, based on the simple life of animals and people on the Inis Mór he knew so well. Subsequently, he returned to Ireland, but he would never again devote himself there to any cause but his own. He maintained his devotion to Communism, making a trip to Russia in 1930, but his 1931 book *I Went to Russia* (written, he tells us in his introduction, to make some fast money) is as much a portrayal of his feelings of detachment from the Russian people and his inability to be more than a spectator to Communism as it is a record of devotion to it.

Like Billy Carleton come to Dublin, Liam O'Flaherty was very much a champion of his own cause after storming the Dublin literary scene. In 1924 he had obtained the patronage and praise of A.E., published his second novel, *The Black Soul,* and started *To-Morrow,* a radical alterna-

tive to A.E.'s *The Irish Statesman.* In a letter to Garnett cited by Zneimer, O'Flaherty described the journal as "a platform for myself" (6). But it folded after two issues, O'Flaherty lamenting that the Jesuits were too powerful for freethinkers like himself. At this point he parted company with A.E. After A.E. had praised Gandhi's Indian passive resistance policy as better than Irish violence, Zneimer records, O'Flaherty wrote to the *Statesman* that he "considered the whole policy of passive resistance to be ghostly, associated with philosophy and death and not with the creative vitality of a living people," and comparing Ireland to England in Shakespeare's time: "His race was emerging, with bloodshot eyes, lean, hungry, virile, savage, from the savagery of feudalism into the struggle for Europe. . . . Ours is the wild tumult of the unchained storm, the tumult of the army on the march, clashing its cymbals, rioting with excess of energy"(8). O'Flaherty, the Catholic Gaelic peasant, disdained Protestant, Anglo-Irish Ascendancy writers such as A.E. and Standish O'Grady, whose celebrations of the heroic Irish past he thought little of; the cautious, scholarly O'Grady and the reckless, polemical O'Flaherty were diametrically opposed personalities.

O'Flaherty was busy setting himself apart from A.E., O'Grady, and Yeats, but he admired O'Casey. "He is an artist, unlike the other bastard writers I met here." But he criticized O'Casey's play *The Plough and the Stars* (1926), John Zneimer points out, because "he thought O'Casey did not do Pearse and Connolly and all the patriots of the Easter Rebellion justice. He himself . . . still looked on Easter 1916 as the most glorious gesture in the history of the country and did not want to see its dignity lessened in any way." (9, 11). The play greatly influenced, however, the opening street scenes in *Insurrection.* O'Flaherty tried to draw O'Casey into his rebellious young literary circle, but O'Casey felt, as he explained in his autobiography, that O'Flaherty possessed Yeats's arrogance without his genius. This is certainly true to the tone of some of O'Flaherty's early letters to Edward Garnett, recorded by Zneimer:

> I pat myself on the back. I licked all these swine into a cocked hat. When I came here nobody would speak to me. Everybody hated me. I wound them all round my fingers. I got AE to give me a thundering review. I got all the old women to praise me. Now that I have fooled them I am telling these damned intellectuals what I think of them in choice scurrilous language. (6)

In 1927 O'Flaherty recorded his disenchantment in a final letter to *The Irish Statesman* written in response to a complaint that he was

not writing in his native language, Irish. O'Flaherty scornfully replied that when he had written a play in Irish for a Dublin theatre, he had not been paid for his work. He extended the broad range of his scorn to include all of Ireland, commenting that he no longer had any hope that the country could be transformed into "a civilization and culture that will make us a force in Europe."[10]

O'Flaherty maintained equally passionate, even angry and violent, ideas about writing. In a 1925 review cited by Zneimer, he set forth a violent ideal for the novel:

> In order to be a work of genius, a novel must offer something more than a perfect style, the imprint of a cultured mind, and gentleness of soul. . . . It must be a relentless picture of life, as lashing in its cruelty as the whip of Christ when there are moneychangers to be beaten from the Temple, as remorseless as the questions of a jealous lover. It must have the power to invoke great beauty or great horror in the same breath as it calls forth laughter from the lips. (9)

The fact that Christ carried no whip into the temple when he rebuked the moneychangers is a telling comment on O'Flaherty's imagination: he would have him do so. For O'Flaherty, passion and primitive energy are everything in writing. Concerning his characters, he wrote, Zneimer reports, that he saw his role as being "to listen and reproduce their passions: because all passion is beautiful" (25). Like Wordsworth, he believed in "the spontaneous overflow of powerful feelings." He was no careful stylist: he wrote quickly and commented to Garnett that he felt that slow attention to style would hinder his artistic statement. Like the Greek Nikos Kazantzakis, he was a follower of many causes and a writer of energy and passion, a practitioner of Henri Bergson's ideal of *élan vital*. Seán Ó Faoláin called him an "inverted Romantic," a felicitous description: following naturalism, O'Flaherty emphasized the entrapped, tragic fate of his characters, but solace and beauty were always to be found in primitive Nature, the unifying principle beyond innocence and despair.

To understand OFlaherty's literary orientation, it is at least as necessary to appreciate that he is a Man of Aran as to know his literary influences. At the end of *Shame the Devil*, he chooses, as John Zneimer puts it, "his exile, his native rock, his Aran: 'A godless hermit, I began my communion with the cliffs, the birds, the wild animals, and the sea of my native land.'" (38). His motifs and beliefs — according to which life is portrayed as pagan, primitive, a struggle of man and beast for the survival of the fittest — hearken back to the old way of life he knew so well

on Aran, as much as to the writings of Dostoevski, Zola, and the natural-
ists. For life on Aran was, and is, primitive; Synge felt that Inis Meáin,
the neighbor island to Inis Mór, must have been the most primitive place
in Europe. O'Flaherty compared his characters to animals and very often
wrote about animals, not merely because Zola and the naturalist writers
he admired did that, but because primitive animal life on Inis Mór was
what he knew most intimately from his childhood. "His concentration . . .
on stories of wild animals and birds," Patrick Sheeran writes, "is not surprising in view of the frequency with which animal tales occur in the folklore of the region" (48). And his intimate experience of Aran peasant life
thoroughly colored his best historical novel, Famine.

Famine was published in 1937, the same year that Ireland won its first
constitution. The novel won great critical and popular acclaim. O'Flaherty
was seen as shifting from his critique of the seamier side of Irish Republicanism contained in political novels such as The Informer to a patriotic
portrayal of the Famine. However, in both cases O'Flaherty was simply
being realistic: he had painted 1920s Republicanism the way he had known
it, and now he was portraying famine the way he imagined it had been
in the 1840s based on the way it was on Inis Mór in his childhood. Sheeran
points out that on the Aran Islands during O'Flaherty's youth, "People
actually died of hunger in conditions as bad as those obtaining in the
years of the Great Famine. The exactitude of Liam O'Flaherty's historical
novel Famine has sometimes been wondered at. What requires an effort
of the historical imagination for others was for him a living reality" (20).
Sheeran writes that there was famine on Inis Mór in 1894, 1895, 1897,
1898, 1905, and 1906 (21). In Famine O'Flaherty drew on his intimate experience of peasant life and death during famine times.
        As for the Great Famine, O'Flaherty knew it through the vast
body of folklore surrounding it, which was especially alive on the Arans,
even in the 1930s. Sheeran notes that "it is generally agreed . . . among
folklorists that the seaboard of Galway had more unrecorded folktales
in 1935 (when the Irish Folklore Commission replaced the more amateur
Irish Folklore Institute) than had all the rest of Western Europe" (46). Ana-
lyzing Famine folklore, Roger McHugh adds that Famine "has something
of the simple and forceful quality of these oral accounts."[11] O'Flaherty
recaptures the "ominous season of mist, of storms of rain and wind alternating with periods of vast and terrible stillness" that McHugh describes

as dominating tales about the beginning of the Famine in 1845. "It was a fearful sight. The sky had not cleared after the rain. It was dark and lowering, with a scant drizzle falling here and there from some shreds of cloud, that hung like floating rags across the sky." [12]

O'Flaherty's instinct is not lyrical, but dramatic; each of his historical novels opens not with the slow, deliberate descriptions found at the beginning of most Irish historical novels, but with a bang. Such is his opening description of the scene near Crom, County Galway, where his story is set: "The cocks had just heralded the break of day when the first clap of thunder burst above Black Valley" (5). The Great Hunger does not begin until midway in the novel. O'Flaherty establishes a foreboding context for it during his early chapters. Well before the potato blight strikes, we meet the already half-starved children of Sally O'Hanlon:

> They devoured even the skins of the potatoes and what was left of the salt and water. They scraped the bottom of the dish with their grimy fingers, to pick out any tiny morsel that had got wedged between the woven willow rods. When there was absolutely nothing left, they sat huddled together by the empty dish, snuffling and wiping their noses on their sleeves. (38)

Even then "the wind was beginning to have the tang of winter in it" (39); Mary Kilmartin has an emigration dream about an angel delivering her to America (53); and the visionary priest, Father Geelan, is "afraid that something is going to happen in Ireland that will make our race wanderers on the face of the earth like the ancient Jews. I dream of many things. And in my dreams I see woeful destruction coming" (123).

When the blight hits, O'Flaherty's graphic descriptions of its results are very true to the folklore described by McHugh: the people's initial hope in 1845 that it will pass and their belief that the government will bail them out; their desperate attempts to salvage enough unspoiled potatoes and parts of potatoes to make up a meal; and their resignation in the face of a second, more disastrous blight in 1846 which they believed was the will of God, "a punishment for waste, a scourge sent from God because of the abuse of plenty," as McHugh puts it. There emerges from Famine folklore as well as from O'Flaherty's novel "a picture of the Irish peasant clinging to a ramshackle social structure whose main prop was snapping while he was bewildered, frightened and totally unequipped with any means of diverting disaster." [13]

After the potato crop — their only crop — spoiled, the peasants had to turn to overpriced Indian meal supplied to gombeen shopkeepers by

the government, or to whatever they could scavenge. McHugh reports a survivor saying, "I heard my own mother to say she saw the people travelling miles to the graveyards to gather the nettles that grew there," and notes that "the indiscriminate use of nettles and of berries is sometimes recalled as having caused disease and death." The people resented the hoarding and overpricing of the Indian meal, the "yellow meal," by the shopkeepers, and McHugh adds that "another strong reason for the bitterness is the association of any form of food-distribution with proselytising work." In *Famine* the parish priest, Father Roche, warns the peasants against going to the Protestant Father Coburn for relief. As McHugh points out, "Local conflicts between Protestant and Catholic clergymen now increased and local traditions recall many of their circumstances; sermons against and curses laid upon 'soupers' and their adherents by local priests." Welfare relief works introduced by the government were likewise resented. In *Famine* the relief works, buried in bureaucracy, are portrayed as useless and ineffective. Writes McHugh: "The useless nature of such works, together with the circumstances of labour upon them, *ó dhubh dubh agus obair chruaidh agus ualaí troma* (from dark to dark with hard work and heavy loads) helps to explain the general dislike of them which exists."[14]

The final scene in *Famine* is a brief description of the last survivor in the valley, old Brian Kilmartin, trying to bury his wife and dying himself in the process. The Gaelic writer Seosamh MacGrianna had published a Famine story in which the protagonist drags a corpse to burial and dies on top of it, "Ar an Trá Fholamh" ("On the Empty Strand"), in his 1935 collection *An Grá agus an Ghruaim (Love and Dejection)*. Both narratives are true to the vivid memories of Famine deaths in Irish folklore. Recalled one informant: "My father told me that he saw a man carrying his brother's corpse on his back from Bailieboro to Moybologue graveyard. He had no one to help him and he had to dig the grave and bury the corpse himself."[15]

O'Flaherty's knowledge of Famine folklore was reinforced by his reading of the Reverend J. O'Rourke's book *The History of the Great Irish Famine of 1847 with Notices of Earlier Irish Famines* (1875). "Of all the early histories of the event," Sheeran writes, it "is by far the most concerned with the plight of the ordinary people. He prepared himself for writing his book by speaking to many of those who had lived through the terrible years of '45-'47 and includes vivid details from their accounts. Among other matters, his description of people eating dogs and dogs eating people is dramatized in *Famine*" (205). Equally if not more importantly, he was provided with a political, an ideological, context in which to view the Famine by a second book: James Connolly's classic socialist

critique of modern Irish history, *Labour in Irish History* (1910). O'Flaherty's friend Peadar O'Donnell noted of him in *The Bell* in 1946: "More
than any other Irish writer he has *consciously* adopted Connolly's vision
of the conquest as a bullock-whacking savagery under which the people
were enslaved and degraded, and of the re-conquest as the struggle of
those same people to fight their way back to their inheritance over a long
and bloody road." The socialist O'Donnell was convinced that because
of his adoption of Connolly's vision as well as his intimate knowledge
of Irish life, O'Flaherty "is our greatest novelist."[16]

Like Connolly, O'Flaherty rejected the simple nationalist idea that
the Famine was a direct result of the exterminating strategy of England.
Both believed, as Sheeran notes, that "it was the social system rather than
the Government that was at fault" (209). Connolly and O'Flaherty blamed
a hierarchical, capitalist system that had its roots in British imperialism
but whose key agents were Irish landlords, bailiffs, shopkeepers, and priests.
Connolly emphasized the Famine and the Land War as the key chapters
in the story of the conversion of Ireland from feudalism to capitalism —
emphases reflected in *Famine* and *Land*. The third great chapter in modern
Irish history, of course, Connolly lived out himself: insurrection, the "blood
sacrifice" of 1916 in which Connolly attempted to merge Irish nationalism and socialism. O'Flaherty also shared Connolly's disdain for Daniel
O'Connell's middle-class stance and its impotence in the face of famine.
In *Famine* O'Connell is lampooned in the figure of McCarthy Lalor, an
O'Connellite who gives a blustering speech in (significantly) Father Roche's
parish churchyard. Clearly, O'Flaherty adopted Connolly's rejection of
O'Connell rather than the heroic O'Connell of Irish folklore.

O'Flaherty's sharp socialist critique raises the tone of *Famine* above
pathos and bathos to anger and passion. It also, unfortunately, frequently
intrudes: the narrator cannot resist adding textbook-styled explanations
of the dramatic events he describes.

> When government is an expression of the people's will, a menace to any
> section of the community rouses the authorities to protective action. Un-
> der a tyranny, the only active forces of government are those of coercion.
> Unless the interests of the ruling class are threatened, authority remains
> indifferent. We have seen how the feudal government acted with brutal
> force when the interests of the landowner were threatened, even to the
> extent of plundering the poor people's property. Now it remains to be
> seen what the same government did when those poor lost, by the act
> of God, all that was left to them by the police and Mr. Chadwick — the
> potato crop which they had sown. (324)

O'Flaherty is capable of following effectively graphic, passionate descriptions of realistic characters and actions with awkward narrative intrusions: Old John Hynes the gombeenman was upset and "The following incident will show how deeply he had felt" (175). Concerning the quality of the novel, James Plunkett's opinion seems truest: "*Famine* page by page seems a badly written book but its totality is extraordinary."[17]

Perhaps the most important concept O'Flaherty got from James Connolly was what Sheeran calls "Irish history as the destiny of the people rather than of a few 'great' men" (207). This was consistent with the already well-established convention in the historical novel later outlined by Georg Lukács in Scott: that the events of history would be played out among a varied, contrasting, panoramic set of fictional characters, with a Waverley or Morton dominating but with the "big names," the actual historical leaders, withdrawn to the background. Seen in this light, O'Flaherty's portrayal of a panorama of characters in *Famine*, as opposed to his focus upon a single alienated hero in the earlier novels, is not anomalous, as John Zneimer calls it. In *Famine* O'Flaherty is simply following the conventions of its genre, the historical novel. The convention is continued in *Land* and *Insurrection:* Parnell, Davitt, and Pearse are all briefly glimpsed as part of the historical background in front of which O'Flaherty's fictional characters play out their parts. In *Land,* Davitt is literally withdrawn in a scene that epitomizes this convention:

> Lettice was unaffected by the hysteria of the multitude. Even while she looked toward the platform with a look of rapture in her eyes, as Davitt began to speak, she was waiting anxiously to hear the voice of the man she loved.
> "To confiscate the land of a subjugated people," Davitt cried passionately, as he gesticulated with his solitary arm, "and bestow it on adventurers is the first act of unrighteous conquest, the preliminary step to the extermination of servitude of an opponent race. The landlord garrison that England established in this country centuries ago is today as true to the object of its foundation as when it first cursed our soil."
> Lettice suddenly felt a touch on her arm. Then she heard Michael whisper her name close to her ear. She turned swiftly and saw him bending over her. He was smiling in a way that made her heart stop beating. He took her by the hand and bade her follow him. They went farther up the slope through the crowd. Soon they were alone and the voice of the speaker down below in the field became indistinct.[18]

A similar critical confusion has existed about O'Flaherty's use of his knowledge of contemporary characters and events in his treatment of history. Zneimer, for example, questioning O'Flaherty's historicity, finds

it odd that he portrays the same polarities in history that he saw at work in his own day. That, of course, is the whole point: like other historical novelists, O'Flaherty was interested in the continuum between the past and present. He sought to make sense of the past in light of the present.

Famine is O'Flaherty's best historical novel, not only because of its passionate, uncompromisingly tragic view of Irish history, but because it contains superior characterizations of a wide range of people who think, talk, and act believably. The center of the novel is the Kilmartin family: old Brian and Maggie; her indolent brother, Thomsy Hynes; the eldest son, Martin, and his wife, Mary; and the consumptive second son, Michael. The story is a family chronicle of the passing of power from old Brian, paterfamilias and proud possessor of ten rocky acres, to Martin and Mary, whom Brian resents at first because she is a mere weaver's daughter but who gains his admiration as she demonstrates her determination to eke out survival on the stony, sacred land. The tragedy of Famine ennobles its characters: that is the novel's significance. Trapped in the Great Hunger, Brian swallows his pride and cooperates with Mary, finally handing her a chunk of mortar from above the family fireplace to take with her to America as a symbol of the family's survival. Pathetic Thomsy Hynes emerges from indolence to become the folk hero of the novel, chasing after Martin, who has gone off with the Young Irelanders, and returning with Famine folktales. Only Martin and Mary and their baby survive the Famine, their passage to America financed by Young Ireland. Michael dies of consumption, Brian and Maggie starve at the homestead, and Thomsy goes up the mountain to expire in the midst of a revolutionary vision.

> He lay down on the earthen floor and then the bubble burst. Now there was no more pain and the roar of the water was distant. It was soft and melodious, receding into the distance, where the man with yellow hair stood on the mountain top, his naked sword flashing in the spears of the rising sun. Now the great horde of marching people called him and he went with them, marching through the sweet-smelling heather to the summit of the promised land. (409)

Surrounding the Kilmartins is a cast of characters carefully selected to demonstrate the volatile polarities that O'Flaherty felt were at work in Irish society. Chadwick is the landlord's agent, a caricature, a demented devil who is as perverse in his determination to exact the rent from a starving peasantry as he is in his pursuit of his unusual sexual desires with Mary's younger sister Ellie, whom he turns into a whore after she comes to work at the Big House. At the opposite extreme are the rebels: the visionary Father Geelan and the Young Irelanders whom Martin

joins. In the middle are Father Roche, the parish priest who cares for his people but will tolerate no threat to law and order; the Reverend Mr. Coburn, the well-meaning but ineffectual Protestant parson; and Dr. Hynes, the gombeen shopkeeper's son.

The real protagonists of the novel are the peasants, captured in several strong minor characters living and dying beside the Kilmartins: Patch Hernon, who loses his land and goes mad; Kitty Hernon and Sally O'Hanlon, both of whom wage desperate, ultimately unsuccessful struggles to save their children, Sally finally committing euthanasia; Mr. Gleeson, the weaver, who vows vengeance on Chadwick after Ellie's humiliation; and Patrick Gleeson, his son, who exacts it, killing Chadwick in an ambush. The peasant world of the novel is created through accurate, effective use of dialogue. No Irish writer knew rural Irish peasant speech better than O'Flaherty.

> "Fine boys! God bless them," said Mrs. Gleeson. "And how are the others, Kitty? You poor creature, you have a house full of mouths to feed."
>
> "Ah! musha," said Kitty plaintively, "how would they be with the hunger? Since the cow died on us in spring it's little they've had. May the Lord look down on us. Now this disease has taken nearly all our praties. God only knows what's going to happen to us, unless the Divine Saviour takes pity on us." (85–86)

Dr. Hynes is the most pivotal and in many ways the most interesting character in the novel, because he vacillates between its societal polarities. As a young medical student, he despised the peasants, but now, burdened by his guilty knowledge of his gombeen father's exploitation of his own race, he seeks to be a part of them. Struck by Mary Kilmartin's beauty, he vows to be loyal to the people, but instead, duped by the devil, Chadwick, he falls into a debauched triangle with Chadwick and Ellie Gleeson. Finally, inspired by Father Geelan, he rejects Chadwick, denouncing both him and his own father, and devotes himself to a life of service to the desperate, dying peasantry. He eventually contracts the "famine fever" himself and dies. His shift of sympathy—from the powers that be to the people, from law and order to defiance of it—is the central one in the novel, the one O'Flaherty wants his readers to follow.

In this sense, *Famine* is by no means objective, nor intended to be; O'Flaherty has an axe to grind. In *Shame the Devil* he had declared that "the strongest driving force of our times is the driving force of the revolutionary proletariat" and bid all writers to "carry the wild rose of insurrection" and "sing us a wild song of revolt."[19] In *Famine* he condemns

the power structure at work in Irish society as well as Daniel O'Connell's nonviolent stance, with Father Roche, implausibly enough, thinking to himself that "the demagogue O'Connell had professed himself a pacifist and a loyal subject of Her Majesty. . . . Now that blood was going to rot in starved bodies; bodies that would pay for the sin of craven pacifism the punishment that has always been enforced by history" (328). O'Flaherty's strident endorsement of violent rebellion is very far indeed from the careful, moderate appeal of the Banim brothers to British sympathies.

Most of the peasant characters in *Famine* die; the novel is both naturalistic and realistic, both tragic and historically true. In it O'Flaherty begins a naturalistic motif continued in *Land* and *Insurrection:* the comparison of doomed, trapped protagonists to animals. Examples of this motif abound. From one side of society, Chadwick declares about the peasants, "Famine! I'm going to root them out like a nest of rats" (172). At the other side of society, Brian Kilmartin dies, at the end of the novel, accompanied only by his own crippled dog, in a scene worthy of Jack London and in sentences reminiscent of Hemingway.

> The old man lay still with his arms stretched out.
> The dog became silent and lay down on his belly. Then he raised his snout and sniffed the air. He shuddered. Then he dragged himself along the ground until he came to the old man's naked foot. He smelt it. He rose slowly to his feet, raised his mane slightly, and advanced, an inch at a time, smelling along the old man's naked shins and thighs. He started and growled when he came to the shirt. Then he made a little circuit, lay down on his belly once more, and dragged himself, whining, to the head. He smelt the face. He whined. He smelt again. His mane dropped.
> Suddenly he raised his snout, sat back on his haunches, and uttered a long howl. Then he lay down on his side and nestled against the old man's shoulder. (448)

Thus, at the end of the novel, man and animal are joined in a death scene that epitomizes O'Flaherty's presentation of the Famine as a naturalistic, tragic disaster.

THE ROMANTIC-NATURALISTIC HERO of *Land* (1946) is Michael O'Dwyer. "Poor Michael! He was one of those on whose foreheads tragedy is written for even the least intelligent to read," Elizabeth St. George declares after

he is shot to death in a Fenian raid on the evil landlord Captain Butcher near the end of the novel. She adds, "Of course, one cannot feel sorrow in the ordinary way for one so strong and so certain of his purpose. It would be like a common sparrow mourning a royal eagle that has fallen in all its glory" (345). O'Dwyer is primitive man, a "primitive creature," according to the description of his own wife, Lettice St. George, who tells Raoul, her father, "He sees beauty only in danger. . . . He said that Cape Horn was beautiful, simply because his ship nearly foundered there in a storm." Raoul replies: "Danger is to him what tragedy is to a poet, the ultimate beauty. You have convinced me that I was right in thinking that he is a born leader of men" (82). O'Dwyer is an animal-man who attempts to break the oppression of peasants trapped like animals, suffering eviction: "Women and children stood in silent groups watching the column from a distance. They were half-naked. Hunger and fear made their faces look nearly as savage as the earth. Stunted animals also watched in silence" (208–9).

In *Land* O'Flaherty attempts to merge an enlightened gentry, represented by the St. Georges, and a courageous, rebellious peasantry, embodied in O'Dwyer: the Parnell-like freethinker Raoul, lately returned from France to his ancestral home near Manister, County Mayo, joins forces with O'Dwyer against a repressive Ascendancy caricatured in the figure of Captain Butcher, a snorting Englishman towing a bloodhound on a leash; and Lettice, Raoul's angelic daughter, marries O'Dwyer and gives birth to a son who will replace his rebel father and carry on the cause. Even before he marries them off, O'Flaherty brings the peasant hero O'Dwyer and the Ascendancy heroine Lettice closer together by making O'Dwyer well educated and well traveled and having Lettice convert to Catholicism, declaring about "the people" that "I want to feel that I belong to them, that I am of their blood and they of mine, that I belong to their earth and their history" (63). It is inevitable that O'Dwyer and Lettice fall in love and marry, as inevitable as any love match in a nineteenth-century historical novel. Once they are married, Lettice exclaims, "Oh! Michael, we now belong completely to one another and to the people" (224). Belonging to "the people" is the yardstick by which O'Flaherty's characters are measured, as in *Famine* where Dr. Hynes gains favor by overcoming his disdain for the peasantry and sacrificing himself to them. In *Land*, the St. Georges align themselves with the people; even Raoul's stodgy sister Elizabeth ends up, somewhat implausibly, collecting and dispersing clothes for the peasants. Captain Butcher, who is just what his name suggests, is the character most removed from "the people"—and therefore the ultimate evil. Like Chadwick in *Famine*, he gets his just deserts.

The problem with all of this is that in *Land* O'Flaherty is dealing in stereotypes; he seems more interested in character-types than in characters. Michael O'Dwyer is a Hollywood hero and Butcher, a Hollywood villain. *Famine* had been dedicated "To John Ford," director of the Hollywood version of *The Informer*, whose popular success seems to have affected O'Flaherty considerably. In *Land*, it is as if he is writing his own script for the popular film he hoped it would become rather than the novel it should have been. The American book blurb declared: "In *Land*, Liam O'Flaherty, the spokesman for Irish liberty, again expresses his own passionate devotion to the cause of Ireland and her people." *Land* is no less partisan a novel than *Famine*, but it lacks its depth and its integrity. Aiming at Hollywood and New York, O'Flaherty avoids in *Land* the realistic peasant characters who dominated *Famine*. His book blurb announces that "with unconcealed partisanship, he champions the cause of the evicted Irish people in their attempt to win back their land from absentee owners and their representatives," but the only peasant characters in the novel are minor, stock characters like the St. Georges' cook, Annie Fitzpatrick, and their laborer, Tim Ahearn: a bit of local color for the Hollywood screen.

In an important sense, Michael O'Dwyer is no real peasant at all: he doesn't talk like one. He is "above" peasant speech even though a Gael himself, like John Banim's Edmund O'Donnell in *The Boyne Water* who emerges from the glens of Antrim speaking standard English. In O'Dwyer's case his standard English, palatable to a popular audience, is explained by his upbringing in the hands of a nasty, wealthy uncle in Dublin and years of travel in America. "Relieved of the embarrassment caused by my presence, my uncle bought a large house in the most fashionable part of town, engaged a staff of servants and began to entertain on a grand scale" (222). No peasant syntax, this: O'Dwyer is Tarzan, the knightly savior of the natives. His brand of Fenianism is purer than that of Ó Faoláin's Leo Donnel, for whom it was an escape, a channel for anger and rebelliousness. To O'Dwyer Fenianism means "liberation," a beautiful courting of danger and a noble, just war against evil landlords.

Interestingly, O'Flaherty covers roughly the same period of history in his three historical novels that Ó Faoláin had traversed in *A Nest of Simple Folk:* from the Famine to the Easter Rising. In 1915 Father Brown had noted of novels of "the days of the Land League": "We may omit consideration of the novels that deal with the last named period. They belong to politics rather than to history."[20] By 1946, however, the Land War of 1879–80 was history to O'Flaherty—even though, as in *Famine*, he sometimes draws on his youthful experiences on Inis Mór to invigorate *Land*. For example, he has O'Dwyer lead a Fenian raid on Butcher's cattle that

has them plunging ritualistically to their death, a death as beautiful in its simple tragedy as the one graphically described in his Gaelic short story, "Bás na Bó" ("The Cow's Death"). They "leaped gracefully to their doom sailing through the void as in a dance, with heads erect and tails outstretched" (329). This episode is based on an incident in which O'Flaherty's father, "as chief of the local branch of the Land League, had driven a land-grabber's cattle over the three hundred foot high cliff of Dun Aenghus." And the *Galway Express* in 1898 reported a showdown between the Royal Irish Constabulary and Inis Mór peasants very similar to the one in *Land* organized by Michael and Lettice.[21] O'Flaherty emphasizes that during the Land War the peasantry feared another Great Famine but had replaced their forebears' resignation with a commitment to political activism. This seems historically true, for the Land League of Davitt and Parnell had an immense popular following and invented the word "boycott." In *Land* Raoul organizes a campaign of "isolation" against Captain Butcher much like the actual one waged against the real Captain Boycott of Ballinrobe, County Mayo, in 1880.[22]

O'Flaherty not only draws on history, he interprets it, interjecting Marxist political-science explanations as he had done in *Famine*. For example, he notes of the gentry: "Representative of the decaying feudal class, then being destroyed by the rising power of capitalism, they felt angry and perplexed owing to the strange apathy toward their interests of a government that had hitherto been completely at their service" (46–47). To O'Flaherty, as to James Connolly, the Land War was the middle chapter in the story of the war against British and Anglo-Irish imperialism: in *Famine* the proletariat lay down dead, crushed by the upper hand of the ruling class; in *Land* they fought back against the landlords and won significant gains; in *Insurrection* they exploded against the Empire. Connolly threw in his lot with Irish Republicanism in 1916, sending out his Citizen Army with the Volunteers, because he believed that the interests of Irish Republicanism and socialism had merged against a British Empire engaged in a World War that Connolly saw as imperialistic and inimical to the cause of international socialism.

The hero of *Insurrection* is Bartly Madden, who, like O'Dwyer, is a primitive man, the ideal soldier aching for action and devoting himself totally to "the Idea" of blood sacrifice against the Empire. Bartly is a Connemara peasant who has lost all his money and can't face a penniless return to his fiancée. Passing through Dublin on his way back home from London, Bartly stumbles into the Rising and joins it because he has nothing better to do and wants some action. "He certainly looked the type of man that is ideally fitted by nature to be a soldier."[23] He is excited

by the phallic power of the gun, which he grips with "sensuous delight" after he wakes up with it in his hands in Mrs. Colgan's flat. She tells him, "With a lovely gun like that in your fist, you can go and join the lads in the Post Office" (41, 44). At the beginning of the novel, the desperate but determined Mrs. Colgan and the down-and-out, penniless Bartly adopt each other in a sequence reminiscent of the liaison of Micil and An Bhean Ruadh (The Big Redheaded Woman) in Pádraic Ó Conaire's Gaelic novel *Deoraíocht (Exile)* (1910). Like Ó Conaire's Micil, Bartly Madden is a picaresque as well as a naturalistic hero.

Mrs. Colgan wants Bartly to join the Irish Volunteers in order to look after her sixteen-year-old son, Tommy, among the rebels in the General Post Office. With a gun in his hands and nothing better to do, Bartly is happy to accept the role of protector. More than that, he becomes a devoted rebel. At first sight of the Volunteers, "Although ignorant of his purpose, he felt sympathetic towards them, sensing that their dark rapture had its origin in a tragedy similar to his own" (10). Like Leo Donnel, Bartly gains from the rebels an outlet for his natural rebelliousness. He hears Pearse read the Proclamation of the Irish Republic, and his soul is on fire.

> At that moment, Madden thrust his head forward and stared in rapture at the poet's face. . . . For the first time in his life, his mind had conceived an abstract idea that lit the fire of passion in his soul. Although the words that he heard were beyond his comprehension, their sound evoked the memory of all that had exalted him since childhood. Like music, they carried him away into enchantment. (29–30)

He attaches himself to Kinsella, a Volunteer leader who is Pearse's type, and follows him in utter devotion to "the Idea." Fighting through all of Easter Week while the city of Dublin falls all around him, at the end Bartly charges straight into the enemy line, in his own individual blood sacrifice, and is shot dead. There the novel ends: "All around the little square, people stared in silence from doors and windows at the dead body that lay prone, with a rifle slung across its back and each outstretched hand gripping a pistol" (248).

The strength of *Insurrection* is its concentration upon bleak, graphic description of action. The opening street scenes in which Bartly and Mrs. Colgan watch looters attack the Dublin shops while Pearse reads his noble Proclamation seem right out of O'Casey's *The Plough and the Stars;* the looters celebrate their spoils in broad Dublin accents. *Insurrection* is a better novel than *Land:* it is more graphic in its descriptions of action and

makes more use of talk from the proletariat to whom O'Flaherty professed to be devoted. However, the concentration upon action in the novel is at the same time its downfall. Bartly Madden finally seems to be simply an animal who acts; he is not a believable person. In *Insurrection* O'Flaherty continues the animal motif that runs through *Famine* and *Land.* "A government is really a complex kind of animal. The various groups of citizens are its limbs and organs. Just as a wounded animal will bite off its foot . . ." (159). The wounded British monster hits back with artillery, and, "Like rabbits flushed from a warren by a ferret, people were fleeing northwards from the quays, in terror of the bursting shells" (163). O'Flaherty's battles are full of "wounded creatures" (39). As for Madden, "Like a rabbit that stands hypnotized by a weasel's deadly stare, an attraction that was stronger than his inherited fear held him motionless" (39).

Curious is O'Flaherty's transference of images of rural Aran animal life to urban guerrilla warfare in Dublin, which becomes an inferno, a den of madness, a chaos in which people continually move about "like an army of marauding ants that had come across rich spoil" (63). It is worth noting, incidentally, that *Insurrection* is the first important Irish historical novel with a totally urban setting. Before 1916, it seemed that Irish nationalism was a predominantly rural affair: a rural focus was evident in the novels that treated Antrim, the Boyne, Wexford, and other nationalist battles fought in the Irish countryside. But in 1916, the rebels marched through the streets of Dublin. Following O'Flaherty, Iris Murdoch and James Plunkett also dealt with Dublin.

Much has been made in the criticism of O'Flaherty's novels about his development of the character-types of soldier, saint, and poet: O'Dwyer, Father Kelly, and Raoul in *Land;* Madden, Kinsella, and Stapleton in *Insurrection.* The Fenian, renegade priest Father Kelly in *Land* seems to Raoul to encapsulate all three types: "The soldier, the poet and the monk represent what is finest in man. They represent man's will to power, to beauty and to immortality. They alone among men are capable of complete love, because they love the unattainable. Their love is never tarnished by possession. Before all three of them, I always bow low. When I bowed to you, I bowed to all three" (75–76). John Zneimer views the characters of Kinsella and his friend Stapleton in *Insurrection* as an artificial imposition of the saint and poet types upon the novel, arguing that O'Flaherty was more interested in the abstract, ideal character-types than in the development of realistic characters (141–43). There is some truth to this; like Madden, Kinsella and Stapleton are not adequately developed as characters. Viewed through Madden's simple eyes, they both die for the cause after a theoretical discussion about the beauty of revolution. But Kinsella and

Stapleton also have a realistic, historical basis: Kinsella, identified as a secondary-school teacher and a selfless leader who knows the rebel cause is doomed, is obviously a fictional version of Pearse; and Stapleton, a dreamy poet suffering from a terminal illness, is clearly meant to reflect Joseph Plunkett. As with Raoul in *Land*, who was "quite as dangerous as Parnell," O'Flaherty's strategy is the conventional one of the historical novelist: he leaves the big names of history in the background and develops fictional characters who are meant to reflect them.

O'Flaherty's basic approach in all three of his historical novels is to show how his protagonists react to major historical crises like trapped animals but are ennobled in their tragic devotion to the cause. His ethic here is very close to that of Theodore Dreiser (whom O'Flaherty admired) in his socialist phase: the naturalistic hero must die but the cause will live on; socialism is the solution. Disaster is always looming on the horizon in O'Flaherty's novels, and they open and close with a bang. But he is no nihilist; the cause is Savior.

O'Flaherty is the most partisan of Irish historical novelists. His is not the glorious "middle way" of Scott but the one true faith of Irish Republican socialism. His politics can alternately strengthen and damage his novels, and his writing is dramatic one moment and lumbering the next. At his best, in *Famine*, the intensity of his vision creates a historical novel that is, even with its faults, perhaps the best of the genre in Ireland. While his peasant predecessor William Carleton could only escape from history, O'Flaherty combined Carleton's intimate grasp of peasant life with a close knowledge of Irish history and a determination to capture the bitter tragedy of it.

8

The 1960s: Macken, Murdoch, Ó Tuairisc

ROM THE PUBLICATION OF O'FLAHERTY's *Insurrection* in 1950 to the appearance of Walter Macken's *Seek the Fair Land* in 1959, there was a gap of nearly a decade in the Irish historical novel. Irish novelists seemed to reflect the general mood of the country during this period, which was marked by a new determination to look ahead rather than behind in time. Under the prime ministership of Eamon de Valera, John Costello, and Seán Le Mass, Ireland appeared determined to move ahead and take its place in the modern world. Irish neutrality during World War II had established a reputation for objectivity in international affairs, and during the 1950s Ireland began to take an increasingly active role in the United Nations, leading to its crucial participation among U.N. peacekeeping forces in Africa and the Mideast during the 1960s. Meanwhile, a new effort to modernize the country's own domestic economy was evident, especially during the administration of Seán Le Mass. These developments served to render the murky Irish past irrelevant, at least for a time.

By the early 1960s, Ireland had gained a new security and a comparable prosperity that allowed its people (and its writers) to look to the past with a kinder, more detached view. In contrast, the bitter O'Flaherty had been convinced that Ireland was still trapped during the 1930s and 1940s by the volatile, divisive politics of Irish history, lending to his his-

155

torical novels a distinctly contemporary flavor. But to Irish historical novelists of the early 1960s, it seemed that the Irish past was truly past. They looked upon it with more distance and more nostalgia — and their readers, sharing these attitudes, eagerly embraced their novels.

Since 1959 there has been seen in the Irish historical novel an explosion of productivity and popularity similar to the one at the beginning of the century. From Walter Macken to the Americans Leon Uris and Thomas Flanagan, popular paperbacks have been much available — in drugstores and train stations as well as in bookstores and libraries — and much read. "Perhaps it was indicative of a changing social and literary situation in Ireland," Richard Fallis writes in *The Irish Renaissance* that "the 1960s saw the publication of a good many historical novels in Ireland, novels of considerable literary craftsmanship, but books directed toward the new middle class. That middle-aged middle class, actively involved in the economic expansion that marked Irish life during the decade, had matured after the years of the 'troubles,' and perhaps it found satisfaction in big novels on the Irish past." He adds that "perhaps the novels' popularity stemmed from the impression they give of creating imaginary ancestors for modern, middle-class Irish people gradually becoming urbanized and out of touch with their own long communal history."[1] And, it ought to be added, the popularity of recent Irish historical novels has extended beyond Ireland to Britain, the United States, and elsewhere. In comparison with the historical novels of the Irish Renaissance, these recent novels have reached a more international and more diverse audience as likely to include a housewife in Detroit or Liverpool as a businessman in Dublin, a farmer in Sligo, or a teacher in New York.

Or perhaps it is more accurate to say that they have reached a variety of audiences. The historical novels published during the 1960s by Walter Macken (1915–1967), Iris Murdoch (1919–), and Eoghan Ó Tuairisc (1919–1982) found readerships differing markedly in scope and character: Macken's novels have attracted "a fairly wide, Book-of-the-Month Club, upper-middle-brow audience,"[2] as Robert Hogan puts it, in Ireland, England, and America; Murdoch, although born in Dublin, has been perceived for good reasons as a British philosophical novelist aiming at a more intellectual, academic readership and attracting the attention of scholars, who have almost totally ignored Macken; while Macken's fellow Galwayman Ó Tuairisc, achieving that rarest of feats, a good Irish historical novel in Irish, necessarily reached by far the smallest readership: literate speakers and students of modern Irish. These authors' publishers, naturally, reflect these distinct readerships: Macken's historical novels have been kept in continual paperback circulation by Pan Books in cooperation with

Macmillan of London; Murdoch's *The Red and the Green* was published in cloth by Chatto and Windus of London and Viking Press in New York; whereas Ó Tuairisc's *L'Attaque* was virtually unobtainable during the years after its initial publication in 1962 until the 1980 paperback edition by Mercier Press in Cork.

A professor in England would most likely read *The Red and the Green*, not *L'Attaque* — which the average Irish member of Connradh na Gaeilge would read while steering clear of Murdoch. Both readers might well read Macken. Macken, Murdoch, and Ó Tuairisc present sharply contrasting studies in language, style, tone, and approach; in these respects their historical novels are more divergent than those of any other single period in the development of the genre. Yet they share most of the major conventions of the historical novel introduced by Scott and practiced by Irish writers from the Banims through Eilís Dillon, even though, as was the case with O'Flaherty, Scott was not a noticeably major or direct influence upon them. Each writer focuses upon a fictional, representative protagonist (or protagonists), withdrawing actual historical personages, the "big names" of history, to the background, for the most part. A Daniel O'Connell, a General Humbert, a Sir Charles Coote will occasionally appear — just as General Walker in Banim and Claverhouse in Scott appeared. But the focus is on fictional protagonists and on a panorama of characters deliberately selected in order to portray the polarities at work in Irish history. Each novel uses dialogue and different dialects in order to underline these polarities. Each author chooses a particular crisis in Irish history and develops the reactions of the novel's characters to the crisis, utilizing conventions of character, plot, and setting to reinforce them. Each seeks to understand the past in terms of their own present, always responding to the mythos of modern Irish history which opposes the Irish and the English. Given the considerable differences among Macken, Murdoch, and Ó Tuairisc, these common elements illustrate all the more the persistent mode of the Irish historical novel.

L IKE EOGHAN Ó TUAIRISC, Walter Macken was a Galwayman who became fluent in Irish and wrote several plays in Irish for the Taibhdhearc, the Irish-language theatre in Galway. In his novels, however, while maintaining an interest in the Gaelic world, Macken did not write in Irish as did Ó Tuairisc nor in the distinctively Irish-English idiom of O'Flaherty, but rather in a standard, "easy" English idiom. Concerning Macken's first his-

torical novel, *Seek the Fair Land* (1959), the reviewer for the *Times Literary Supplement* thought it "worth noting that the author, writing in the most westerly city of Europe, uses an amalgam of American and metropolitan English."[3] It is odd that a speaker and writer of Irish would so ignore its flavor, its residue, in Anglo-Irish speech. Macken conveys the Irishness of his characters' speech mostly through individual words —"'What is to prevent one of those people burying a *scian* in you?' Murdoc asked" —rather than through the Anglo-Irish syntax of O'Flaherty, Ó Faoláin, or MacManus ("Grumbling about their quarters they were then").[4]

Why Macken chose to write in his particular "metropolitan" idiom we cannot know, because, due to a lack of scholarly attention, very little is known about Macken in general. We know that he was born on May 3, 1915, in Galway City, son of Agnes Brady Macken and Walter Macken, a carpenter, who died in his son's youth. He attended the Patrician Brothers' primary and high schools in Galway, was a clerk on the county council, and became involved in the Taibhdhearc at the age of sixteen or seventeen. "He played there until he was twenty-one," Robert Hogan notes, "when he eloped to London with the daughter of a local newspaper editor and thereafter sold insurance for two years. When Frank Dermody, the Taibhdhearc's director, went on to the Abbey, Macken returned and stayed nine years, acting, producing, and writing plays in Irish."[5]

His Irish plays were not published, however; only his plays in English were. Like O'Flaherty, Macken was undoubtedly influenced in his decision to switch to English by the bleak outlook of publishing in Irish. Elsewhere Hogan adds:

> Macken's greater growth as a dramatist was limited mainly by his considerable success as a novelist and his increasing fascination with fiction. Some of his books found a wide audience in America, and many of them are kept in print by an English popular market paperback firm. Macken's fiction, like his plays, hangs between entertainment and art—say, between the excellent popular novels of a Maurice Walsh and the serious work of a Liam O'Flaherty. Macken's books . . . have usually well-drawn, if somewhat simple, characters, strong plotting, and an easy and often evocative style.[6]

Macken's early English plays were an attempt to do for Galway what O'Casey had done for Dublin.[7] In his dramatic work he had shown an increasing interest in fuller characterizations more suited to fiction and had already indicated the historical bent he would follow in his novels. His play *Twilight of a Warrior* (1956) was concerned with the aftermath

of the Troubles. He had collaborated with Liam O'Flaherty on a dramatic adaptation of *The Informer*, which was completed in 1952 but never produced.[8] O'Flaherty was clearly an influence on Macken, who adopted a very different style but explored some of the same themes in his historical novels — most notably the passivity of the common people in the face of famine in *The Silent People* (1962), much as in O'Flaherty's *Famine*.

Macken wrote eleven novels, three of which were historical novels: *Seek the Fair Land* (1959), about the 1650s, the Cromwellian period; *The Silent People* (1962), on the years of O'Connell and the Famine (1826–47); and *The Scorching Wind* (1964), extending from before the Easter Rising into the Anglo-Irish and Civil wars (1915–22). Although these novels deal with three distinct periods and thus cannot tell a single, unified story, as MacManus's trilogy does, Macken wrote them in succession and they are linked thematically, like O'Flaherty's trilogy, and are more uniform stylistically (and qualitatively) than the O'Flaherty novels. Macken even goes so far as to use two of the same names, Dualta and Dominick (the spelling of which varies), in each novel: Dominick is the protagonist of *Seek the Fair Land* and Dualta, his young benefactor; Dualta, the hero of *The Silent People*, has a young son, Dominick, at the end; and Dominic and Dualta are the brothers whose story dominates *The Scorching Wind*. Each novel presents a hero fleeing from English pursuers: the common theme is of an Ireland on the run. The shared world of the three novels is further suggested whenever characters think about history: Daniel O'Connell seems to Dualta in *The Silent People* to be like one of the old Gaelic chieftains, and he gives a feast much like that of the chieftain Murdoc in *Seek the Fair Land*; in *The Scorching Wind*, old men at a funeral talk about Wolfe Tone, Robert Emmet, and Daniel O'Connell, and Dualta and Dominic think about the Gaels of old as they pass through the mountains of Connemara.

Macken's popularity is due to his "easy" style, his emphasis upon action, and his romantic approach, which in some ways recalls that of the Banims. His novels may well appeal to an "upper-middle-brow" audience as Hogan suggests, but an Irish friend of mine assures me that he read and enjoyed them when he was about twelve. The paperback covers have a youthful appeal, suggesting that Father Brown's dictum about educating "the youth of the nation" to Irish history was part of Macken's (or at least his publisher's) intent.

It is also clear that Macken wanted to accommodate his work to foreign readers. Like the Banims, Macken was writing for a British publisher, and as with their novels there is always an expository, educational frame to his — what Eoghan Ó Tuairisc describes as the "this-is-history"

approach.⁹ Each of Macken's historical novels is introduced by a "Historical Note" that is both expository and didactic, both informing readers of
key historical facts and preparing them for an Irish nationalist interpreta-
tion of the facts, as for example at the beginning of *Seek the Fair Land:*

> When Murdoc and Dominick meet in Chapter One, Drogheda is
> invested by Irish insurgent forces who rose in rebellion in 1641 against,
> among other things, (a) the forcible plantation of Ulster by Scots and
> English; (b) the Act of Supremacy, whereby to be a judge, lawyer or
> government official required an oath that the King of England was Head
> of the Church — an impossible oath for Catholics; (c) the Act of Unifor-
> mity, whereby Catholics could be fined or imprisoned for not attending
> Protestant services; (d) the militant anti-Catholic attitude of the Parlia-
> ment in England who were already in opposition to King Charles and
> determined to remove all Catholic landowners, Irish and Anglo-Irish,
> from their estates.
>   By Chapter Two, Cromwell is investing Drogheda with his Iron-
> sides, King Charles has been executed, and Irish and Anglo-Irish, Catho-
> lic and Protestant, are partly united in a last despairing effort to avert
> a terrible destruction by a gloomy and pitiless enemy. (3)

In 1959, Macken no longer needed to write an apologia for Irish nationalism, as the Banims had done in the 1820s. His is an all-out attack on
the British historical repression of the Irish, concerning which he could
assume that his average British reader might be as critical as he was.

While changing its tone, Macken shares the Banims' expository
didacticism; he also adopts a romantic approach similar to theirs. Like
their heroes, his are larger than life. In the development of his protagonists, Macken is part realist and part romancer. His heroes struggle with
realistic, historical problems, but at the same time they have some of the
virtual anonymity of the old knights. Dominic in *The Scorching Wind,*
for example, is never assigned a surname; his namesake in *Seek the Fair
Land* has a surname, but it is never clear what he did for a living before
the holocaust at Drogheda. The point seems to be that either Dominic
might be *any* Dominic in Ireland during these particular periods of history. Furthermore, Macken's endings are romantic. Like the Banims' protagonists, Macken's heroes escape from the nightmare of history at the
end. In *Seek the Fair Land,* at the end of the Cromwellian war, Dominick
goes home to live in peace with his daughter and son-in-law, recalling
the ending of Banim's *The Last Baron of Crana;* similarly, at the end of
The Silent People, Dualta, in spite of the Famine, walks the road home

with his wife and child ("We will survive"); and even at the end of *The Scorching Wind*, although Dominic has just found his brother dead in the Civil War, he finally gets the girl.

Consistently, Macken's historical heroes are reluctant rebels on the run. Each is forced into a rebellious, fugitive posture. Dominick MacMahon in *Seek the Fair Land* finds his wife dead in the Cromwellian blitz on Drogheda in 1649; he escapes with his daughter and son and a priest, fleeing westward through the countryside. Dualta Dane in *The Silent People* is struck in the face with a horsewhip by the landlord's son in the opening scene of the novel; after he dumps his assailant from his horse, he must leave his Galway town in a hurry, running south toward Clare, where he becomes an agrarian rebel. In *The Scorching Wind* Dominic, called the "reluctant rebel" by his brother, slowly becomes involved in the rebel cause during the Anglo-Irish War and is "convinced" through the experience of torture at the hands of the British; after the Treaty of 1921, Dominic the reluctant rebel has transformed himself into a die-hard Republican who opposes his brother's cooperative, Free-State accession to the Treaty.

While Macken's protagonists are forced into rebelliousness, there is at the same time a counter-motive in the novels, a higher lesson: the peace beyond tragedy. The clearest example is the plot of *Seek the Fair Land*. Dominick MacMahon's journey from Drogheda to the "fair land" of the Galway mountains in the company of his children and his friend Father Sebastian achieves a dual purpose for Macken: it allows him to show a series of scenes of Cromwellian horror all across the country, and it facilitates Dominick's development in contact and conversation with Father Sebastian. For Dominick's journey, he finally learns, is a spiritual one more than a geographical one. Provoked into rebellion, he is gradually converted toward pacifism by Father Sebastian. As a priest Sebastian is necessarily an outlaw himself; he accepts Dominick's protection, caring for his children in return. By the time he is captured and killed by Cromwell's forces, Sebastian has become a Christlike figure. Burnt at the stake, he passes on his voice to Dominick's formerly mute son, significantly named Peter, who stands on a rock and offers up a prayer for Sebastian. Dominick is transformed by the experience and is determined to live in peace. He has found the "fair land" of the soul: "that would be the real fair land, deep down in yourself" (299). His spiritual peace is reinforced by the setting: "Not that this physical one wasn't fair too. The mountains were all purple-tinged and they ranged all around him protectingly, and below him was the white sand of the shore, and the heaving sea was stained with many colours" (299).

Macken's other protagonists undergo similar transformations. Dualta in *The Silent People* has joined Cuan McCarthy and the Whiteboys in the 1820s, but he is moved by Daniel O'Connell's pacifist war of words and numbers against British supremacy. The noble O'Connell exerts an influence on Dualta similar to that of Father Sebastian. Dualta parts ways with Cuan, settling down on a farm and teaching in the schoolhouse. Although Dominic in *The Scorching Wind* doesn't learn his pacifist lesson until his brother's death at the end of the novel, he is reluctant to involve himself in wanton violence throughout the Anglo-Irish War. In the Civil War he is a Republican and his brother is a Free-Stater, which is synecdochic of an Ireland at war with itself at the same time that it is realistic, because many Irish families were in fact bitterly divided during the Civil War. When his brother dies, Dominic leaves the war. "'You see,' he said, struggling for the words, 'it can become too much for the individual. Like this. Just little men, with love, and brothers. You see, men with brothers.'"[10] He abandons the rebel cause in order to make peace with himself.

Macken's heroes undergo journeys that always include Galway, Macken's home. Dominick MacMahon's odyssey is from Drogheda to Galway; Dualta Dane flees Galway for Clare; Dominic in *The Scorching Wind* leaves Galway to go underground during the Anglo-Irish War but repeatedly returns. Each experiences a geographical run for survival that becomes a romantic and spiritual quest for freedom and peace.

The pacifist theme of Macken's novels sets him sharply apart from O'Flaherty, who ridiculed pacifism and disdained Daniel O'Connell. Macken is less willing than O'Flaherty to glorify violence. It might be said that O'Flaherty is the better writer and Macken the better moralist. While O'Flaherty's central historical protagonist is the animal-man turned rebel, Macken's pivotal figure is more often the schoolteacher: Dominick MacMahon in *Seek the Fair Land*, who is never called a schoolteacher but who is introspective and left shelves full of books behind in Drogheda; Dualta's crafty, resigned Uncle Marcus in *The Silent People*, who sends him on his way out of trouble to Clare; and Dominic's and Dualta's father in *The Scorching Wind*, who is arrested because he taught Irish nationalism for years in the schoolhouse and who dies of pneumonia contracted in jail. And the priest and the pacifist politician educate Macken's rebels. In these respects Macken is much closer to MacManus than to O'Flaherty. The education of Dominick MacMahon by Father Sebastian is much like that of Donnacha MacConmara by Father O'Casey. For Macken and MacManus, the Church is not the repressive agent it generally is in O'Flaherty and Ó Faoláin, but rather an outpost of peace and liberty. Of course, this is clearer in the seventeenth- and eighteenth-century world, in which the

Church itself was an outlawed institution, portrayed by Macken (in *Seek the Fair Land*) and MacManus, than it would be in the nineteenth- and twentieth-century world, when the Church gained the security that led to an often reactionary stance. Yet Macken does not touch upon the conservatism of the church in his nineteenth- and twentieth-century novels, as do O'Flaherty and Ó Faoláin.

It is noteworthy that Macken is the only Irish historical novelist treated in this study who deals with the two most common historical characters in Irish folklore, Oliver Cromwell and Daniel O'Connell. The images in folklore of Cromwell as devil and O'Connell as silver-tongued advocate are reflected in Macken's novels. In *Seek the Fair Land* the image of Cromwell as devil is reflected in the figure of his follower Sir Charles Coote, Lord President of Connacht, who combines cruelty and sexual perversity, much like the land agent Chadwick in O'Flaherty's *Famine*. When Dominick MacMahon first meets Coote, he is engaged in torturing a young noblewoman who has refused to pay her Cromwellian tribute. Coote has the woman stripped and bound in front of a fire. He is sweating and "his fingernails were long and dirty" (120). "He had long eyelashes, a small mouth. He was delicately built, like a young woman. His gestures were feminine, like his walk" (110). Years earlier Dominick had seen Cromwell himself invoking the Lord against the Irish, and now it is clear to him that Coote embraces the same religious perversity: "'She refused tribute,' said Coote, 'and referred in malodorous terms to the personal appearance of the Lord Protector, a crime for which we all pray that the Lord will forgive her.' He was grinning" (120). As the reviewer for *Time Magazine* put it, Macken's Coote is "a fine, blood-curdling villain . . . a chap so dark-eyed and nasty that readers will cheer when he is knifed to death in the next-to-last chapter by an incensed Irishman."[11] It is significant, however, that it is not Macken's protagonist who does the deed, but rather the defiant old Gaelic chieftain Murdoc O'Flaherty, who dies in the encounter.

Macken's Daniel O'Connell is as positive as his Coote/Cromwell is negative. O'Connell is more visible in *The Silent People* than are major historical personages in other Irish historical novels, except for Carleton's Redmond O'Hanlon and O'Grady's Red Hugh O'Donnell. Macken's Dualta meets O'Connell several times. The first time he felt that "it was strange to see the lines drawn in a newspaper or a magazine, the cartooning and caricaturing of the real, suddenly become reality before your eyes. There it was, the thick curly hair with the reddish tint, dusted with grey, intelligent blue eyes and an impudent snub nose."[12] He is both demagogue and demigod. O'Connell proceeds to refute Cuan McCarthy's violent views: "There has been too much blood spilled, without need. Listen, I have called

a nation into existence, all of them, not a few here and a few there with pikes in the thatch, but a whole people. I will imbue them like a yeast in a cake so that they will rise and swell, and become so peacefully big and cohesive, so morally strong, that they will have to be handed what they want" (123). He wins Dualta over, and Dualta helps him in his successful campaign against the landlord's man, Vesey-Fitzgerald, in the Clare election of 1828. Much later, when Dualta seeks out O'Connell at the beginning of the Famine in 1845 and finds him dying, he sees that "the great voice was silent" and that therefore all of Ireland would now be silent and passive. As soon as he leaves O'Connell, "While Dualta rode the long road home, he was impressed by the great silence" (286). Here Macken departs from the folkloric image of O'Connell as flawless advocate in order to capture his actual last, desperate days in the face of Young Ireland and the Famine. His portrait is a very sympathetic one.

Macken's basic approach to Irish history, according to which he endorses both Irish nationalism and moderate pacifism, could have been obtained only at the remove of many years, during the relatively comfortable period, both politically and economically, in which he was living and writing. In the 1960s both author and audience could enjoy unprecedented prosperity and detachment. Macken emphasized always the struggle of the common people, a struggle of which his Irish readers could be proud. We read about the struggle in standard English, but these common people often speak, we are told (as by the Banims), "in Irish." Macken's style and appeal are cosmopolitan; his ethic is Catholic and nationalist. The "fair land" to which Macken and his readers, like Dominick MacMahon, would like to escape, is, however little they may actually use the language, a Gaelic one, the "Beanna Beola," somewhere in the green-blue mountains of Connemara.

MACKEN's historical Ireland, like that of Carleton, MacManus, and O'Flaherty, is predominantly a peasant society. In sharp contrast, the world of Iris Murdoch's *The Red and the Green*, like that of Le Fanu and O'Grady, is the Anglo-Irish Ascendancy. Like Macken's *The Scorching Wind* (1964), *The Red and the Green* (1965), published on the verge of the fiftieth anniversary of the Easter Rising of 1916, explores the historical conflicts at work during that period. Both Macken and Murdoch were born around the time of the Rising. But there the similarities between these two authors and their novels seem to end. Macken was a lifelong Galwayman, an Irish

speaker, a strictly popular novelist; Murdoch was an early and permanent emigré to Britain, a member of the Ascendancy, an academic, intellectual, philosophical novelist. Murdoch has been much studied by scholars; Macken has been ignored by them. Yet Macken's historical novels were met by a more positive popular reception than was *The Red and the Green*, as a comparison of reviews in periodicals illustrates.[13]

Murdoch was born in Dublin on July 15, 1919, "of Anglo-Irish 'settler' stock that has been in Ireland for centuries, but thinks of itself, she says, as *the* Irish."[14] She was educated at the Badminton School in Bristol and at Somerville College, Oxford (1938–42), receiving a first-class honors degree in classics. She served as an assistant principal in the Treasury (1942–44), as a fellow at Cambridge (1947), and a tutor in philosophy at Oxford (1948), marrying a fellow of New College, Oxford (1956). As Donna Gerstenberger writes:

> Although Iris Murdoch was born in Dublin within a few years of the Easter Rising and the caesarian birth pangs of modern Ireland and grew up with an awareness of Ireland's difficult definition and existence, her family life, her early schooling at Badminton, her employment by the English government and UNESCO, her training at Oxford and Cambridge, and her interest in modern continental philosophers have all contributed to the creation of a body of writing not particularly definable as Irish. If there are roots in her fiction, the main ones seem to be English, although the recurrence of Irish characters in Murdoch's novels and the extensive treatment of the Easter Rising in *The Red and the Green* make explicit a persistent consciousness of Ireland as a force in her fictional world.[15]

Moreover, *The Red and the Green* is clearly an Irish historical novel in terms of its subject matter as well as many of the conventions it adopts. The Irish literary influences apparent in Murdoch's work are fellow travelers among the Ascendancy: Le Fanu, O'Grady, and Yeats. Her novel *The Unicorn* (1963) was a Gothic novel influenced by the work of Le Fanu.[16] In *The Red and the Green*, the antiquarian Christopher Bellman expresses opinions remarkably like those of O'Grady: "Ireland's real past *is* the ascendancy. Ireland should turn back to the eighteenth century."[17] Arguing that Anglo-Irish leaders of the eighteenth century would have worked with English leaders to relieve the Great Famine, Bellman calls the romantic Pearse an "idiot" and echoes O'Grady's nostalgia for the Anglo-Irish "Patriot Parliament" of Grattan and Flood. Similarly, throughout the novel there are echoes of Yeats, especially at the end, where the tone and

even the language of the 1938 "Epilogue" to the Rising are very close to Yeats's pronouncement that the leaders of 1916 have been transformed, that "a terrible beauty is born."

As in Macken's novels, a new sense of distance from history is evident in *The Red and the Green*. Writing in the 1960s, Murdoch has the detachment necessary to explore her main theme: the conflicts between energy and order, rebellion and law, eros and impotence, among an Anglo-Irish family fifty years earlier. But in contrast to Macken's chronologically sprawling novels, *The Red and the Green* is focused upon just a few days before and during the Rising in April 1916. This permits an interesting comparison of the novel to O'Flaherty's similarly focused *Insurrection* — a comparison which yields, for the most part, contrast more than semblance.

Like O'Flaherty's Bartly Madden, Murdoch's Pat Dumay is a rebel who has totally devoted himself to the cause, developing a happy, lustful attachment to his gun. So happy had he been to get a gun in the famous Howth gun-running episode of 1914 that "marching back with his rifle on his shoulders, Pat could have wept with emotion" (88). Yet while Pat and Bartly are on the surface similar characters, their authors' characterizations of them are quite different: O'Flaherty treats Bartly's consciousness from the inside, while Murdoch views Pat mostly from the outside, maintaining a strict detachment from him. Bartly is O'Flaherty's protagonist, while Pat is merely one among Murdoch's motley crew of characters. Because of this difference in narrative perspective and emphasis, O'Flaherty's characterization of Bartly is sympathetic whereas Murdoch's critique of Pat is negative.

Like Patrick Pearse, Pat's hero and the historical figure whom he is clearly meant to reflect, Pat appears to be a latent homosexual; he hates women.

> Pat had little use for women. He connected them with the part of himself which disgusted him. He found them somehow muddled and unclean, representative of the frailty and incompleteness of human life. He despised the stupidity and frivolity which characterized their talk, and he was positively nervous of being touched by one. He did not, in fact, like being touched by anybody. The human touch reminded him of a fact which he preferred to forget, that he was incarnate. (84)

Ruth Dudley Edwards' recent biography of Pearse documents his similar aversion to women and messianic attachment to the cause as passionate fulfillment.[18] Pat Dumay represents a new twist to the familiar figure of the rebel in the Irish historical novel: he is neither chivalric hero as in

Banim, Carleton, Le Fanu, and O'Grady, nor dissolute defier like Ó Faoláin's Leo Donnel (who seeks out sex rather than avoiding it), nor animal-man as in O'Flaherty, nor rebel as penitent as in MacManus and Macken. Pat's is a new kind of defiance: the cause replaces sex.

Indeed, sex is a prime problem for most of the male characters in *The Red and the Green*. In this novel by the first female and first foreign (of half-foreign) writer considered in this study, there is more sex and more talk about sex than in any other Irish historical novel considered herein. All of the novel's major male characters are sexually frustrated. In a "comic-opera" scene late in the novel, the Anglo-Irish major Andrew Chase-White, the Irish rebel Pat Dumay, the Ascendancy antiquarian Christopher Bellman, and the "spoiled priest" Barnabas Drumm all appear together at the home of the promiscuous noblewoman Aunt Millie. All of them want her and none of them can have her. As all of these characters are related to each other one way or another, there is also an air of incest about all of this.

Murdoch is primarily interested in the inner workings of the Anglo-Irish Ascendancy, and so the clash of "Red" and "Green" is confined to her Anglo-Irish cast of characters. She cites Anglo-Irish precedent when Pat Dumay's brother Cathal sings of British Red and Irish Green:

Sure 'twas for this Lord Edward died and Wolfe Tone sunk serene,
Because they could not bear to leave the red above the green. (116)

Murdoch's title also suggests Stendhal's *Le Rouge et Le Noir*, and Pat Dumay has something of the decadent, driven quality of Julian Sorel. Her literary inspirations, indeed, were traditional, nineteenth-century ones; she was a great admirer of Scott.[19]

It is odd that with all of the scholarly work that has been done on Murdoch, none has analyzed *The Red and the Green* as a historical novel. Several critics note that it is one but none considers what that means. The epitome of misunderstanding on this point is Frank Baldanza's. In his book on Murdoch he writes that *The Red and the Green* "is inevitably called a 'historical novel,' although the term needs to be used with many qualifications. It is 'historical' in the sense that a famous public event occurs at the climax and affects the lives of the characters, but it is not 'historical' in the sense that it either gives any thorough review of public events (aside from the random dinner-table discussions of private citizens) or treats the experience of famous public persons."[20] That Murdoch does not "treat the experience of famous public persons" but instead focuses upon fic-

tional characters is, of course, the whole point; as we have seen, this is what historical novelists, beginning with Scott, generally do. Through her characters Murdoch does indeed give a "thorough review of public events." Pat Dumay and his relatives talk and think for page after page about Pearse, Connolly, and the preparations for and details of the Rising.

Much of the criticism on *The Red and the Green* quite rightly focuses upon character conflicts in the novel; character is always Murdoch's prime concern. Weldon Thornton, for example, points out that the novel's characters seek an elusive balance between energy and order, passion and control, always desiring the qualities in others which they feel to be lacking in themselves.[21] Pat Dumay's cousin Andrew Chase-White is jealous of Pat's resoluteness and courage – qualities we discover to be deceptive. Christopher Bellman seems to possess British restraint and good sense, but then he perishes on his way to join the rebels in the General Post Office. Barney Drumm seeks courage by participating in the Rising and then shoots himself in the foot. Aunt Millie seeks true individuality and discovers merely roles, a facade. These character conflicts possess a broader political, historical significance. The most important conflict is that between Andrew Chase-White and Pat Dumay, for they are really the Red and the Green of the novel, and they never understand each other.

Andrew the Anglo-Irish major and Pat the Irish rebel are cousins, a significant fact; they represent Murdoch's exploration of the contradictions inherent in her own Anglo-Irish family heritage. At the beginning of her novel, Murdoch seems to be speaking for herself when she notes that the scene at Howth Head was for Andrew "intensely familiar and yet disturbingly alien. It was like a place revisited continually in dreams, both portentous and fleeting, vivid to the point of necessity, but not entirely real" (4). As was the case with Murdoch herself, "Andrew's family were Anglo-Irish, but he had never lived in Ireland, although he had spent most of his childhood holidays there" (4). As perhaps for his creator, "Ireland remained for him a mystery, an unsolvable problem: and a problem which was in some obscure way disagreeable" (5)

This initial tone of detachment is one that persists throughout the novel and is not fully overcome by the epilogue, in which it is revealed that Pat Dumay and Christopher Bellman died in the Rising, Andrew in the war on the Continent, and Cathal Dumay at the hands of Black and Tans in 1921 (in, Murdoch inaccurately notes, the "Civil War") – and that the rebels were heroes after all. Murdoch's history is generally accurate, her critique of Pearse in the form of Pat is perceptive, and her characterizations are lively and interesting. The plight of Andrew and Cathal Dumay, British soldier and Irish would-be rebel, handcuffed together by Pat

late in the novel, ineffectually groping down a Dublin street just in time to hear Pearse's Proclamation, is an apt image of the divided status of the Anglo-Irish family. Too often, however, the Easter Rising emerges from *The Red and the Green* as a problem to be studied, an event to be analyzed; no character *lives* it quite the way Bartly Madden does in *Insurrection*.

MACKEN's *The Scorching Wind* and Murdoch's *The Red and the Green* were not the only Irish historical novels to celebrate the fiftieth anniversary of the Easter Rising, nor were Murdoch and O'Flaherty the only authors to focus so closely upon the chronology of the event. Eoghan Ó Tuairisc's 1966 novel in Irish *Dé Luain (Monday)*, Ó Tuairisc noted, "was designed to commemorate the 50th anniversary of 1916, and deals with the opening hours of the Revolution in Dublin, minute by minute, from midnight Easter Sunday to noon on Monday. Though it won the Butler Prize, it has never been as popular with readers as *L'Attaque:* it is too complex, having dozens of perception centres in the weave of it, whereas *L'Attaque* has only the one. Very few Irish readers have sufficient mastery of the language to enjoy such a shifting spectrum of mood, action, and persona." *Dé Luain* is now virtually unobtainable. Much more successful was *L'Attaque* (1962), Ó Tuairisc's novel on 1798 in Mayo, which, as the only clearly successful Irish historical novel to have been written in the Irish language, certainly deserves to be included in this study.

Several other of our authors – Carleton, Ó Faoláin, MacManus, O'Flaherty, Macken, James Plunkett, Eilís Dillon – knew Irish, and both O'Flaherty and Macken, as we have seen, did some writing in Irish. But only Ó Tuairisc wrote a historical novel in Irish – or, I should say, a *good* historical novel in Irish. Pádraic Ó Conaire had published *Brian Óg*, a hero tale of the Jacobite-Williamite war, some forty years earlier, but it was, as Ó Tuairisc himself noted, "a piece of pure Romantic bumph, never rising above the 'brave young Irishman plying his sword upon callous enemy for the sake of the old sod.'" The hero, Brian Óg, manages a heroic escape at the end. King James is on the scene as historical hero; he is not withdrawn to the background. *Brian Óg* was not really a serious Irish historical novel, but a children's story, as the simple cover and large print of its most recent paperback edition indicate.[22] It is no fair example – neither of what Ó Conaire as serious artist could do nor of what the historical novel in Irish could be. Ó Conaire's serious work – his novel *Deoraíocht* (1910) and stories such as "Nóra Mhárcais Bhig" – was a pio-

neer achievement in modern Gaelic fiction, presenting a vividly naturalistic and picaresque vision. Like Carleton in English, Ó Conaire in Irish was capable of great and graphic fictions about his own contemporary world, but when looking at history he could not go beyond fulsome romance.

Yet, Ó Tuairisc wrote, "There is some particular quirk in the Irish character, and consequently in pre-Famine Irish history, that it is impossible to delineate adequately in English — adequately, that is, to one who knows the literature of the country in both languages." He added that "unlike English, Irish, in its stylistic detachment, can be heroic without being inflated, or plain silly." A telling example of this difference is Brendan Behan's play The Hostage: its Irish original, An Giall, was a quiet, lyrical play; in English, it became vaudeville theatre. This is not because Irish is a simple, naive language — to the contrary, Ó Tuairisc celebrates "that ambiguity — that poetry of language in which all opposites are possible — which is an innate modality of the Irish language."[23] He argued that novels such as Brian Óg failed because earlier Gaelic novelists "lost the connection with the sagas and epics of the pre-1600 literature, and were attempting to import the novel into Irish, going on English models."

Ó Tuairisc's enthusiasm for early Irish epic much preceded his appearance on the literary scene in the 1960s. Born Eugene Watters in Ballinasloe, County Galway, in 1919 (the same year as Murdoch), he studied Irish throughout his schooling and developed a deep interest in early Irish literature during his degree work at St. Patrick's Teachers' Training College in Drumcondra and at University College, Dublin, where he studied not only "the ancient Irish battle-sagas of the Ulster cycle" but Homer, Virgil, and Beowulf as well. During World War II he held a commission in the Irish army, "training a battalion in mobile and guerrilla warfare . . . in case of invasion," thereby learning "to know soldiers intimately" and getting "a glimpse of what real fighting might be like — particularly with volunteer bands against professionals, which is mainly the situation in L'Attaque." He then taught for a number of years in Dublin primary schools, "the best training in the world for a writer: with young children he learns to make his ideas concrete, make language enjoyable as language, and take the hi- out of history." In 1961 he "gave up teaching to go wholetime as a creative writer . . . in Irish and English, writing in Ireland, mainly on Irish themes, and publishing in Ireland — and taking the financial consequences."

L'Attaque, "begun Feb. 1961, writing day and night, and finished in June," was its author's "first long-distance work in Irish," and perhaps his most successful one. It won the Club Leabhar, Gradam an Direachtais,

and Hyde Memorial awards. "My English name, 'Eugene Watters,' was practically wiped out, and I have been 'Eoghan Ó Tuairisc' ever since." Following *L'Attaque*, Ó Tuairisc wrote a number of other works of historical interest, in both Irish and English: *Dé Luain* (1966); *The Hedge-schoolmaster* (1975), a novel for the schools; *Infinite Variety* (1976), "the story of Dan Lowry's Music Hall in Dublin, 1879–1897"; and *An Lomnochtáin*, a novel about "a childhood in the Civil War period." Mercier's 1980 paperback edition of *L'Attaque* has marked a resurgence of popularity for its author: Mercier's editor, Caoimhín Ó Marcaigh, noted the year before Ó Tuairisc's death that he had become "something of a cult figure."[24] Ó Tuairisc's translation of stories by Máirtín Ó Cadhain, *The Road to Bright City* (1981), has recently been released, and at the time of his death he was working on *Fornacht do Chonac*, a play on "the effects of the 1916 violence in modern times"; *Lá Fhéile Míchíl*, "a drama of the Civil War"; and *Carolan*, a play "based on the life of the blind harper of the eighteenth century."

The paperback book blurb for *L'Attaque* notes:

Is minic a thugtar "úrscéal stairiúil" ar an leabhar cáiliúil seo ach níl sa mhéid sin ach rangú ginearálta. Is mó d'eipic nó de shaga atá i *L'Attaque*.

[This celebrated book is often called a "historical novel" but that's only a general classification. There's more of the epic or saga in *L'Attaque*.][25]

Yet it is clear that while *L'Attaque* is laced with epic influences, it is above all a realistic, sometimes experimental novel that fits squarely in the tradition of the Irish historical novel in the twentieth century. Ó Tuairisc outlined to me his major influences: "the epic style of the Classics, of Anglo-Saxon, and particularly of the Irish 'historical' sagas of the Old Irish and Medieval period, as seen in such fictionalized history as *Táin Bó Cuailgne*, *Cath Rois na Rí for Bóinn*, and even in the would-be historical *Leabhar Gabhála* ['The Book of Invasions']"; and "a second and even more powerful influence," Tolstoy's *War and Peace*, which gave Ó Tuairisc artistic courage as it did Eilís Dillon a decade later. Concerning early Irish authors, Ó Tuairisc noted that "all these writers (the 'synthetic historians'), in common with the rest of the medieval world, had no compunction about weaving the actual facts of history into a myth or a poetic fiction: such poiesis, of course, included prose as well as verse." There were early Irish sagas about recovering the *Táin*, just as *L'Attaque* is in part a novel that reasserts, as we shall see, the vision of the *Táin*. But the mythic world of early Irish epic was overwhelmed in *L'Attaque* by Tolstoy's realism, "the

human quality which . . . is invariably absent in Irish epic. Tolstoy's soldiers are not the half-divine heroes of the *Táin*, but the down-to-earth, haymaking, hungry, bored and humorsome soldiers I had known in the Army of Ireland." Thus, *L'Attaque* is colored by Tolstoy's realism as well as by the *Táin*'s myth.

Reacting to the *Táin* and Tolstoy, Ó Tuairisc observed a "conflict between the heroic and the anti-hero . . . concentrated in my prime character, Máirtín Dubh Caomhánach, bearing the name of the Royal House of Leinster . . . and now a turfcutter in the bogs of Connacht." Ó Tuairisc's source for the story of the Mayo rising of 1798 was Richard Hayes's *The Last Invasion of Ireland* (1937), in whose introduction it is noted that the story "is one of high adventure, with not a few epic qualities."[26] Hayes presents the facts surrounding the rising in the autumn of 1798 and explores its popular reverberations. Ó Tuairisc noted that he was "attracted by the theme of the impact of a dynamic, revolutionary, atheistic force upon a static peasant population who by sheer tribulation and passive resistance had survived a hundred years of a penal colonial regime coldly calculated to keep them socially, politically, and intellectually poor and impotent. Violence was rare amongst them, and their language had nothing of the sharp impact of the French word *attaque*."

In *L'Attaque* he explores some of the traditional societal polarities at work in the Irish historical novel—leaders and followers, gentry and peasants—but here he is primarily interested not in the conflict between the English and the Irish, but in tensions entirely on the Republican side: the French in the midst of the Irish, and Irish peasant soldiers led by "the Protestant and Presbyterian gentry . . . who had been inspired to an anti-colonial Republicanism by the example of the American Revolution." In the novel he presents these tensions linguistically. Irish and French soldiers grapple with the others' language as they address each other: "'Parlez-vous, Jackser!' chaith an Foghlaeir chuige. 'Sláinte, Paidí!' arsa an Francach" (50). The Protestant leader Robert Craigie's letter home to his wife in lofty, patriotic language is followed by the peasant Pádraig Ó Flannagáin's earthy, humble, reassuring note to his mother (57–62).

The novel opens with Máirtín Caomhánach's reluctant entry into the rising. Recently married to Saidhbhín, daughter of a wealthy man and the pride of the area, Máirtín is happy in the daily ritual of home life: cutting turf in the field with Saidhbhín, dinner, and the sweet privacy of their bed. With the arrival of the French in Killala, Máirtín experiences "an mórshaol amuigh ag briseadh isteach air [the big world outside breaking in on him]" (18). As a Volunteer he must go to join the rising, but he's reluctant. Their parting is a sad, tender one, and Saidhbhín is upset

by it, like Nora Clitheroe in O'Casey's *The Plough and the Stars.* Máirtín's initial attitude is "Damnú air mar phíce! [Damn the pike!]" (15). Throughout the early stages of the rising, Máirtín and his Leitrim mates maintain a lively pessimism about their chances. When Craigie (whom Máirtín never liked) announces, "ionsaí eile [another attack]", Máirtín thinks to himself, "Ionsaí eile. Ní hea, a chailleach, ach eirleach eile [Another attack. No, old hag, another slaughter]" (113). No Cúchulainn, this; rather than bluntly assert his hero to be another Cúchulainn, as did Standish O'Grady with Red Hugh O'Donnell, Ó Tuairisc often uses the *Táin* for ironic purposes. When Máirtín and Taimí MacNiallais drive cattle down a glen toward British guns, hoping to flush them out, the cattle freeze, turn, and scatter; reality supplants myth.

> Chas an meall dlúite mairteola ar chrúba sceimhle, thug fogha adharc-íslithe ar son an Liberté trí ranganna na réabhlóidithe ar ais nó go ndeachaigh idir phíceadóiri agus bheithígh ina dTáin Bó Cuailgne ar sraoille reatha soir siar roimh réadachas neamheipiciúil ordanás an Rí Seoirse.

> [The mass of beef pulled together in a clutch of terror, made an attack for the sake of *Liberté* back through the rebel ranks until they were between the pikemen and the beasts in the *Táin Bó Cuailgne*, struggling, running hither and thither before the epic military realism of King George.] (110)

The French and Anglo-Irish revolutionary leaders don't think much more of their makeshift Irish peasant forces than the peasants do of them: these are not the masses of eager Irish revolutionaries General Humbert had been led to expect, but a band of untrained, unarmed, and, for the most part, unshod farm laborers. General Blake gives Craigie a commission simply because his troop of Leitrim men are the only ones around with shoes already on their feet.

Nonetheless, Humbert courageously leads on his motley forces — taking a back road to avoid the British forces on the main road — and Máirtín and his mates become heroes in spite of themselves in the famous "Races of Castlebar" in which both the militia and the population of the town madly fled *en masse* before Humbert's army. Ó Tuairisc captures their flight in long, fleeting, fluid sentences, ending the story with a single sentence: "Tá an Táin déanta" (139). "The raid has been completed" is the literal translation, but it also suggests, as Ó Tuairisc explained to me, "'The ancient *Táin*, long lost, has been recovered, and now written.' That's just the way I felt when I put down the last full stop." In order to emphasize

the unlikely but therefore all the more impressive heroism of peasants like Máirtín Caomhánach, Ó Tuairisc strategically ends with Republican victory in the Races of Castlebar, rather than continue to the defeat that followed — much as Murdoch ended in the midst of the Easter Rising, adding an epilogue that celebrated its heroism. Ó Tuairisc's '98 rebels emerge more positively than do Michael Banim's or William Buckley's '98 Wexford rebels — an accurate contrast, since there was not the kind of carnage in Mayo (at least until afterwards) that there was in Wexford. And he concludes with victory —"Tá an Táin déanta" — partly in order to celebrate his own victory in using Irish to write a historical novel. Ó Tuairisc has succeeded in entering the mainstream of the genre shaped by Scott and Tolstoy, while presenting the Gaelic world within its own linguistic tradition, not divorced from it as were other historical novelists, who only alluded in English to those who spoke "in Irish."

There is great stylistic variety in L'Attaque; indeed, if there is a fault to the novel, it is that the work is not longer, in order to allow for more graceful, less abrupt transitions between contrasting sections. (Brevity is a rare shortcoming in a historical novel!) L'Attaque includes short, staccato sentences describing battle scenes as well as epic catalogues and long, fluid flights of imagination; the narrative alternates between an outer, objective, realistic point of view and an inner, subjective, dreamlike perspective. A good example of this variety in perspective occurs when Sonaí Bán MacReachtain dies. He repeatedly hears the song "Cár chodail me aréir?" [Where did I sleep last night?] in which no one recognizes the singer of the song. Having been wounded in his Adam's applie, he sees in a vision his wife ironically crying, "Mo ghrá do sciúch!" (100), which means, "Bless your voice," or literally, "My love, your throat!". He fades between reality and dream —"Luigh sé faoi mheisce na cuimhne" (102) [He lay drunk with memory] — before dying. He hears French —"Parlaí bhú maim seil?" (102) — with the words spelled in Irish, recalling the comic games Myles na Gopaleen used to play on English in Irish within the pages of the Irish Times.[27] Meanwhile, his burly, earthy comrades stand over him lamenting their increasingly desperate plight in the face of oncoming British forces, and the Realpolitik of the novel continues: "Réab clogarnach nua isteach ar an tormán [A new clatter burst into the tumult]" (104). Objectivity supplanting subjectivity, the nightmarish battle resumes.

L'Attaque was the best Irish historical novel of the early 1960s — indeed, one of the most interesting of all Irish historical novels — because of its remarkable blend of realism and experimentalism, pessimism and heroism, all in Irish, the language of the peasantry. Many Irish historical novelists celebrated the peasantry, the "common people"; only Ó Tuairisc

wrote successfully about their history in their own historical language. He shows them with all their pessimism and all their contradictory impulses, and in his view they emerge as heroes nonetheless.

Ó Tuairisc's language could not be much more different from Murdoch's proper, Anglo-Irish voice, full of "rather" and "vaguely," or from Macken's cosmopolitan, standard, popular idiom. Yet for all of their divergences, all three authors attempt to assert a panoramic fictional vision in the midst of the violent facts of Irish history. They focus on representative protagonists — Macken's Dominicks and Dualtas, Murdoch's Pat Dumay and Andrew Chase-White, Ó Tuairisc's Máirtín Caomhánach — who grapple with the extreme forces at work in Irish history. Interestingly enough, these protagonists share a somewhat ambivalent attitude about involving themselves in that history: Macken's heroes retreat at the end, Murdoch's Pat and Andrew finally see how ridiculous their opposed military postures are, and Ó Tuairisc's Máirtín is very reluctant to go off to war in the first place. None of these are the fanatics that O'Flaherty's nationalist heroes are. Their ambivalence reflects the position of these authors who, at the safe remove of the 1960s, were able to be detached about Irish history and ambivalent about its violence, their protagonists joining the war at one moment and retreating from it the next. It is as if the Irish historical novel came almost full circle: just as O'Flaherty's open, extreme nationalism was in sharp contrast to the cautious, moderate didacticism of the Banims a century earlier, the somewhat ambivalent attitudes of Macken, Murdoch, and Ó Tuairisc, mixing nostalgia and detachment, differ considerably from those of the polemical O'Flaherty. Writing in the midst of the Irish struggle for freedom, the Banims had felt they needed to be cautious in presenting its history, so as not to inflame the English. Returning to the struggle for freedom decades after it seemingly had been settled, Macken, Murdoch, and Ó Tuairisc were moderate about it not because they had to be but because they could afford to be.

9

The 1970s: *Plunkett, Dillon, Flanagan*

IRISH HISTORICAL NOVELS proved to be even more popular in the 1970s than they were in the 1960s. Increasingly so, in fact: the popular success of James Plunkett's *Strumpet City* (1969) and Eilís Dillon's *Across the Bitter Sea* (1973) and *Blood Relations* (1977) was surpassed by that of Thomas Flanagan's *The Year of the French* (1979), which did extremely well in the huge American market as well as in Ireland and Britain. In addition, popular film adaptations are in the works. In 1980 Irish television aired a very successful multi-part adaptation of *Strumpet City* starring Peter O'Toole and Cyril Cusack, and now a similar version of *The Year of the French* has been done. Thus, there is the very real possibility that a second, perhaps even larger audience, many of whom have never read the novels, will see the films.

Irish historical novels of the 1970s were not as divergent in their appeal as those of the 1960s. Anybody and everybody in the English-speaking world might read Plunkett, Dillon,and Flanagan. Among the 1970s novels there are none of the linguistic and societal barriers that separate students of *The Red and the Green* from readers of *L'Attaque*. The 1970s readership was wider; it was Walter Macken's type of readership. Of course, the novelist's sense of audience varies, just as does the quality of the novels. When asked about the Harlequin-romance-styled

covers for the American paperback editions of her novels, Eilís Dillon wrote:

> Every writer dimly envisages his audience but a didactic purpose is the kiss of death. I am aware now that my novels do indeed help to educate the youth of the nation but the audience I had in mind was one that I am much better pleased to have satisfied. These are highly-educated, sophisticated men and women, some of them historians, and if I had not succeeded with them I would have regarded my efforts as having been a failure. The English editions of the two books you mention had jackets chosen by me, with reproductions of paintings by Jack B. Yeats, the poet's brother. They were very far from comic book jackets and these I find unpleasant and disturbing. However, the world has become accustomed to having a vulgar standard of book jacket on paperbacks and not much attention is paid to them. The English paperbacks were not as offensive as the American ones, and they are still in print in large numbers there. In England, where most of my books are published, there is not the same attempt to take in all audiences with every book. There are plenty of literate people, especially in Ireland, and this causes a levelling up of standards instead of the reverse, which I am afraid happens here.[1]

The 1970s writers continue the conventions of the historical novel. They are not directly influenced by Scott, but for the most part they follow the model for the genre outlined by Lukács in Scott, a model most successfully exploited in Plunkett's *Strumpet City* and Flanagan's *The Year of the French*. *Strumpet City* permits an interesting case study of just how persistent Lukács' Scottian model has proven to be. A consideration of it in light of Lukács' critical theory is particularly interesting, for while the nineteenth-century authors of whom Lukács writes were essentially bourgeois writers, James Plunkett (1920–), like Liam O'Flaherty before him, has absorbed a twentieth-century socialist critique which Lukács shares. In applying his Marxist approach to Scott, Balzac, Stendhal, and Tolstoy, Lukács can do little more than try to trace a movement toward socialism in these writers, and "show how the historical novel in its origin, development, rise and decline follows inevitably upon the great social transformations of modern times."[2] Plunkett, however, has already absorbed socialism, and it can be argued that his work, or, say, that of the Russian historical novelist Mikhail Sholokhov, is closer to Lukács's critique than the nineteenth-century novels with which Lukács is concerned. This and

the fact that *Strumpet City* is the best Irish historical novel of recent years earn it generous consideration.

S*trumpet City* grew out of Plunkett's own involvement with the Workers' Union of Ireland, which he had joined as a young clerk in 1938, at the age of eighteen. In April 1946, Plunkett became a branch and staff secretary for the union, working under Jim Larkin until Larkin's death in 1947. The fact that in the novel he ignores the late, less glamorous stage of Larkin's career, during which he knew him, in favor of a focus upon his Great Strike of 1913 (in which William Martin Murphy and his Employers' Federation locked out Larkin's striking workers for months) is parallel to the avoidance of Daniel O'Connell's later career in Irish folklore. Early stories such as "Working Class" and "The Mother," as well as contributions during the 1940s and early 1950s to various socialist papers and humorous magazines such as *Passing Variety*, reflect the young writer's concern.[3]

In January 1955, Plunkett visited the Soviet Union as part of a delegation of Irish writers and artists invited by the Soviet secretary of arts. His breakthrough as a writer came that same year with the publication of his volume of short stories *The Trusting and the Maimed* and his radio play *Big Jim*, which celebrated Larkin's achievement. It was also the peak time of anti-Communism in Ireland, for the waves of McCarthyism had rippled across the sea from the United States. It is not surprising that a *Catholic Standard* columnist attacked Plunkett, along with Anthony Cronin and others, pointing out that he had "returned only recently from Russia" and leaving it to his readers to meditate upon the murky implications of that fact. This columnist struck a resonant chord with his readership, and the call came from the *Catholic Standard* and from other quarters for Plunkett to be forced to resign his position in the Workers' Union. The union, however, refused to bow to pressure. When Plunkett left his post in August 1955, he did so quite voluntarily in response to an offer to take on the job of drama assistant in Radio Éireann.

These events clearly represent a turning point in Plunkett's career. At this time an important direction in his thought and his work became clear to him, and the concrete realities of his situation can be seen to have been crucial in this respect. His entrance into the world of radio and, later, television—he became one of Radio Telefís Éireann's first two producers

in 1960 — provided him with new outlets for his creative abilities. At the same time, the success of *Big Jim* and, at least as importantly, Plunkett's own involvement with the events of his time, caused him to begin to turn more and more to history as a panorama for his drama and his fiction.[4] *Big Jim* was subsequently rewritten, expanded, and adapted for the stage in the shape of *The Risen People*, which was produced successfully at The Abbey Theatre in 1958. Not long after that, Hutchinson, the London publisher, suggested to Plunkett that he write a novel of similar historical interest, and so his work for the next decade was cut out for him.

Although he was born seven years after the 1913 lockout (of which his own father was a victim), Plunkett was saturated with accounts of it from Larkin himself and from his many other union contacts. His own union, the Workers' Union of Ireland, published a documentary account entitled *1913: Jim Larkin and the Dublin Lockout* in 1964 while he was working on *Strumpet City*. The novel itself is permeated by a documentary realism, a thoroughly accurate view of this time when, in "September 1913," Yeats lamented that men could only "fumble in a greasy till / And add the halfpence to the pence / And prayer to shivering prayer." Plunkett's vision of this dark period is strengthened by an attention to detail indicating that he did his homework as a historian very thoroughly.

The texts of *Big Jim, The Risen People*, and *Strumpet City* provide a remarkably clear and extremely interesting record of a literary transformation in the works, from radio to stage to novel.[5] Like Standish O'Grady with Red Hugh O'Donnell, Plunkett continually reworked the story of Jim Larkin and the lockout, withdrawing Larkin himself to the background when he moved from documentary play to historical novel. In *Big Jim*, Larkin had been a realistic character; in *The Risen People*, "more a presence, a chorus, than a flesh and blood character," according to his character description; in *Strumpet City*, more an influence in the background than an active character. In his approach to Larkin, Plunkett realized that "you either write a biography or else you don't write about the person, but you write about their influence."[6] While withdrawing Larkin to the background of *Strumpet City*, Plunkett also wrote, in the midst of his work on the novel, such a "biography," as if to compensate: an essay entitled "Jim Larkin" for the book *Leaders and Workers*, in which he noted that "James Joyce spoke of Dublin as the centre of paralysis. It was a total paralysis, blinding conscience and soul. It remained to Jim Larkin to see the slum dweller as a human being — degraded, yet capable of nobility, perceptive, capable of living with dignity, capable, even, of music and literature — Jim Larkin's great task was to create a new social conscience."[7] In *Strumpet City*, Plunkett found that he was writing not about Larkin

but about the dignity and the revolutionary potential of the Dublin working class. He never read Lukács, but he would agree with Lukács' central
thesis about the relationship of the leader and the common people, and
about revolution as a transforming force:

> The important thing for these great writers [was] to lay bare those vast,
> heroic, human potentialities which are always latently present in the people
> and which, on each big occasion, with every deep disturbance of the
> social or even the more personal life, emerge "suddenly," with colossal
> force, to the surface. . . . They wished to show that the possibilities for
> this human upsurge and heroism are widespread among the popular
> masses, that endless numbers of people live out their lives quietly, with-
> out this upsurge, because no opportunity has come their way to evoke
> such an exertion of powers. Revolutions are thus the great periods of
> mankind because in and through them such rapid upward movements
> in human capacities become widespread.[8]

Interestingly, Plunkett got his sense about the relationship of the
great leader to the big revolution neither from Scott nor from Lukács but,
like Liam O'Flaherty, from James Connolly. As an epigraph to *Big Jim*,
Plunkett attached a quotation from Connolly about 1913 that echoes
Lukács' idea about revolutions:

> There are times in history when we realise that it is easier to convert
> a multitude than it ordinarily is to convert an individual: when indeed
> ideas seem to seize upon the masses as contra-distinguished by ordinary
> times when individuals slowly seize ideas. The propagandist toils on for
> decades in seeming failure and ignominy, when suddenly some great event
> takes place in accord with the principles he has been advocating, and
> immediately he finds that the seed he has been sowing is springing up
> in plants that are covering the earth. To the idea of working class unity,
> to the seed of industrial solidarity, Dublin (in 1913) was a great event
> that ennobled it to seize the minds of the masses, the germinating force
> that gave power to the seed to fructify and cover these islands.[9]

Plunkett's Marxist view of the strike, informed by Connolly and Larkin,
was quite remote from the politics of Walter Scott and much closer to
the stance of Liam O'Flaherty.

When asked about literary influence, Plunkett noted, "I was never
a Scott fan but I must have read Banim at some time in the remote past.
. . . Frank MacManus was one of my teachers in Synge Street School so

I knew his work very well at one stage." *The Risen People* was written largely under the inspiration of Sean O'Casey. But the strongest Irish literary influence on *Strumpet City* was O'Flaherty's *Famine*, which Plunkett thought "page by page seems a badly written book but its totality is extraordinary." Frank O'Connor and Seán Ó Faoláin were his closest mentors, but the socialist inspiration for an Irish historical novel comes from *Famine*, and *Strumpet City* shares a number of significant features with O'Flaherty's novel.[10]

Like O'Flaherty exploring the broad range of rural Irish society during the Famine, Plunkett made a conscious attempt in *Strumpet City* to present a broad cross-section of Dublin society of the time, from the working class to the upper classes. He has commented that the novel

> is a picture of Dublin in the seven years, 1907 to 1914. Against the backcloth of social agitation, it is about the attitudes of various strata of society — from Dublin Castle and people of property down to the destitute poor and the outcasts. Joyce wrote about the moderately middle class, and O'Casey about the slums of the period. I was concerned with finding a form in which all the elements could fit.[11]

Like Eoghan Ó Tuairisc in *L'Attaque*, Plunkett was primarily interested not in the English-Irish polarity, but in the contradictions within Irish society. In the novel we meet an impressive cast of working-class characters: Fitz, the striking foreman with leadership abilities; his wife, Mary, concerned for home and family; Pat, Fitz's mate, an amateur socialist philosopher reminiscent of O'Casey's Young Covey; Hennessy, a scrounging, displaced gentleman, plagued by poverty and by his wife; Mulhall, one of the Larkinite faithful, a hard man with his fists; Keever, who becomes a stool pigeon for the employers; and Rashers Tierney, folk hero and the poorest of the poor. Rashers is much like O'Flaherty's Thomsy Hynes — the tragicomic proletarian who is ennobled in death.

Strumpet City very effectively contrasts the extremes of society, the working class and the upper class, but its treatment of the middle class is sparse. This was natural in writing about so polarized a period. The best developed characters in the book are either from the top of society — Yearling and Father O'Connor — or from its dregs — Rashers and Pat. Father Giffley is one exception to this rule; an alcoholic priest, he is a world unto himself. Sympathetic to the working class, he is unable to overcome his self-pity and his alcoholism. The upper-class Yearling's sympathy for the working class, however, is fulfilled when he aids Larkin's movement; the genteel Mrs. Bradshaw helps the Fitzpatricks behind her own capitalistic husband's back; and even the conservative Father O'Connor finally feels

joined to the working class when performing Rashers's last rites. The working-class cause is the yardstick by which Plunkett measures his characters; his partisanship is unconcealed. The "good" upper-class characters are the ones who side with the working class, such as Yearling. Between the extremes of upper class and working class, there is no middle class to speak of in the novel, not only because of the polarization of the period but because of Plunkett's own political stance. This omission exemplifies the distance of the partisan Irish historical novel from Scott's novels. Plunkett avoids middle-class figures, whereas they are always Scott's protagonists, dramatizing Scott's bourgeois solution to politico-economic problems, showing the reader his glorious "middle way." But for Plunkett and O'Flaherty, there can be no "middle" way; the only way for them is the socialist way. Nor, given the realities of history, can Plunkett and O'Flaherty continue Scott's happy endings: *Strumpet City* and *Famine* end in humane despair rather than Scott's bourgeois forward progress.

In early stories such as "Janey Mary" and "The Plain People," Plunkett had already demonstrated his ability to write convincingly about the working class, but *Strumpet City* shows that he could accurately represent the thinking of the upper classes as well, even though he did not share it himself. This accuracy about the upper classes is explained partly by his reliance upon Arnold Wright's book *Disturbed Dublin: The Story of the Great Strike of 1913*, which was published in 1914, having been commissioned by William Martin Murphy's Dublin Chamber of Commerce as the employers' defense of the stance they had taken. It is a book, as Plunkett has noted, in which "the social thinking of the period is typified." Plunkett has noted that Wright's book was the single most useful historical document he came across while researching *Strumpet City*. Wright argued that the worker's low standard of living and energy level had tended to reduce their value in the labor market, and therefore we should be "chary of playing the role of critic to employers who have to utilise this damaged material."[12]

Plunkett has made clear his response to Wright:

> In other words, hunger reduces stamina, so you scale down the wages. An employee was not a human being, he was an instrument. If he was sick or physically debilitated, he was a damaged instrument. As to the man who failed to find any employment whatever, it was God's, not society's business to provide. God, despite concrete evidence to the contrary, was still popularly believed to feed even the sparrows.[13]

Wright's book reads throughout as if it had been written by Father O'Connor of *Strumpet City*. The great attention paid to Father O'Connor and

Yearling would almost seem to suggest that Plunkett's new fascination with the Dublin upper class had become foremost in his mind. On the other hand, upper-class characters — Father O'Connor, Yearling, and the Bradshaws — are few, while working-class characters — such as Rashers, Hennessy, Fitz, Mary, the Mulhalls, Pat, Lily, and Keever — are comparatively numerous.

Father O'Connor's characterization is the most complex of the novel; indeed, Plunkett makes his priests come alive like no other Irish historical novelist has done. Father O'Connor comes in contact, at one point or another, with virtually every other figure in the book, and he certainly comes off as the novel's most confused character. His chief tension is between his pride and attachment to upper-class comforts, on the one hand, and his desire to rid himself of pride and to serve others unselfishly, on the other hand. He moves voluntarily from his comfortable parish to Father Giffley's working-class parish, but feels contempt for the poor, rather than unselfishness and love. He must survive not only his own confusion but also the contempt of his parish priest.

Things reach a boiling point when he discovers weak Rashers Tierney, whom he had hired as church boilerman, asleep in the basement of the church.

> "Tierney," he called.
> He was tempted to kick at the prostrate horror. Was the whole of Ireland possessed by Drink; had it become an unwashed wretch on a slag-heap, grasping an empty bottle by the neck? What right had any creature to spurn God's gifts of mind and health in this way, put out God's sun — quench his stars and obliterate the lovely face of His Creation? Father O'Connor felt fury blazing in the arteries of neck and temple.[14]

When accused of stealing whiskey, Rashers gives the priest his curse and receives his walking papers in return. At this point and at many others, Father O'Connor is very distant indeed from the poor he had intended to serve. Ironically enough, he feels close to the poor only when he goes to minister to the decaying corpse of Rashers, a victim of the pneumonia and starvation that had afflicted him when the priest had found him asleep in the church basement.

> He looked down at the ravaged body without fear and without revulsion. Age and the rot of death were brothers, for rich and poor alike. Neither intellect nor ignorance could triumph over them. What was spread on the straw before him was no more than the common mystery, the everyday fate, the cruel heart of the world. (521)

Plunkett finds a completely different character in Yearling, who holds a post on a large company's board of directors, along with some unusual ideas. Yearling embraces the advantages of his own wealth, yet he finds himself supporting Larkin and his movement. He functions much like Dr. John Hynes in *Famine:* he is the pivotal figure, the character who moves from Ascendancy conservatism to an advocacy of "the people." He is "a combination of generosity and culture" (310). In the course of his peculiar friendship with Father O'Connor, Yearling is revealed as a man of singular lucidity and good humor. He casts aside the prejudices of his own class, quietly choosing to help Larkin's movement, and is therefore rejected by some of his rich associates. He may seem a very unusual character, but he would not have been by any means unique in 1913. When Plunkett has Yearling meet an artist working in Liberty Hall and subsequently help with Larkin's scheme to send Dublin working-class children on holiday to the homes of British union members, Plunkett is drawing straight from history, for intellectuals and artists — people such as Francis Sheehy-Skeffington, Countess Markiewicz, George Russell, and George Bernard Shaw — did indeed play supporting roles in Larkin's movement. In the case of the holiday scheme, of course, Larkin had to contend with massive opposition led by priests, like Father O'Connor, who were convinced that the plan was a threat to the Catholic faith and morals of the children. Larkin's (and Father Giffley's) response was that "it's a poor faith that can't stand up to a fortnight's holidays."

Plunkett also draws straight from history with his account of the collapse of a row of tenement houses that had been left unrepaired by their landlord. Holding this incident in mind, Plunkett wanted to come to grips in fiction with the attitude of the landlord in question, whom he calls Mr. Bradshaw. A contrast is drawn between Mr. Bradshaw, who knows the right people in the right places and wants nothing to disturb his comfortable world, and his wife, who is troubled by a quiet, deep sense of guilt, which she soothes by helping Fitz and Mary behind her husband's back.

Many aspects of the working-class world presented in *Strumpet City* are drawn directly from Plunkett's own experience, whether it be firsthand or secondhand. Plunkett has told me that Rashers Tierney is based on a fellow he knew about called "Johnny Forty Coats," and that Mulhall is based on Barney Conway, who was a hard-fisted, highly respected right-hand man to Larkin. Mulhall loses his feet in an industrial accident and becomes a powerful symbol for Fitz: "He peeped behind the screens at the great body that would march in no more processions and battle no more through cordons of police. He would never let down the

trust of that ageing and wounded man" (336). Plunkett told me that Fitz is a fictional representation of Larkin as a young man. He is the fictional character who reflects the major historical person, following the convention introduced by Scott. Like Fitz, Larkin first distinguished himself as a trade unionist by joining a strike even though he was a foreman, which put him in an unusually vulnerable position. Fitz mirrors Larkin's leadership qualities and his unflagging dedication to the cause. Fitz and the other working-class characters in the novel, however, are much more than mere parts of a cause. Plunkett was trying not only to recapture the events of the lockout, but also to do justice to a class of people he knew and liked.

> They were very rounded people. . . . They had ideals; they knew there was a better world, to be got by sheer slog in most cases. They debated problems, and they read because they had to do this. They needed the drive, the faith that they could change things. They were relaxed about it, but they had that belief that they could change things if they concentrated hard enough. That meant that many of them took an interest in the political world and then in the artistic world.[15]

I mentioned earlier that in *Strumpet City* Larkin is more a symbol than a flesh-and-blood character. His name does not appear at all until the thirty-eighth page of the novel, and it is even later that we are given a first glimpse of the man, when Fitz meets him briefly and realizes who he is only after he is gone. We are not given our first physical description of Larkin until page 479, when Father Giffley makes his pathetic gesture of help, and even then it is only a fleeting glance: "He saw a man of about thirty-five years of age, big physically, with a face which had a strong jaw and deep circles of tiredness under the eyes. A lock of brown hair fell across the forehead and had a streak of grey running through it." Larkin appears here as a face in a painting, a figure in the backdrop to the action of the book, like Napoleon in *War and Peace*. Plunkett's approach is close to the one Lukács found in Walter Scott: "Scott does not stylize these [historical] figures, nor place them upon a Romantic pedestal; he portrays them as human beings with virtues and weaknesses, good and bad qualities. And yet they never create a petty impression. With all their weaknesses they appear historically imposing."[16] This rings true to Larkin's appearances through the eyes of Father Giffley and to all of his reverberations in the novel.

Lukacs' argument about how the historical novelist interprets the past in light of the present is also echoed by Plunkett. In a speech he pointed out that the story of the 1913 lockout carried implications for his own generation:

That confrontation had effects on Irish society which were to last into our own times. . . . On the one hand it drew liberal and intellectual sympathy to the side of the underprivileged. The revelations of various Commissions of Inquiry concerning wages, housing and public health shocked polite society and prepared the ground for the growth of a new social conscience. It brough Pearse and Connolly into close contact with each other, and in doing so it broadened the concept of what was meant by national freedom. It furnished working-class imagination with its high point of martyrdom. As against all that, its socialist colouring, minimal though it was in reality, so frightened Irish conservatism in State and Church that for more than long enough social change of any kind was regarded with deep suspicion and doggedly resisted.

The implications of 1913 clearly helped motivate Plunkett to write *Strumpet City*. After all, James Connolly had declared that "when that story is written by a Man or a Woman with honesty in their hearts and with a sympathetic insight into the travails of the poor, it will be a record of which Ireland may be proud."[17]

Plunkett had strong feelings about the lockout:

At the turn of the present century the capitalist system appears to have been so confident regarding the rights of private property and so reassured by the power that control over the means of livelihood invested in it, that it felt itself free to operate not only without limitation or restraint, but independently of the common good and the needs of society. Ownership was sovereign. When its assumptions were challenged here in Ireland in 1913 by those whose existence had become unbearable as a result of them, it angrily rejected any attempt of the government to meddle in its affairs and it seemed genuinely shocked when it was urged to yield a little rather than starve a city into subjection.

Plunkett's sympathies are obviously with the cause of labor. Noting also the fact that one chapter about the union in *Strumpet City* begins with the sentence, "In December defeat became a certainty" (486), it would be easy to argue that Plunkett has given the world a biased account of his story. Yet no academic historian would defend the actions of the Employers' Federation in 1913, a year in which the results of great hatred and little room reached epic proportions. Even the reactionary Arnold Wright admitted, "It is impossible to withhold sympathy from classes so depressed as these slum dwellers of Dublin."[18]

But it is important not to allow the history in *Strumpet City* to

overshadow the fiction, for it is a novel, not a secondary historical source. If much of its power derives from straight, effective narrative and dialogue, it is also true that it achieves some fine lyrical moments. In considering this fiction as a whole, its individual parts must not be forgotten. The novel is a tapestry as well as a panorama, a collection of stories, in a sense, as well as one big story. The episodic structure of the novel, in fact, is drawn from the method at work in Plunkett's best short stories. *Strumpet City* concerns itself far more than a short story would, of course, with narrative detail, but parts of the book read like short stories. Chapter 3, Book 1, for example, ends with a short-story downbeat: "The fog rolled over all with ever-shifting movements, so that the city lay submerged and paralysed and the foghorns had it all to themselves. They sang all night to the great and the little, telling them life was vanity and Death the only certainty" (56).

Throughout the novel, Plunkett uses time very effectively when he juxtaposes upper-class and working-class experiences. For example, the novel opens with an expansive description of King Edward's arrival in Dublin Harbor on his yacht in 1907, and then Plunkett begins a second episode by informing us that "Rashers Tierney rose that morning about the same time as King Edward. First the dog barked and then a hand reached down and shook his shoulder. It was very dark in the basement. The form above him could have been Death, or a ghost, or the hangover figure from a nightmare" (17). Rashers may well be the best-drawn character in the book. He is a proud tramp, a Larkinite bard, a dispossessed tin whistler. Rashers bows to no man.

The contrasts outlined in *Strumpet City* move gradually toward an artistic unity, as individual stories blend and characters collide. Godeleine Carpentier writes aptly that "the contrapuntal structure of the novel in which all episodes are skillfully dovetailed, the network of symmetries and contrasts efficiently put forward the fact that, in the end, Larkinism has become part of the personal tragedy of each character."[19] These places where the individual stories come together, where the various episodes are "dovetailed," exemplify some of the techniques Plunkett had learned writing short stories. The ending to the first chapter of the book, for example, in working toward its chordal effect, utilizes the same sort of collage that ends a story such as "The Trusting and the Maimed" (whose narrative alternates between a man dying in a Wicklow field and a homing pigeon futilely flying into Dublin without his rescue note, having dropped it). In the novel, Plunkett juxtaposes Yearling, Mr. Bradshaw, Mary, and Rashers, thus moving from the upper class to the working class.

"We musn't detain you," Mr. Yearling said.

They took their leave and went out through the gate. Mr. Bradshaw put the heavy chain on the hall door and began his nightly task of winding each of the clocks.

The rockets made a playground of the sky for an hour on end, while Mary watched from her bedroom window, thinking of Fitz, speaking silent messages to him, living again the moments of their day together. As they burst and drew successive cheers from the watching crowds, Death kept its ordained appointment with the little boy in his strange hospital bed. The night sergeant suffered the news quietly. He had been expecting it since early evening. Rashers, exhausted by the day, sat on his straw bed in the dark and told the dog about him.

"He was kind, Rusty," he said. "Imagine that. I met a kind sergeant today, the first kind policeman in history."

The dog raised itself in response to Rashers' voice, placed its paws on Rashers' knees and, sniffing delicately, began to lick the dried blood on the side of his face. (45)

The final collage of *Strumpet City* ends with Father Giffley, the alcoholic priest. Rashers Tierney is dead, Fitz and Yearling are leaving Ireland — Fitz, because the army is the only job he can find; Yearling, because "nothing would ever happen in Ireland again" — and the other characters in the novel are left paralyzed in Dublin. Father Giffley, confined to a madhouse, is also paralyzed, yet it is he who leaves us with some final thoughts and a last, lyrical message:

Should the Devil ever become greatest then he would become God in turn and the order of creation would be changed in an instant. Not changed simply as from that moment, but right back to wherever and however it had had its beginnings. But in God and Divine Order there is no Becoming, no passive Potentiality. All Is. No Was or Shall Be. The Devil hadn't a hope. Poor devil. Amen.

He decided to commit something to the sea, a thing he had been fond of doing as a child. He found a pencil and tore a page from his pocket diary and scrawled:

"Time takes all away. This was written by a madman on the shores of a mad island."

He put the note in the bottle, pushed in the cork, and threw the bottle as far as he could into the sea. Not very far. He could see it bobbing up and down. He had to squint to do so. His eyes were not very good. (524)

Father Giffley emerges as a peculiar hero, or anti-hero. Throughout the novel he has seen things very clearly—so clearly, in fact, that he has been rendered useless by what he has seen. He is an educated priest of working-class origins who wants to help his people in real terms, but his own cynicism and an encrusted, arch-conservative church hierarchy have maimed him from the start. He tries to overcome the bitterness that mounts in him one night as he walks drunkenly through the streets of his parish, and finally he presents himself to Larkin. Larkin, a teetotaller with a nose for drink, thanks him for his offer of help, but tells him that "it wouldn't be wise for either of us" (480), and Father Giffley sees his own ridiculousness. He and Yearling had been the only two characters in the book with a potential for overcoming their own class limitations. At the end of the novel, however, both number among the bitter and the maimed.

The conclusion of *Strumpet City* may present a bleak, bitter visage, but it is nonetheless informed with a certain nobility: "There was no defeat in the faces he passed" (494). When Rashers declares to his dog that "God never shut one door to us but he closed another" (rather than "opened another" as the popular saying has it), he is staking out his own independence and pride as much as expressing his bitterness: "When I can no longer fend for myself, then God, let me die" (435). Even though he dies alone in his room from starvation and the assorted maladies associated with poverty, Rashers never loses his dignity; in fact, informed by Plunkett's lucid humanity, his stature is enlarged in death. *Strumpet City* is, along with *Famine*, the greatest of Irish historical novels not only because it portrays history panoramically and accurately, but because characters like Rashers live on in the imagination, independent of the facts of history. The novel comes alive as literature, thanks to the vibrancy of Rashers, Yearling, and Father O'Connor, at the same time that it is remarkably faithful to history in both its detail and depth. With these simultaneous strengths, *Strumpet City* is what a historical novel ought to be.

T̄HE GREAT POPULAR SUCCESS of *Strumpet City* marked the beginning of a new wave of Irish historical novels in the seventies. Thomas Kilroy's *The Big Chapel* (1971), like Francis MacManus' *The Greatest of These* (1943), dealt with the ecclesiastic controversies in the town of Callan, County Kilkenny, during the 1870s—a minor, internal conflict rather than a major, national one. Eilís Dillon's *Across the Bitter Sea* (1973) and *Blood*

Relations (1977) explored nationalist history: the Fenians, the Easter Rising, the Anglo-Irish War. The blurb from *The Daily Mirror* on the paperback cover of *Across the Bitter Sea* predicted "a bestseller, a runaway success like another Irish novel, 'Strumpet City', a few years ago."[20]

Like Seán Ó Faoláin, Francis MacManus, and Walter Macken before her, Dillon adopted the strategy of historical novel through family chronicle, the history of the Irish people as viewed through the history of an Irish family. Seán Ó Faoláin, as we have seen, initiated the family-chronicle approach to the Irish historical novel, and several features in Dillon's novels suggest Ó Faoláin's influence. *Across the Bitter Sea* covers the same period (1851–1916) as *A Nest of Simple Folk*, both novels include family trees, and in both the protagonist is a Fenian who survives to witness the Easter Rising. In *Blood Relations* the informer Henry Gould, guilty and unpunished, is much like Ó Faoláin's John Hussey, and Dillon's Aunt Jack brings her secret, illegitimate daughter home to live with her much as Leo and Julie Donnel's "nephew" Johnno is adopted in *A Nest of Simple Folk*. If *Strumpet City*'s precursor is *Famine*, *A Nest of Simple Folk* is the closest antecedent to *Across the Bitter Sea* and *Blood Relations*.

Dillon has noted, "James Stephens, Yeats, Joyce of course, Sean O'Faoláin and Frank O'Connor, Synge, Daniel Corkery—these all affected me strongly," adding:

> I have never read Banim nor even Standish O'Grady. I found Liam O'Flaherty somewhat too crude in English though I admire his Irish short stories very much. I found Francis MacManus a little too simple in adult life though I liked his book about Donnacha Rua when I read it at the age of sixteen or so. . . . Scott was never a great influence on my work. I had written a number of novels of contemporary Irish life before using an historical background and by the time I began on this my influences were international, French, German, above all Russian. Stendhal and Balzac delighted me by the way they handled their background, keeping the history out of sight except insofar as it affected their characters. Tolstoy gave me courage to lengthen scenes and occurrences. (January 21, 1981)

Dillon shows here that she was inspired by Ó Faoláin's generation of Irish writers and, in turn, by their Russian and European models.

Dillon was born on March 7, 1920, the same year as Plunkett, in Galway, Walter Macken's hometown. "James Plunkett and Walter Macken are contemporaries of mine," she explains, "so it looks as if we were all formed by the same outside influences within Ireland. I find myself more at ease with Plunkett and Iris Murdoch than with Macken . . . though

he was a close personal friend of mine — I refer only to his work" (January 21, 1981). Yet her historical novels — covering many years and featuring romantic heroes who are realistic, yet larger than life — are more like Macken's than they are like *Strumpet City.*

Though Dillon, like Murdoch, devotes more attention in her novels to sex than do their Irish male colleagues, her heroines are not aggressive about sex like Murdoch's Aunt Millie, but passive.

> He gripped her still closer, his hands moving down her sides, all over her body, his mouth feeding on her mouth, until slowly, slowly he felt her go limp and knew that he had conquered her, and tearing her nightdress down about her breast and waist, he laid her on the white-covered bed. After that she resisted no longer and spoke only once. (*ABS*, 96)

Dillon's plot is the love triangle, the woman who loves two men. In *Across the Bitter Sea* Alice MacDonagh marries Samuel Flaherty but her first love is Morgan Connolly, whom she marries after Samuel's death. Similarly, her mother, Mary, had lived with George Flaherty (Samuel's father) but married Thomas MacDonagh. In *Blood Relations,* the sequel, Molly Gould loves Sam Flaherty (grandson of the elder Samuel), but when he runs off to fight in the Easter Rising she has sex, in a weaker moment, with Peter Morrow and ends up marrying Nicholas de Lacy, bearing Peter's son thought by everyone to be Sam's. And Sam, Peter, and Nicholas are friends, as are Morgan and Samuel in *Across the Bitter Sea.*

Dillon's plot is not really as risqué as this brief summary might make it sound. While seeking to entertain her readers with love stories, Dillon attempts at the same time to educate them about Irish history from a point of view that is clearly "Irish Nationalist" (as the listing for "Politics" under her entry in *Contemporary Authors* has it). Like Walter Macken's novels, Dillon's are easily accessible to a wide variety of readers, including some of "the youth of the nation." Just as footnotes were used by Banim, appendices by O'Grady, historical forewords by Macken, and a list of "principal characters" by Flanagan, Dillon includes her own educational, expository addition: a glossary of terms (such as gombeen man and sleeveen). The strength of an O'Flaherty or a Plunkett, on the other hand, lies partly in what they *don't* do: they don't explain; they tend to show rather than tell Irish history.

Dillon has been very scrupulous about her historical facts. Daughter of a university professor and wife of two others — she married Vivian Mercier after Cormac Ó Cúilleanáin's death — Dillon did her historical homework carefully. When asked about the history in her novels, she commented:

I checked and cross-checked every incident throughout the writing of both books and would not have considered any other course. For 'Across the Bitter Sea' I went back first to 1798, where I found an explanation of old George Flaherty's mentality. My reading then included Jonah Barrington and dozens of more reliable biographers and social historians. For the actual period of the book I read biographies of John O'Leary, George Moore, five of Parnell, one of Fintan Lalor, one of James Stephens, O'Donovan Rossa's memoirs and literally hundreds more, including as much contemporary fiction and belles letters as I had time for, so as to get the feel of the times. (May 11, 1981)

She scorns her American contemporaries Leon Uris and Thomas Flanagan because they "were so inaccurate in their facts that they have scarcely justified their incursion into the history of another country than their own. Taking liberties with history in fiction seems to me somewhat unprincipled but you will be told that Scott did it. One wonders whether that justifies it" (January 21, 1981). She was particularly angry about the inaccuracies in Uris' bestseller, *Trinity* (1976).

In *Trinity* a kind of vulgar flamboyance seems to have been used to heighten tension and to introduce an hysterical note. . . . For instance, *Trinity* begins with a wake. Uris must have heard that there was a lot of drinking at wakes in Ireland, so he makes this one into a sex orgy as well, with young people creeping up to the loft in pairs throughout the night of the wake. He doesn't seem to have heard of wake games, though this is how those people would have spent the long hours of the night. He says the poteen was made and sold by widows traditionally; not so. Making poteen requires the attention of someone who can remain out in a remote place for a couple of days at a stretch, and the product was and is then sold by its manufacturer. Uris has the family saying the rosary and he makes it last more than half an hour. It takes ten minutes at most. He must have heard of the long-drawn-out prayers known as "the trimmings of the rosary," additions that had nothing to do with it at all and that varied from one family to another. He has everyone dropping to their knees at the sound of the Angelus bell, while on their way home from work, at the cross-roads near the church, and again on another occasion actually in the fields. In fact the Angelus was and is said in a standing position if people happen to be at work. He describes how the recitation of the rosary caused the boy to vomit, a reaction I have never heard of before. When he comes to the rich he is equally at sea. Victorian employers, even nasty ones, would never have used filthy language, and the word "horseshit" which is frequently used only reached the shores of Ireland a few years ago. . . . It would be tedious to list all the massive errors in this book, especially in his loath-

ing and lack of knowledge of the Catholic church and its doings. (May 11, 1981)

Dillon's statement about the conventional withdrawal of the "big names" of history to the background of her novels is interesting and unusually direct: "The main characters are invented, Morgan Connolly and Alice and Samuel Flaherty, but they constantly meet real historical characters in the course of the narrative. This was done on the principle . . . that it is difficult if not impossible to convey a real sense of a person who has actually lived — that fiction is more credible than truth, in fact" (May 11, 1981).

The problem with the history in Dillon's novels is not its accuracy but rather its uneven integration with the private plot. Chapters of love story alternate with chapters of public history. This approach and the span of *Across the Bitter Sea* across sixty-five years mean that much of the novel reads like a history survey: we get from Parnell to Larkin, for example, in twenty pages. "A novel with unity is always more satisfying," Dillon admits, "and the shorter span of 'Blood Relations' was therefore easier from the artistic point of view. Besides, 'Across the Bitter Sea' had taken in so much that it seemed more sensible to confine the second book to a single series of incidents" (May 11, 1981). Even though *Blood Relations* is limited to 1916–24, in it Dillon skips the Civil War altogether: "Three years after the terrible day of Peter's death, in the spring of 1924, Molly and Nicholas were still living at Woodbrook. The Civil War was over and the country had settled down to an uneasy peace" (*BR*, 431).

Dillon is the only Irish historical novelist considered in this study who presents Irish history predominantly from the perspective of a female protagonist. Iris Murdoch's Aunt Millie is by no means the protagonist of *The Red and the Green;* most of her novel's main characters are male, and Frances's epilogue is extraneous to the main action. But Alice Mac-Donagh dominates *Across the Bitter Sea,* and Molly Gould dominates *Blood Relations.* They are traditional, passive heroines, but then it might be argued that their passivity and powerlessness are true to the average Irish woman of the time. Complicated with gender is caste: Alice MacDonagh, for example, marries the kindhearted landlord Samuel Flaherty partly because he can make her comfortable. Alice and Molly have their romantic encounters with rebel lovers, and much of Dillon's narrative is devoted to their meditations while waiting for their rebels to come home to them. Molly Gould, for example:

> She was expected to live through those days as if nothing special were happening, as if it were possible to bear them like a lady, when she was

burning with a pain that must surely kill her. It didn't kill her, because that sort of pain rarely does. Instead she waited, with the family, for news from Dublin, as if she had no more to lose than anyone else, as if her whole life were not in the balance. (*BR*, 25)

The heroes of other Irish historical novels travel, and the reader travels with them. Dillon's heroines stay at home, for the most part, and her reader stays there with them. Her male characters are simple, flat creations. The noble Fenian Morgan Connolly, for example, leaves as a peasant and returns to Alice as a rich man, like Heathcliff, with no explanation of how he made his fortune. But Dillon's women are full of confusion and complexity; the strong characterizations of Alice MacDonagh in *Across the Bitter Sea* and Molly Gould in *Blood Relations* outweigh these novels' shortcomings. Since Irish history was populated not only by men, but by women, Dillon's novels provide in their narrative perspective a valuable counterpoint to the rest of Irish historical fiction.

THE MOST EXTRAORDINARY DEVELOPMENT during the late 1970s that was relevant to the Irish historical novel came not from Ireland at all, but from America: the immense popular success of Leon Uris' *Trinity* (1976) and Thomas Flanagan's *The Year of the French* (1979). The Irish historical novel had always been popular and Americans had been trying their hand at it since the late nineteenth century, but Uris' and Flanagan's books reached a mass readership unprecedented in its size, especially in the United States, where *Trinity* hovered at the top of the bestseller lists for two years. Like most earlier Americans who wrote historical novels about Ireland, Flanagan is an Irish-American who closely identifies himself with "the old country," and he is also a scholar who knows its literature, including its historical novels, very well. In contrast, Uris is a non-Irish popular novelist who had already established himself as an author of bestsellers about other countries. *Trinity* does not merit any extended analysis: as an attempt at an Irish historical novel, it fails critically as much as it succeeded popularly. But since so many American readers unfortunately base their sense of what Ireland, Irish literature, and the Irish historical novel are all about upon their reading of *Trinity*, it must be mentioned and assessed in passing here.

    Trinity distorts the most important conventions of the Irish historical novel. It sets up opposites — Protestants against Catholics in Northern Ireland between the late nineteenth century and the Easter Rising — but

they are presented in extremely simplistic ways. Uris' hero, Conor Larkin, is a Catholic superman who is opposed by devilish Protestant oppressors. One has to return to the heroes of nineteenth-century Irish historical novels — to Torlogh O'Brien, Redmond O'Hanlon, and Red Hugh O'Donnell — in order to find a more overblown romantic hero. When Protestant employers encourage violence, that is presented as demonic, but when Catholic Republicans execute a "heinous" informer, that seems well deserved. *Trinity* encourages a simplistic, pro-Catholic, anti-Protestant view of the Irish crisis. As Wayne Hall asked: "Sectarian labels aside, precisely where do Leon Uris' rhetorical and political solutions differ from those of Ian Paisley?"[21]

Trinity is also very inaccurate in its use of language. Uris is consistent in his misunderstanding, for example, of the use of "after" in the Anglo-Irish present-perfect verbal construction, according to which "What are you after finding out?" ought to translate as "What have you just found out?", not "What would you like to find out?" as it does for Uris.[22] He has the great Parnell inviting an adolescent Conor Larkin to "drop by" (a distinctively American phrase) his hotel in order to borrow his copy of Thomas Paine's *The Rights of Man*, thus implausibly pulling Parnell out of the background of the fictional world of the novel, where he ought to remain, according to the conventions of the historical novel. At the same time he unaccountably changes Patrick Pearse's name to "Garrett O'Hara," even though *he* remains in the background.

In its foggy use of language, its simplistic, romanticized presentation of history, and its confusion about what to do with real historical characters, *Trinity* seems to be not an evolved twentieth-century historical novel at all, but a return to nineteenth-century romance. Certainly it has fulfilled psychological needs for Irish-American readers looking for simple, dramatic explanations of how "the Irish problem" came to be. Its lively, appealing plot, full of fantastic heroes, beautiful heroines, and demonic antagonists, would entertain just about anybody looking for an escape — and so it has. As an attempt at an Irish historical novel, it illustrates almost everything such a novel should *not* be.

Fortunately, Uris' fellow American Thomas Flanagan has written a better historical novel than *Trinity* because he knows Ireland better. Born Thomas James Bonner Flanagan in Greenwich, Connecticut, on November 5, 1923, Flanagan is proud of his Fenian ancestry. *The Year of the*

French is dedicated "In memory, as always, of Ellen Treacy of Fermanagh and Thomas Bonner of the Fenian Brotherhood."[23] After his book *The Irish Novelists, 1800–1850* was published in 1958, Flanagan taught at Columbia University, and in 1973 he became professor and chairman of the English department at the University of California at Berkeley, before moving to his present position as professor at the State University of New York at Stonybrook.[24]

Flanagan's training as an academic shows in *The Year of the French,* whose several first-person narratives are based on contemporary accounts of the 1798 rebellion in Mayo, which Flanagan assiduously researched. Like *Trinity, The Year of the French* has been a great popular success, and it won the National Book Critics' Circle Award.

Flanagan began his career writing about *The Boyne Water,* making mention of its gilt-edged successors. Now they include his own novel. When asked in a public forum if he was perhaps haunted, during the writing of his own novel, by any of the Irish novelists whom he had studied, Flanagan replied: "The fast answer is that I'm American, not an Irishman. On the other hand it's clear that *The Year of the French* is an Irish novel, not an American novel." Privately, he said that he had read, in addition to the writers discussed in *The Irish Novelists,* Sir Jonah Barrington and Francis MacManus.[25]

It is clear that Flanagan immersed himself in and modelled his first-person narratives on contemporary accounts of 1798. The best bibliography of these accounts is contained in Thomas Pakenham's *The Year of Liberty.*[26] They include diaries by United Irish leaders, British officers, clerics, and other "eyewitnesses" such as those presented by Flanagan. His narrator Arthur Vincent Broome was obviously inspired by Bishop Joseph Stock of Killala and his *A Narrative of What Passed at Killala, in the County Mayo, and the Parts Adjacent, During the French Invasion in the Summer of 1798* (1800), a title mimicked by Flanagan: "*An Impartial Narrative of What Passed at Killala in the Summer of 1798.*"

The Year of the French was not the first Irish historical novel about '98 in Mayo to be modelled partly on Bishop Stock: Emily Lawless and Shan F. Bullock had done the same thing in *The Race of Castlebar* (1913).[27] The nature of Flanagan's stylistic mimicry might be suggested through a comparison of the following passages from Bishop Stock, Sir Jonah Barrington, and Flanagan:

> As I know that inaccurate accounts of remarkable events must at length be taken for true, and be adopted by the historian, if he is not supplied with better, I feel myself drawn against my liking by the very imperfect

narratives I have yet seen of what passed at Killala, while foreign and domestic enemies possessed that town in the summer of 1798, to state to you as much as fell under my observation at that critical period. (Stock)

Never was there an era in the history of any country which, in so short a space of time, gave birth to such numerous and varied circumstances as did the memorable year 1798 in Ireland: nor was there ever yet an event so important as the Irish insurrection, but has afforded a veracious — or, at least, a tolerably impartial account. (Barrington)[28]

My present purpose . . . is to offer as fully and as impartially as I can, yet without idle digression, a narrative account of those events which, a few years ago, bestowed upon our remote countryside a transient celebrity. (Flanagan, 17)

Like John Barth responding to Ebenezer Cooke in *The Sot-Weed Factor*, Flanagan obviously modelled himself on, but took liberties with, his sources. The content of his Broome narrative resembles Stock's, but its style is closer to Barrington's.

Flanagan's use of multiple first-person narrators is at once his novel's strength and its weakness. It is an interesting and unusual extension of the convention in the genre of presenting history from several points of view. At the same time this approach is occasionally confusing, as we move from one narrative to another, and ponderous, as an individual narrative drones on. But Flanagan does achieve a panoramic effect similar to Plunkett's contrapuntal attention to multiple characters. He presents a variety of points of view — a clergyman, a United Irishman and his wife, a schoolmaster, and an aide to General Cornwallis — but these narrators, it must be noted, come from the educated and upper-class strata of society. There are no peasants here, neither among the first-person diaries (which an eighteenth-century Irish peasant could not have been expected to write) nor among the major characters in the third-person sections of the novel. The literate, predominantly upper-class points of view presented in *The Year of the French* make for a sharp contrast and valuable complement to *L'Attaque*, in which Eoghan Ó Tuairisc recreated the very same events from the point of view of illiterate, Gaelic-speaking peasants.

Flanagan's hero, Owen MacCarthy, is a peasant by origin, but as a gifted Gaelic poet he feels alienated not only from his English-speaking superiors, but from his Irish-speaking inferiors as well. He refuses to recite one of his poems in a pub because

It was an intricate poem and it depended upon allusions, hints, the small gestures of remembered names. These poor cowherds, matted hair,

breeches streaked with the dung of cattle, would be puzzled and embar-
rassed. As though a velvet-coated gentleman had flung himself into the
room to call for punch. (169–70)

MacCarthy is the most compelling character in the novel and the chief
voice of Flanagan's theme about the inevitability and futility of the Mayo
rising. Unfortunately, an overdependence on the first-person narratives
tends to take the focus away from MacCarthy.

Flanagan's despairing theme, which is voiced by several other characters besides MacCarthy, including the United Irish leader Malcolm El-
liott, takes him in a different direction than Ó Tuairisc, beyond the obvious linguistic and narrative contrasts. Because Flanagan's theme is despair,
futility, and defeat, not epic courage and victory as in Ó Tuairisc, he extends his story well beyond the great victory at Castlebar (which occurs
less than halfway through the novel and receives relatively short shrift)
to the series of devastating defeats that followed it. Both authors are interested in the meeting of the French and the Irish, and both illustrate General Humbert's resourcefulness among an unprepared, untrained Irish
peasantry. But Flanagan goes on to show a scornful French departure from
Mayo and Humbert's cynical chat with the British General Cornwallis in
Dublin and his determination never to return to this "most unhealthy country" (567). L'Attaque ends with the noble declaration, "Tá an Táin déanta."
The Year of the French ends with the Gaelic schoolteacher Sean McKenna's deflating thought, after lamenting MacCarthy's death, that "the linen
which I brought back with me from Killala is badly bleached, and I will
think carefully before I have further dealings with Johnston of Sligo" (638).

The Catholic landlord and historian George Moore, brother of
John Moore (the young man whom Humbert peremptorily appointed "president" of the short-lived "Republic of Connaught"), is an interesting character who occupies a pivotal position in the novel somewhat similar to
that of Dr. Hynes in Famine and Yearling in Strumpet City. He disdains
the rebellion and discourages his brother's participation but loves him and
mourns his death at the end of it. The only thing he hates more than
violence is the arrogance of the Protestant Ascendancy. He acidly rejects
his Protestant neighbor Cooper's request to help put down the rebellion
and takes gleeful note of Cooper's quick defeat by the French at Kilcum-
min, even though he opposes the rebellion.

The real hero of the novel, however, is Owen MacCarthy, namesake of the despairing peasant who is the protagonist of William Carleton's story "Tubber Derg" (about which Flanagan wrote in The Irish
Novelists). Like Francis MacManus' Donnacha MacConmara, Owen is a
Gaelic poet and sometime-schoolteacher, down on his luck, who witnesses

'98. Donnacha shrinks from the rising in Wexford and repents his sins. In contrast, Owen becomes a reluctant rebel in Mayo and never repents his sins—or rather, he sends the priest "out of here with his ears burning" (607) when he does confess, the day before his hanging, his epic indulgence in sex, drink, and rebelliousness. His more pious friend Sean McKenna decides that the tragic Owen's sin is a too great love:

> There is in Owen a great love of our earthly existence and it is perhaps because of it that he is so fine a poet. What are the worst of his sins, the wild ways and even the girl at the gable end, if not that love speaking out? I truly believe that his love is so strong that he cannot understand his sinfulness. God help him and make allowances for him. (609)

Owen loves his world and sees it go up in flames; against the devastation of war, his poetry is impotent.

Even the law-abiding Reverend Broome is driven toward despair by the brutal crushing of the rising in Mayo, wondering, "Does man learn from History?" (616). "Heavy curtains will be drawn, to hold back the limitless silences of the Mayo night. We know parts of a world only, parts of a history, shards, bits of broken pottery" (635).

Flanagan is much more accurate about Irish history and culture than is his countryman Uris, and the high quality of his writing makes *The Year of the French* the best of its kind since *Strumpet City*. The achievement of these two novels as compared to the commercialism of *Trinity*—together with the uneven quality of such recent novels as Peter Everett's *A Death in Ireland* (1980), Neil Jordan's *The Past* (1980), and Morgan Llywelyn's *Lion of Ireland* (1981)—prompts an inevitable and unanswerable question: Where will the Irish historical novel go from here?

Conclusion

O
N EASTER SUNDAY NIGHT in 1976, the sixtieth anniversary of Easter 1916, I sat in a pub (since destroyed by explosives) in a Catholic area of Belfast, observing the spirited festivities centered on the microphone where religion, politics, and history were fused. I heard prayers, ballads, poems, and stories, all celebrating a unified vision of the Irish Catholic cause in Northern Ireland. In a foolish moment, I muttered to the friend who had brought me there that he ought to "get up there and recite Robert Emmet's speech from the dock," the Irish patriot's immortal words uttered before his execution in 1803. Well aware of the significance of that speech in the mythology of Irish nationalism, but possessing neither the ability nor the willingness to recite it (or anything else), my friend grunted in negative reply to my jest and, surrounded by the din of the pub, we returned to more pressing matters. But a few minutes later it was announced, much to my amazement and my friend's understandable chagrin, that he would now oblige the audience with Emmet's speech. An awkward moment passed — during which our continued friendship was in some doubt — before another acquaintance rescued us by walking to the microphone, explaining that my friend was indisposed, and reciting W. B. Yeats's "Easter 1916" with some fervor.

Yeats's poem served just as well in this instance as Emmet's speech; in the popular Irish nationalist mythology, literary and historical texts are

interchangeable. Poem and story as well as ballad and speech – to say nothing of personal and communal experience – continue to inform the Irish nationalist and to teach his children how to think about Irish history and politics. While the history of Ireland has shaped its literature, it is equally clear that Irish literature has reverberated in history, for life has often sought to imitate art in Ireland. Having staged his apocalyptic play *Cathleen ni Hoolihan* in 1902, with Maud Gonne in the lead, Yeats later wondered, in his poem "The Man and the Echo," "Did that play of mine send out / Certain men the English shot?" The answer is that it probably contributed. Listening to our savior recite "Easter 1916" in 1976, I could not help but meditate upon the continuing effects of such texts on contemporary Irish nationalism.

More germane to the Irish historical novel is the testimony of H-Block prisoner Joseph Maguire, cited by Tim Pat Coogan in *On the Blanket*, about how he and his mates relieved the tedium of life in Long Kesh prison: "Then you have stories and songs. Some of the memories are fantastic. One man, Bobby Sands, memorised *Trinity* by Leon Uris. That took eight days to tell. The lads are very good to each other. . . . You are all in there because you want to be there." Having recited *Trinity*, Bobby Sands was later the first of ten prisoners to die in the 1981 Long Kesh hunger strike over prison conditions and political prisoner status. Coogan points out that "it is too easy to die now in Northern Ireland" because of the continued reverence for "the physical force tradition in Irish history."[1] This tradition is celebrated in large part in the Irish historical novel – and certainly in Uris' attempt at one.

In an article entitled "In Troubled Ireland, the Enemy Is History," Thomas Flanagan argued that the Irish "have memories, imagination, a passionate involvement in history, traditions of rebellion, of sympathy for desperate causes, of a human, illogical respect for martyrdom. Perhaps, being Irish, such things are central to their sense of identity. Britain has served them ill, and perhaps herself as well, by conspiring with the IRA to bestow upon them so ambiguous an icon as the body of Bobby Sands."[2] The Irish writer cannot escape the nightmare of history, nor could Bobby Sands escape *Trinity*. Thus has fiction pathetically influenced life: not only is history relived in the historical novel; the historical novel resounds in history.

Trinity illustrates the continuing popularity of the mythos of Irish nationalism, but in its inaccurate, twisted view of history it is a very long way indeed from the moderate Sir Walter Scott or, for that matter, from the partisan but conscientious Irish writers. At the end of *The Boyne Water*, Scott's disciple John Banim implored his audience to seek understanding

and a peace that would heal the deep wounds of the Irish past. In contrast, *Trinity* has aggravated present-day wounds. Like Yeats wondering if his play sent out "Certain men the English shot," writers such as Leon Uris would do well to think about the likes of Bobby Sands. Twentieth-century Irish historical novelists have been equally partisan but fortunately much more accurate than Uris in their depictions of modern Irish history. The best of them do not reduce that history to the simple, biased, distorted categories that Uris presents. Their novels seek to explore the conflicts embedded in Irish history in ways that encourage thought.

The violence of Irish history should not be continued or relived, but rejected. I believe that the reader of the Irish historical novel ought to become an advocate of peace. This alternative assumes, of course, an intelligent reader who can see through the romantic distortions of history and glorifications of violence that dominate Uris' novel and most nineteenth-century Irish historical novels, and who can understand the bitter conflicts more conscientiously explored by John Banim in *The Boyne Water*, William Buckley in *Croppies Lie Down*, Seán Ó Faoláin in *A Nest of Simple Folk*, Liam O'Flaherty in *Famine*, Francis MacManus and Walter Macken in their trilogies, Eoghan Ó Tuairisc in *L'Attaque*, James Plunkett in *Strumpet City*, Eilís Dillon in *Across the Bitter Sea* and *Blood Relations*, and Thomas Flanagan in *The Year of the French*.

The predominance of twentieth-century novels in this list underlines a conclusion that has become obvious in the course of this study: twentieth-century Irish historical novels are clearly superior to those of the nineteenth century. While the Irish historical novel certainly benefited from the impetus and popularity of the novels of Sir Walter Scott, which set forth the basic model for such a novel, it came to focus increasingly on the events of Irish history from a uniquely Irish perspective. The nineteenth-century novels indulge in a certain amount of romantic excess, distortion, and escapism, fabricating a chivalric, noble hero who wins the day. The later novels come to focus more and more on all classes of Irish society, and the peasantry and proletariat become increasingly portrayed in a realistic and sympathetic manner that does not hide the unhappy endings of Irish history.

The superiority of the later novels is due to changed social and political conditions as well as to more sophisticated literary sensibilities and political views: for the Irish writer in the twentieth century, all was truly changed, changed utterly. The defensive posture of nineteenth-century Irish historical novelists – who were overawed by Scott, often wrote for English publishers, and lacked confidence in the sympathy of their readership – was abandoned in the twentieth century by novelists who were

more confident of their Irishness as writers and more liable to be inspired by their fellow Irish writers or by Continental masters such as Turgenev, Tolstoy, and Stendhal than by Scott, Carlyle, or Tennyson. Similar to the Irish rebel who felt that Britain's difficulty was Ireland's opportunity, the Irish writer came to realize that greater, more original work was to be done by abandoning the earlier, nearly total adherence to British models. Twentieth-century Irish historical novelists perceived that their subject matter was not quite the same as Scott's. They were as likely to be inspired by Tolstoy's impassioned vision of Russian history as by Scott's moderate view of Scottish history — much as Gaelic peasant writers turned to Maxim Gorki rather than anyone in British literature.

But even the twentieth-century novelists, while departing from Scott's moderate view of history and eschewing his happy endings, which nineteenth-century novelists had imposed on Irish history, continued to follow other important conventions of the kind of novel he introduced. All of the Irish historical novelists considered in this study sought to portray Irish history as rife with conflict, divided by sharp societal extremes which were reflected in contrasting customs, dialects, and beliefs. All of them presented a hero meant to be representative of the Irish people as a whole and reflecting the author's own views. As Irish writers became more sure of their Irishness and more open about their nationalism, their heroes became less passive and more partisan, whether they died for the cause, as did O'Flaherty's, or retreated from it, as did Macken's. Like Scott, Irish historical novelists, writing for a popular audience, drew upon popular versions of history as preserved in folklore. Whether naming their novels after ballads, as did John Banim and William Buckley, rewriting the popular versions of Oliver Cromwell and Daniel O'Connell, as did Walter Macken, or utilizing folklore about peasant life, as did Liam O'Flaherty, Eoghan Ó Tuairisc, and several others, Irish historical novelists continually responded to the mythology of Irish history. This mythology consistently celebrated the good, noble struggle of Irish heroes in the face of evil, overpowering English dominance. Like any mythology, the Irish one was not always factually "true," but it nonetheless reflected essential truths about the historical experience of the people who created it. Moreover, peasant folklore, such as the Famine tales used by Liam O'Flaherty, preserved many important details about Irish life that were not recorded in the formal annals of history. Irish folklore informed historical novelists in fruitful ways, just as Scottish folklore had fed Scott. Only when reduced to stereotype by a writer such as Uris was the folklore of Irish history more false than true.

The development of the Irish historical novel was an evolution

out of the works of Scott and his early Irish imitators rather than a rejection of them. The more developed Irish novelist of the twentieth century looked quite different from his nineteenth-century Irish forebear, who had been caricatured as an ape by English cartoonists, but he was still much the same animal, and his recognition as artist and man could not have come without the painful struggle of his literary ancestor. Without the agonizing efforts of William Carleton (who believed that he looked like Scott) before him, Liam O'Flaherty could never have set forth his angry, uncompromising views. Without the tenuous attempts of John Banim to educate his readers, the more pointed didacticisms of Walter Macken and James Plunkett would have been unthinkable. If Standish O'Grady had not undertaken his noble if often misdirected trip into Irish saga, Eoghan Ó Tuairisc might never have attempted his own, far more accurate journey. Recent Irish historical novelists are not apt to recognize themselves in their forebears. The influence of Scott, Banim, Le Fanu, Carleton, and O'Grady upon them is not an immediate one, but an evolutionary one, according to which the descendants have markedly changed, while preserving many of the features of their predecessors.

By understanding this evolution, we can see that the Irish historical novel developed in a gradual, intelligible fashion. A huge critical literature on Yeats, Joyce, and Beckett often seems to suggest that Irish literature is some kind of mutant, exiled phenomenon, with the Irish writer at odds with Irish life and largely divorced from Irish history (even though obsessed with it). The development of the historical novel in Ireland is clearly to be understood in the context of the country's changing social and political conditions, as reflected in the novelists' own lives. The history of the Irish historical novel makes sense; similar sense, one feels, ought to be made of the whole of modern Irish literature as a distinct and coherent body of work, developing in history. Irish historical novelists have imaginatively recreated the greatest crises in this history, bringing them to life in a way that the history books cannot do. It is to their credit that, faced with Irish history's great hatred and little room, the best of these novelists have achieved great clarity.

Notes

Introduction

1. James Joyce, *Ulysses* (New York: Random House, 1961), 31, 34. Mr. Deasy calls Stephen a Fenian: "You fenians forget some things" (31). He is not, of course, a Fenian, but here he must react like one.

2. W. B. Yeats, *The Collected Poems of W. B. Yeats* (New York: Macmillan, 1956), 249.

3. W. C. Zellars, *Scott and Certain Spanish Historical Novels* (Albuquerque: University of New Mexico Press, 1930); Avrom Fleishman, *The English Historical Novel* (Baltimore: Johns Hopkins University Press, 1971).

4. Thomas Flanagan, *The Irish Novelists, 1800–1850* (New York: Columbia University Press, 1958); and Donald Davie, *The Heyday of Sir Walter Scott* (London: Routledge and Kegan Paul, 1961). As we shall see, Flanagan names John Banim as author of *The Croppy* even though it is clear his brother Michael wrote it. Davie almost ignores the Banims altogether (except for a brief, condescending reference on p. 94), deciding instead that Le Fanu's *The Cock and Anchor* and *Torlogh O'Brien* "come nearer than any other Irish novels to challenging Scott on his own ground," yet assuring us that "these are not truly historical novels but thrillers in fancy dress."

5. Steven J. Brown, *Ireland in Fiction: A Guide to Irish Novels, Tales, Romances, and Folk-lore* (1919; reprint, Shannon: Irish Universities Press, 1969). See also his article "Irish Historical Fiction," *Studies: An Irish Quarterly Review of Letters, Philosophy, and Science* 4 (1915): 441–63, and 5 (1916): 82–95, where he groups it by historical period dealt with and attempts to gauge its impact on the "youth of the nation."

6. Fleishman, *English Historical Novel*, 9.

1—The Model: *Scott's Historical Novel*

1. See James T. Hillhouse, rev. by Alexander Welsh, "Sir Walter Scott," in *The English Romantic Poets and Essayists: A Review of Research and Criticism*, ed. Carolyn Washburn Houtchens and Lawrence Huston Houtchens (New York: New York University Press, 1966), 149–50.

2. Sir Walter Scott, "General Preface to the Waverley Novels," in *Waverley* (Boston and New York: Houghton Mifflin, 1912), 1:xxi. Subsequent quotations from *Waverley* and its preface are cited parenthetically in the text.

3. See George Levine, "Sir Walter Scott: The End of Romance," *Wordsworth Circle* 10 (1979):147–60.

4. D. J. O'Donoghue, *Sir Walter Scott's Tour in Ireland in 1825, Now First Fully Described* (Dublin: O'Donoghue and Gill, 1905), 12. Subsequent quotations are cited parenthetically in the text.

5. Davie, *Heyday of Sir Walter Scott*, 71, 66; Avrom Fleishman, *The English Historical Novel* (Baltimore: Johns Hopkins University Press, 1971), ix.

6. Davie, *Heyday of Sir Walter Scott*, 65.

7. Mark Twain, Chap. 46 in *Life on the Mississippi*, 1883; reprinted in *Scott: The Critical Heritage*, ed. John O. Hayden (New York: Barnes and Noble, 1970), 537–39.

8. See William Montgomerie, "Scottish Ballad Manuscripts," *Studies in Scottish Literature* 4 (1967): 15–16.

9. David Daiches, "Sir Walter Scott and History," *Études Anglaises* 24 (1971): 460.

10. See Duncan Forbes, "The Rationalism of Sir Walter Scott," *Cambridge Journal* 7 (1953): 17–32; and Fleishman, *English Historical Novel*, 39–46.

11. See Coleman O. Parsons, *Witchcraft and Demonology in Scott's Fiction* (Edinburgh and London: Oliver and Boyd, 1964).

12. Fleishman, *English Historical Novel*, 21.

13. Parsons, *Witchcraft and Demonology*, 71–72.

14. William Hazlitt, *New Monthly Magazine* (April 1824); reprinted in *Scott: The Critical Heritage*, ed. John O. Hayden (New York: Barnes and Noble, 1970), 279–89.

15. Samuel Taylor Coleridge, letter to Thomas Allsop, April 8, 1820; reprinted in *Scott: The Critical Heritage*, ed. John O. Hayden (New York: Barnes and Noble, 1970), 180.

16. David Brown, *Walter Scott and the Historical Imagination* (London and Boston: Routledge and Kegan Paul, 1979), 2–3. Henri Gibault agrees with Brown: "La véritable impulsion devait venir des écrits de Daiches et de Lukács." "Études sur Walter Scott," *Études Anglaises* 24 (1971): 511.

17. See, e.g., Robert French, "Sir Walter Scott as Historian," *Dalhousie Review* 47 (1966): 159–72; James Anderson, "Sir Walter Scott as Historical Novelist," *Studies in Scottish Literature* 4 (1967): 29–41, 63–78, 155–78; 5 (1968): 14–27, 83–97, 143–66; and D. D. Devlin, "Scott and History," in *Scott's Mind and Art*, ed. A. Norman Jeffares (Edinburgh: Oliver and Boyd, 1969), 21–52.

18. Daiches, "Sir Walter Scott and History," 464.

19. Georg Lukács, *The Historical Novel*, trans. Hannah and Stanley Mitchell (London: Merlin Press, 1962), 17. Subsequent quotations are cited parenthetically in the text.

20. Lukács was the first to point out this passivity. See also Alexander Welsh, *The Hero of the Waverley Novels* (New Haven: Yale University Press, 1963).

21. Francis R. Hart, *Scott's Novels: The Plotting of Historic Survival* (Charlottesville: University Press of Virginia, 1966), 12.

22. Welsh, *Hero of the Waverley Novels*, 50.

23. See David Murison, "The Two Languages of Scott," in *Scott's Mind and Art*, ed. A. Norman Jeffares (Edinburgh: Oliver and Boyd, 1969), 206–29.

24. See Daiches, "Sir Walter Scott and History," and "Scott's Achievement as a Novelist," *Nineteenth Century Fiction* (September 1951); reprinted in *Scott's Mind and Art*, ed. A. Norman Jeffares (Edinburgh: Oliver and Boyd, 1969), 21.

25. Hillhouse, "Sir Walter Scott," 132.

26. Welsh, *Hero of the Waverley Novels*, 150.

27. Northrop Frye, *The Anatomy of Criticism* (New York: Atheneum, 1965), 187, 33.

28. Welsh, *Hero of the Waverley Novels*, 13.

29. Welsh, *Hero of the Waverley Novels*, 14, 15.

2—The Background: *The Mythos of Modern Irish History*

1. See Francis R. Hart, *The Scottish Novel: From Smollett to Spark* (Cambridge, Mass.: Harvard University Press, 1978).

2. Richard M. Dorson, *American Folklore and the Historian* (Chicago and London: University of Chicago Press, 1971), 134.

3. Caoimhín Ó Danachair, "Donall Ó Conaill i mBéalaimh na nDaoine," *Studia Hibernica* 14 (1974): 40. Translations from Ó Danachair are my own.

4. Dorson, *Folklore and Traditional History* (The Hague and Paris: Mouton, 1973), 7.

5. Dorson, *American Folklore and the Historian*, 134; Frank O'Connor, *A Short History of Irish Literature: A Backward Look* (New York: Capricorn Books, 1967), 7.

6. Georges-Denis Zimmermann, *Irish Political Street Ballads and Rebel Songs, 1780–1900* (Geneva: Imprimeria La Sirène, 1966), 10–11.

7. Ibid., 10.

8. See also Steven J. Brown, "Irish Historical Fiction," *Studies: An Irish Quarterly Review of Letters, Philosophy, and Science* 4 (1915): 441–63; and 5 (1916): 82–95. Father Brown, surveying the historical pulp fiction of the nineteenth and early twentieth centuries, is mainly concerned to group it in terms of the historical periods dealt with and to assess its patriotic value to the youth of the nation.

9. J. C. Beckett, *The Making of Modern Ireland, 1603–1923* (New York: Alfred A. Knopf, 1966). Beckett's book is the best survey of the entire period with which I deal. Subsequent quotations are cited parenthetically in the text.

10. Alfred Sheppard, *The Art and Practice of Historical Fiction* (London: Humphrey Toulmin, 1930).

11. *National and Historical Ballads of Ireland* (Np., n.d.), 52.

12. Tommy Makem and the Clancy Brothers, eds., *The Irish Songbook: Collected, Adapted, Written, and Sung by the Clancy Brothers and Tommy Makem* (Toronto: Macmillan, 1969), v.

13. Bö Almqvist, letter to author, November 18, 1980.

14. Seán Ó Súilleabháin, "Oliver Cromwell in Irish Oral Tradition," in *Folklore Today: A Festschrift for Richard M. Dorson*, ed. Linda Dégh, Henry Glassie, and Felix J. Oinas (Bloomington: Indiana University Research Center for Language and Semiotic Studies, 1976), 474.

15. Ibid., 481, 482.

16. Ó Súilleabháin, *Folktales of Ireland* (Chicago and London: University of Chicago Press, 1966), 284.

17. Makem and the Clancy Brothers, *Irish Songbook*, 18.
18. See Maurice Keen, "The Outlaw Ballad as an Expression of Peasant Discontent," in *The Outlaws of Medieval Legend* (Toronto: University of Toronto Press, 1977), 145–73.
19. Zimmermann, *Irish Political Street Ballads*, 24–25.
20. Colm Ó Lochlainn, ed., *Irish Street Ballads* (London: Pan Books, 1978), 73.
21. Among some 116 Irish historical novels described by Steven J. Brown in *Ireland in Fiction: A Guide to Irish Novels, Tales, Romances, and Folk-lore* (1919; reprint, Shannon: Irish Universities Press, 1969), only nine are characterized by Brown as Protestant and Unionist in tone.
22. John Banim, *The Boyne Water* (New York: D. and J. Sadlier, 1866), 553. "The Treaty of Limerick will yet be kept."
23. P. W. Joyce, ed., *Old Irish Folk Music and Songs* (New York: Cooper Square Publishers, 1965), 179.
24. Zimmermann, *Irish Political Street Ballads*, 31. The translation is Zimmermann's.
25. Ibid., 133.
26. See Brown, *Ireland in Fiction*, 327–28. He lists forty-one novels on 1798 in all.
27. F. S. L. Lyons, *Ireland since the Famine* (Glasgow: Fontana/Collins, 1975), 110.
28. Zimmermann, *Irish Political Steet Ballads*, 146.
29. Ibid., 158.
30. Zimmermann, *Irish Political Street Ballads*, 80, 50.
31. Ó Danachair, "Donall Ó Conaill," 65, 66.
32. Ibid., 45.
33. Ó Danachair, "Donall Ó Conaill," 45.
34. See Ó Súilleabháin, *Folktales of Ireland*, 232–33, 231–32.
35. Makem and the Clancy Brothers, *Irish Songbook*, vi.
36. Roger McHugh, "The Famine in Irish Oral Tradition," in *The Great Famine: Studies in Irish History, 1845–52*, ed. R. Dudley Edwards and T. Desmond Williams (Dublin, 1956), 391, 436, 336.
37. Lyons, *Ireland since the Famine*, 4.
38. Ó Súilleabháin, "The Iveragh Fenians in Oral Tradition," in *Fenians and Fenianism*, ed. Maurice Harmon (Seattle: University of Washington Press, 1970), 35–37.
39. Ó Lochlainn, *Irish Street Ballads*, 96.
40. See Herbert Howarth, *The Irish Writers, 1880–1940: Literature under Parnell's Star* (London: Rockliff, 1958).
41. Zimmermann, *Irish Political Street Ballads*, 64.
42. See O'Connor, *Backward Look*; William Irwin Thompson's *The Imagination of an Insurrection* (New York: Oxford University Press, 1967); Malcolm Brown's *The Politics of Irish Literature* (London: George Allen and Unwin, 1972); and Peter Costello's *The Heart Grown Brutal: The Irish Revolution in Literature, from Parnell to the Death of Yeats* (Dublin: Gill and Macmillan, 1977).
43. Makem and the Clancy Brothers, *Irish Songbook*, 136–37.
44. Ó Lochlainn, *More Irish Street Ballads* (London: Pan Books, 1978), 188.

3 – Beginnings: *The Banims*

1. Thomas Flanagan, *The Irish Novelists, 1800–1850* (New York: Columbia University Press, 1958), 188, 189.

2. Patrick Rafroidi, *L'Irlande et le romantisme: La littérature Irlandaise-Anglaise de 1789 à 1850 et sa place dans le mouvement occidental* (Paris: Éditions Universitaires, 1972), 253.

3. Mark Hawthorne, *John and Michael Banim (The "O'Hara Brothers"): A Study in the Early Development of the Anglo-Irish Novel* (Salzburg: Institut für Englische Sprache und Literatur, 1975), 6.

4. See Steven J. Brown, *Ireland in Fiction: A Guide to Irish Novels, Tales, Romances, and Folk-lore* (1919; reprint, Shannon: Irish Universities Press, 1969), 188, 189, 206, 20.

5. See Robert Lee Wolff, "The Fiction of the 'O'Hara Family,'" Introduction to *The Denounced*, by John Banim (1830; reprint, New York: Garland Publishing, 1979), v–lii. Wolff's essay is the best bibliographic source on the Banims.

6. Flanagan, *Irish Novelists*, 175.

7. See Patrick Joseph Murray, *The Life of John Banim* (1857; reprint, New York: Garland Publishing, 1978), 191–92; Wolff, "Fiction of the 'O'Hara Family.'" vii–viii, xxi, xlix n.2; Hawthorne, *John and Michael Banim* 5, 136ff.; Michael Banim, Preface to *The Croppy* (Dublin: James Duffy, 1865).

8. Rafroidi, *L'Irlande et le romantisme*, 191.

9. Both these ballads appear in *National and Historical Ballads of Ireland* (N.p., n.d.), 59, 112.

10. Rafroidi, *L'Irlande et le romantisme*, 195. Barton R. Friedman makes much the same point in an article published since the foregoing was written: "Fabricating History, or John Banim Refights the Boyne," *Éire-Ireland* 17, no. 1 (1982): 39–56. Friedman examines the novel as history, comparing it to Macauley and others.

11. Murray, *Life of John Banim*, 92. Subsequent quotations are cited parenthetically in the text.

12. Flanagan, *Irish Novelists*, 169.

13. Bernard Escarbelt, Introduction to *The Boyne Water*, by John Banim (1865; reprint, Lille: Université de Lille, 1976), 13; James T. Hillhouse, *The Waverley Novels and Their Critics* (1936; reprint, New York: Octagon Books, 1968), 265; Brown, *Ireland in Fiction*, 23; Anna Steger, *John Banim, ein Nachahmer Walter Scott* (Erlangen: Karl Döres, 1935). I am very grateful to my dear friend Michael Birkel of Harvard University for assistance in obtaining and translating this last work.

14. Murray, *Life of John Banim,* 165.

15. John Banim, *The Boyne Water* (New York: D. and J. Sadlier, 1866), 156. Subsequent quotations are cited parenthetically in the text.

16. For example, Banim footnotes "Bannocth-lath" (424) as "good night" instead of "blessing of the day" (Beanneacht an lae) in the original text, and a few anglicized spellings, such as "Yemen-ac-knuck" (353) for Eamon an cnoc, are unnecessarily unfaithful to the Irish. But his versions of the Gaelic speaker's attempts at English, however, aren't bad ("Phwat will hur say?" [81]), and he seems to be sensitive to the considerable variations in Irish speech, as his discussion of the "southern brogue" versus the "northern slang" (421) indicates.

17. Hawthorne, *John and Michael Banim*, 56, 29.

18. In a note to the 1866 edition of the novel, Michael Banim wrote that "the Ossianic remnant embodied in the tale is the literal translation of a poem recited in the Irish tongue for my brother, while he travelled through the country Antrim. And the transcriber assured me that numerous relics of the same character could be obtained in the same locality" (559).

19. Flanagan, *Irish Novelists*, 194.

20. John Banim uses, for example, "Haw may onsasta" (anglicized version of the Scots Gaelic for "I'm very satisfied"), along with numerous phrases from Irish Gaelic, such as "Sheese,

sheese, Sassenagh!" (185), anglicized from "Síos, síos, Sasanach!" which means, "Down, down, Englishman!"

21. Flanagan, *Irish Novelists*, 195.

22. John Banim, *The Denounced* (1830; reprint, New York: Garland Publishing, 1979), 1: vi–vii. Subsequent quotations are cited parenthetically in the text.

23. John Banim, *Boyne Water*, 565 n.

24. Wolff, "Fiction of the 'O'Hara Family,'" xxviii.

25. Michael Banim, *The Croppy: A Tale of the Irish Rebellion of 1798* (Dublin: James Duffy, 1865), 11. Subsequent quotations are cited parenthetically in the text.

26. See Wolff, "Fiction of the 'O'Hara Family,'" xxii–xxiii. He contradicts Flanagan, who had written that Rourke was based upon the famous Father Murphy. Wolff offers fairly convincing evidence that Philip Roche, not Murphy, was Banim's model.

27. Wolff, *William Carleton, Irish Peasant Novelist: A Preface to His Fiction* (New York: Garland Publishing, 1980), 4.

4 – Retreat to History: *Sheridan Le Fanu and William Carleton*

1. See Steven J. Brown, *Ireland in Fiction: A Guide to Irish Novels, Tales, Romances, and Folk-lore* (1919; reprint, Shannon: Irish Universities Press, 1969), 121. In his appendix list of historical novels, Father Brown notes a number of novels treating ancient and medieval Irish history (324–25) that are beyond the scope of my study as I am interested in the treatment of post-1600 Irish history (with which most of the 212 novels listed by Brown are concerned).

2. See ibid., pp. 100, 176, 169, 112, 83, 170, 165, 171, 116, 47, 271, 181, and 57, respectively, for brief descriptions of these novels.

3. Thomas Flanagan, *The Irish Novelists, 1800–1850* (New York: Columbia University Press, 1958), 188.

4. There has been a resurgence of critical interest in each of these writers, although it has not for the most part extended to their historical novels. In each case an excellent, comprehensive book has been published: W. J. McCormack's perceptive critical biography *Sheridan Le Fanu and Victorian Ireland* (Oxford: Clarendon Press, 1980) and Robert Lee Wolff's critical introduction *William Carleton, Irish Peasant Novelist: A Preface to His Fiction* (New York: Garland Publishing, 1980).

5. McCormack, *Sheridan Le Fanu*, 1. Subsequent quotations are cited parenthetically in the text.

6. Browne, *Sheridan Le Fanu*, 17. Le Fanu's brother, W. R. Le Fanu, wrote a book entitled *Seventy Years of Irish Life* in which some of these events are recalled.

7. Robert Lee Wolff, "The Irish Fiction of Joseph Sheridan Le Fanu (1814–1873)," Introduction to *The Cock and Anchor*, by Joseph Sheridan Le Fanu (New York: Garland Publishing, 1979), vi, x.

8. Ibid., xii.

9. Malcolm Brown, *The Politics of Irish Literature: From Thomas Davis to W. B. Yeats* (London: George Allen and Unwin, 1972), 65.

10. McCormack, *Sheridan Le Fanu*, 105.

11. Joseph Sheridan Le Fanu, *The Cock and Anchor: A Chronicle of Old Dublin* (1845; reprint, New York: Garland Publishing, 1979), 2: 287–88.

12. Wolff, "Le Fanu," xiv.

NOTES 213

13. Browne, *Sheridan Le Fanu*, 107.

14. Donald Davie, *The Heyday of Sir Walter Scott* (London: Routledge and Kegan Paul, 1961), 90; Browne, *Sheridan Le Fanu*, 107.

15. I do not accept McCormack's assertion (95) that *Torlogh O'Brien* may have been written before *The Cock and Anchor.* His only evidence is the rapidity with which *Torlogh* appeared serially and his own impression that it is less mature stylistically (which I do not share). I am convinced, to the contrary, that the more political focus of *Torlogh* reflects Young Ireland's influence on Le Fanu from 1845 to 1847, thus supporting the idea that *Torlogh* was written just as it was published: after *The Cock and Anchor.*

16. Joseph Sheridan Le Fanu, *The Fortunes of Colonel Torlogh O'Brien: A Tale of the Wars of King James* (Dublin: James M'Glashan, 1847), 281.

17. McCormack, *Sheridan Le Fanu*, 83, 90.

18. See Wayne E. Hall, *Shadowy Heroes: Irish Literature of the 1890s* (Syracuse: Syracuse University Press, 1980).

19. Phillip L. Marcus, *Yeats and the Beginning of the Irish Renaissance* (Ithaca: Cornell University Press, 1970), 285. Yeats listed *Castle Rackrent* along with Carleton's *Fardorougha the Miser, The Black Prophet,* and *Traits and Stories of the Irish Peasantry* and Banim's *The Nolans* [sic] and *John Doe.*

20. Wolff, *William Carleton*, 3. Subsequent quotations are cited parenthetically in the text.

21. Ibid., 21.

22. Flanagan, *Irish Novelists*, 273.

23. Benedict Kiely, *Poor Scholar: A Study of the Works and Days of William Carleton* (New York: Sheed and Ward, 1948), 177.

24. Flanagan, *Irish Novelists*, 312.

25. William Carleton, "The Late John Banim," *The Nation* (Dublin), September 23, 1843, 794–95. I am thankful to the staff of the Widener Library, Harvard University, for obtaining this article for me.

26. See Kiely, *Poor Scholar*, 178.

27. Ibid., 178.

28. Davie, *Heyday of Sir Walter Scott*, 80.

29. I do not agree with Flanagan that what Carleton wrote after 1856 "has no proper place in literary history" (329).

30. D. J. O'Donoghue, *Sir Walter Scott's Tour in Ireland in 1825, Now First Fully Described* (Dublin: O'Donoghue and Gill, 1905), 10–11.

31. Kiely, *Poor Scholar*, 178.

32. D. J. O'Donoghue, *The Life of William Carleton* (1896; reprint, New York: Garland Publishing, 1969), 2: 287.

33. Kiely, *Poor Scholar*, 177.

34. William Carleton, *Redmond Count O'Hanlon, the Irish Rapparee* (Dublin: James Duffy, 1886), 84–85. Subsequent quotations are cited parenthetically in the text.

35. Flanagan, *Irish Novelists*, 327.

5—The Shift from Romance to Realism: *Standish O'Grady and William Buckley*

1. Ernest Boyd, *Ireland's Literary Renaissance* (1922; reprint, New York: Barnes and Noble, 1968), 374; Thomas Flanagan, "Fact and Imagination in Ireland," talk presented in

the Boston College Humanities Series, October 9, 1980, recorded with permission of Professor Flanagan.

2. I have compiled these figures, as with the figures that follow, by examining Steven J. Brown, *Ireland in Fiction: A Guide to Irish Novels, Tales, Romances, and Folk-lore* (1919; reprint, Shannon: Irish Universities Press, 1969).

3. Steven J. Brown, "Irish Historical Fiction," *Studies: An Irish Quarterly Review of Letters, Philosophy, and Science* 5 (1916): 95.

4. Thomas Fitzpatrick, *The King of Claddagh*, abridged by Una Morrissy (Cork: Mercier Press, 1979).

5. Phillip Marcus, *Standish O'Grady* (Lewisburg, Pa.: Bucknell University Press, 1970), 76. Subsequent quotations from Marcus cited parenthetically in the text refer to this book.

6. Hugh Art O'Grady, *Standish James O'Grady, the Man and the Writer: A Memoir* (Dublin: Talbot Press, 1929), 64-65, 74.

7. Standish O'Grady, undated letter in the Boston College Special Irish Collection; copy of an original in the Healy Collection at Colby College, Waterville, Maine.

8. For an appreciation of Yeats's organizing abilities, see Phillip Marcus, *Yeats and the Beginning of the Irish Renaissance* (Ithaca: Cornell University Press, 1970). Marcus's examination of the practical side of Yeats counters the popular perception of him as merely a starry-eyed dreamer.

9. Ibid., 285-86, 118.

10. William Butler Yeats, "Battles Long Ago," *The Bookman* (London), February 1895, 153; Hugh Art O'Grady, *Standish James O'Grady*, 66, 67.

11. Marcus, *Yeats*, 279; Benedict Kiely, *Modern Irish Fiction — A Critique* (Dublin: Golden Eagle Books, 1950), 59.

12. Wayne E. Hall, *Shadowy Heroes: Irish Literature of the 1890s* (Syracuse: Syracuse University Press, 1980), 177.

13. Standish O'Grady, *Toryism and the Tory Democracy* (London: Chapman and Hall, 1886), 197; Hall, *Shadowy Heroes*, 31.

14. Marcus, *Standish O'Grady*, 88.

15. William Irwin Thompson, *The Imagination of an Insurrection, Dublin, Easter 1916: A Study of an Ideological Movement* (New York: Harper Colophon, 1967).

16. Marcus, *Standish O'Grady*, 87.

17. Standish O'Grady, *Red Hugh's Captivity: A Picture of Ireland, Social and Political, in the Reign of Queen Elizabeth* (London: Ward and Downey, 1889), 1, 3-5. Subsequent quotations are cited parenthetically in the text using the abbreviation *RHC*.

18. Standish O'Grady, *The Flight of the Eagle* (Dublin: Talbot Press, 1945), 185-86. Subsequent quotations are cited parenthetically in the text using the abbreviation *FE*.

19. Standish O'Grady, *Ulrick the Ready, or the Chieftains' Last Rally* (London: Downey, 1896), iv. Subsequent quotations are cited parenthetically in the text using the abbreviation *UR*.

20. Standish O'Grady, "Pacata Hibernia," in *Standish O'Grady: Selected Essays and Passages* (Dublin: Talbot Press, 1918), 157.

21. Hugh Art O'Grady, *Standish James O'Grady*, 38-39.

22. See chapter 9 on Plunkett and, for more detail concerning the evolution of *Strumpet City*, see my article "The Making of *Strumpet City*: James Plunkett's Historical Vision," *Éire-Ireland: A Journal of Irish Studies* 13, no. 4 (1978):81-100.

23. Boyd, *Ireland's Literary Renaissance*, 47.

24. Standish O'Grady, *Hugh Roe O'Donnell: A Sixteenth Century Irish Historical Play* (Belfast: Ardrie, 1902), 27.

25. Thomas Flanagan, *The Irish Novelists, 1800-1850* (New York: Columbia University Press, 1958), 197.

26. For an account of Davitt's advocacy of land nationalization from 1882 to 1902, see my article "Michael Davitt: The 'Preacher of Ideas,' 1881-1906," *Éire-Ireland: A Journal of Irish Studies* 11, no. 1 (1976): 20-22, 27, 32-33.

27. Donald Davie, *The Heyday of Sir Walter Scott* (London: Routledge and Kegan Paul, 1961), 100.

28. Marcus, *O'Grady*, 31.

29. Brown, *Ireland in Fiction*, 242.

30. These figures are based on an examination of Brown, *Ireland in Fiction*.

31. Boyd, *Ireland's Literary Renaissance*, 386; Brown, Irish Historical Fiction," 449; Brown, *Ireland in Fiction*, 44.

32. John Gilbert, *Cork Historical and Archaeological Society Journal* 19 (1913): 172. I am very grateful to Mr. Alf MacLochlainn, director of the National Library of Ireland, who kindly searched out this information for me.

33. Georges-Denis Zimmermann, *Irish Political Street Ballads and Rebel Songs, 1780-1900* (Geneva: Imprimerie La Sirène, 1966), 307-08.

34. William Buckley, *Croppies Lie Down: A Tale of Ireland in '98* (London: Duckworth, 1903), 1. Further quotations are cited parenthetically in the text.

6—The Realistic Visions of Seán Ó Faoláin and Francis MacManus

1. See Steven J. Brown, *Ireland in Fiction: A Guide to Irish Novels, Tales, Romances, and Folk-lore* (1919; reprint, Shannon: Irish Universities Press, 1969), 305. For the Sheehy-Skeffington novel, see 279.

2. Eimar O'Duffy, *The Wasted Island* (Dublin: Martin Lester, 1919). Barry borrows from *A Portrait*: "'Thomas Joseph Creagan, 14 Oakville Avenue, City of Dublin, County Dublin, Leinster, Ireland, Europe, Eastern Hemisphere, Earth, Solar System, Universe. The Year of our Lord 1907.'" Dermot Barry, *Tom Creagan* (Dublin: At the Sign of the Three Candles, 1932), 178; Louis d'Alton, *Death Is So Fair* (New York: Doubleday, Doran, 1938); Michael McLaverty, *Call My Brother Back* (London: Longmans, Gree, 1939).

3. Brinsley MacNamara, *The Clanking of Chains* (London: Maunsel, 1920); Eimar O'Duffy, *The Lion and the Fox* (Dublin: Martin Lester, 1922); Joseph O'Neill, *Wind from the North* (London: J. Cape, 1934); Robert Hogan, *Eimar O'Duffy* (Lewisburg, Pa.: Bucknell University Press, 1972), 42.

4. Francis MacManus, "The Literature of the Period," in *The Years of the Great Test, 1926-39* (Cork: Mercier Press, 1967), 116.

5. Seán Ó Faoláin, *The Irish: A Character Study* (New York: Devin-Adair, 1956), 164-65.

6. MacManus, "Literature of the Period," 123.

7. Steven J. Brown, "Irish Historical Fiction," *Studies: An Irish Quarterly Review of Letters, Philosophy, and Science* 4 (1915): 446; Aodh de Blacam, "Who Now Reads Scott?," *The Irish Monthly* 65 (1937): 486, 491, 499.

8. Donald Davie, *The Heyday of Sir Walter Scott* (London: Routledge and Kegan Paul, 1961), 100.

9. Ó Faoláin, *The Irish*, 162, 164.

10. Ibid., 163.

11. Paul A. Doyle, *Sean O'Faolain* (New York: Twayne, 1968), 19, 23. Subsequent quotations are cited parenthetically in the text.

12. Maurice Harmon, *Sean O'Faolain: A Critical Introduction* (Notre Dame: University of Notre Dame Press, 1967), 33.

13. Doyle, *Sean O'Faolain*, 99.

14. Ó Faoláin, *Vive Moi!* (Boston: Little, Brown, 1964), 329.

15. Ibid., 371.

16. Ó Faoláin, *A Nest of Simple Folk* (New York: Viking, 1934), 131. Further quotations are cited parenthetically in the text.

17. Ó Faoláin, *The Irish*, 120–21.

18. Ó Faoláin, *Vive Moi!*, 329.

19. Harmon, *Sean O'Faoláin*, 170.

20. Ó Faoláin, *The Irish*, 125–26.

21. MacManus, "Literature of the Period," 122.

22. MacManus, "Arrows for the Target," *The Irish Monthly* 62 (1934): 542.

23. Denis Cotter, "MacManus, Francis," in *Dictionary of Irish Literature*, ed. Robert Hogan (Westport, Conn.: Greenwood Press, 1979), 414–15.

24. Sean McMahon, "Francis MacManus' Novels of Modern Ireland," *Éire-Ireland: A Journal of Irish Studies* 5, no. 1 (1970): 130.

25. For a summary of the bitter debate over Cross's *The Tailor and Ansty*, see my article "Tailor Tim Buckley: Folklore, Literature, and *Seanchas an Táilliúra*," *Éire-Ireland: A Journal of Irish Studies* 14, no. 2 (1979): 116–18.

26. James Plunkett, letter to author, January 17, 1981. "Frank MacManus was one of my teachers in Synge Street School so I knew his work very well at one stage."

27. Cotter, "MacManus, Francis," 413.

28. MacManus, "The Novelist of Vast Landscapes. A Note on Sigrid Undset," *The Irish Monthly* 62 (1934): 366; MacManus, "Arrows for the Target," 544.

29. MacManus, *Candle for the Proud* (Cork: Mercier, 1964), 103. Further quotations are cited parenthetically in the text using the abbreviation *CP.*

30. MacManus, "The Background of the Catholic Novel," *The Irish Monthly* 62 (1934): 437; MacManus, "Arrows for the Target," 543.

31. MacManus, "Novelist of Vast Landscapes," 367; MacManus, "The Artist for Nobody's Sake," *The Irish Monthly* 63 (1935): 178; McMahon, "Francis MacManus' Novels," 118; Benedict Kiely, *Modern Irish Fiction – A Critique* (Dublin: Golden Eagle Books, 1950), 83.

32. Carl Bayerschmidt, *Sigrid Undset* (New York: Twayne, 1970), 7; O'Neill, *Wind from the North*, 341.

33. MacManus, "Novelist of Vast Landscapes," 361. I am greatly indebted to my friend, colleague, and former classmate Denis Cotter of Dublin, who first alerted me to Undset's influence on MacManus and to this article.

34. Bayerschmidt, *Sigrid Undset*, 19, 18.

35. See MacManus's "Communism: The Monstrous Parody," "The Conflict and the Hidden Enemy," and "The Shape of Nonsense to Come," in *The Irish Monthly* 63 (1935): 79–85; 64 (1936): 216–23; and 65 (1937): 181–85, respectively.

36. MacManus, "Arrows for the Target," 545; Bayerschmidt, *Sigrid Undset*, 90.

37. Daniel Corkery, *The Hidden Ireland: A Study of Gaelic Munster in the Eighteenth Century* (Dublin: M. H. Gill, 1941), 262, 266, 264.

38. Corkery, *Hidden Ireland*, 273.

39. MacManus, *Stand and Give Challenge* (Cork: Mercier, 1964), 5. Further quotations are cited parenthetically using the abbreviation *SGC.*

40. MacManus, *Men Withering* (Cork: Mercier, 1972), 125–26. Further quotations are cited parenthetically using the abbreviation *MW*.

41. MacManus, "Novelist of Vast Landscapes," 362.

7 — Liam O'Flaherty's Natural History

1. Jim Phelan, *And Blackthorns* (London: Nicholson and Watson, 1944), 7.

2. Paul A. Doyle, *Liam O'Flaherty* (New York: Twayne, 1971), 7.

3. John Zneimer, *The Literary Vision of Liam O'Flaherty* (Syracuse: Syracuse University Press, 1970); Doyle, *Liam O'Flaherty*, 1971; James H. O'Brien, *Liam O'Flaherty* (Lewisburg, Pa.: Bucknell University Press, 1973); Patrick F. Sheeran, *The Novels of Liam O'Flaherty: A Study in Romantic Realism* (Atlantic Highlands, N.J.: Humanities Press, 1976); and A. A. Kelly, *Liam O'Flaherty the Storyteller* (London: Macmillan, 1976).

4. Sheeran, *Liam O'Flaherty*, 94. Subsequent references are cited parenthetically in the text.

5. Doyle, *Liam O'Flaherty*, 15.

6. O'Brien, *Liam O'Flaherty*, 16; Liam O'Flaherty, *Shame the Devil* (London: Grayson and Grayson, 1934), 18, 19.

7. Doyle, *Liam O'Flaherty*, 13, 20.

8. Zneimer, *Vision of Liam O'Flaherty*, 28. Subsequent quotations are cited parenthetically in the text.

9. O'Flaherty, *Shame the Devil*, 21–22, 23.

10. O'Flaherty, "Writing in Gaelic," *The Irish Statesman*, December 17, 1927, 348.

11. Roger McHugh, "The Famine in Irish Oral Tradition," in *The Great Famine: Studies in Irish History, 1845–52*, ed. R. Dudley Edwards and T. Desmond Williams (Dublin, 1956), 436.

12. O'Flaherty, *Famine* (London: Readers' Union, 1938), 107. Further quotations are cited parenthetically in the text.

13. McHugh, "The Famine in Irish Oral Tradition," 395.

14. Ibid., 396, 400, 410, 413.

15. Ibid., 425.

16. Peadar O'Donnell, review of *Land*, by Liam O'Flaherty, *The Bell* (Dublin) 12, no. 5 (1946): 442–44.

17. James Plunkett, interview with Eavon Boland, "Dublin's Advocate," *This Week*, October 12, 1972, 42.

18. Liam O'Flaherty, *Land* (New York: Random House, 1946), 175–76. Further quotations are cited parenthetically in the text.

19. O'Flaherty, *Shame the Devil*, 197, 211.

20. Steven J. Brown, "Irish Historical Fiction," *Studies: An Irish Quarterly Review of Letters, Philosophy, and Science* 4 (1915): 447.

21. See Sheeran, *Novels of Liam O'Flaherty*, 34, 35.

22. See Joyce Marlow, *Captain Boycott and the Irish* (London: Deutsch, 1973), for a historical examination of the Boycott incident and the circumstances surrounding it. A pop-historical approach to it is found in Philip Rooney, *Captain Boycott* (New York: Appleton-Century, 1946).

23. O'Flaherty, *Insurrection* (Boston: Little, Brown, 1951), 5. Further quotations are cited parenthetically in the text.

8—The 1960s: *Macken, Murdoch, Ó Tuairisc*

1. Richard Fallis, *The Irish Renaissance* (Syracuse: Syracuse University Press, 1977), 276, 277.

2. Robert Hogan, *After the Irish Renaissance: A Critical History of the Irish Drama Since 'The Plough and the Stars'* (Minneapolis: University of Minnesota Press, 1967), 65.

3. *Times Literary Supplement* (London), October 16, 1959, 598.

4. Walter Macken, *Seek the Fair Land* (London: Pan Books, 1979), 126. Further quotations are from this edition and are cited parenthetically in the text. *Scian* means "knife." The second quotation is from Francis MacManus, *Men Withering* (Cork: Mercier Press, 1979), 23.

5. Hogan, *After the Renaissance*, 65.

6. "Macken, Walter," *Dictionary of Irish Literature*, ed. Robert Hogan (Westport, Conn.: Greenwood Press, 1979), 406.

7. See Hogan, *After the Renaissance*, 66–67.

8. Paul Doyle, *Liam O'Flaherty* (New York: Twayne, 1971), 132.

9. Eoghan Ó Tuairisc, letter to author, March 27, 1981. "In Walter Macken, I find a little too much this-is-history; O'Flaherty represents a too frail, too black-and-white fatalism." I am deeply and considerably indebted to Mr. Ó Tuairisc for this letter. He took the time to write eleven pages to me about his life and work, a gift made all the more invaluable by the fact there was absolutely no secondary source of information on Ó Tuairisc available to me. All further quotations from Ó Tuairisc are from this letter.

10. Macken, *The Scorching Wind* (London: Pan Books, 1979), 304. Further quotations are cited parenthetically in the text.

11. *Time Magazine*, 74 (August 10, 1959): 78.

12. Macken, *The Silent People* (London: Pan Books, 1980), 119. Further quotations are cited parenthetically in the text.

13. For reviews of Macken, see, for example, *The New York Times Book Review*, November 25, 1962, 67, and the *Times Literary Supplement* (London), October 16, 1959, 598; on Murdoch, *Times Literary Supplement*, October 14, 1965, 912, and *Critic*, 24 (December 1965–January 1966): 63.

14. Frank Baldanza, *Iris Murdoch* (New York: Twayne, 1974), 13.

15. Donna Gerstenberger, *Iris Murdoch* (Lewisburg, Pa.: Bucknell University Press, 1975), 13.

16. See Gerstenberger, *Iris Murdoch*, 40.

17. Iris Murdoch, *The Red and the Green* (New York: Viking Press, 1965), 36. Further quotations are cited parenthetically in the text.

18. See Ruth Dudley Edwards, *Patrick Pearse: The Triumph of Failure* (London: Faber and Faber, 1979).

19. Gerstenberger, *Iris Murdoch*, 78.

20. Baldanza, *Iris Murdoch*, 126.

21. Weldon E. Thornton, "Elusive Balance in Iris Murdoch's *The Red and the Green*," in *The Modern Irish Novel (Excluding Joyce): Papers Presented before the 1980 American Committee for Irish Studies—Modern Language Association Symposium, Houston, Texas*, ed. Herbert V. Fackler (Lafayette: University of Southwestern Louisiana, Office of Institutional Research, 1980), 59–85.

22. Pádraic Ó Conaire, *Brian Óg* (Comhlacht Oideachais na hÉireann, n.d.). First published serially in 1922–23 and in book form in 1926.

23. This recalls the brilliant buffoonery of Myles na gCopaleen (Flann O'Brien, Brian

O'Nolan) as reprinted in *The Best of Myles*, ed. Kevin Ó Nolan (London: Picador, 1977), 278, on "The Gaelic."

24. Caoimhín Ó Marcaigh, letter to author, January 30, 1981.

25. Ó Tuairisc, *L'Attaque* (Cork: Mercier Press, 1980). Further quotations are from this edition and are cited parenthetically in the text.

26. Richard Hayes, *The Last Invasion of Ireland, When Connacht Rose* (Dublin: M. H. Gill, 1937), xv.

27. Consider, for example, the following passage in *The Best of Myles*: "Aigh nó a mean thú ios só léasaigh dat thí slips in this clós, bhears a bíord, and dos not smóc bíocós obh de trobal obh straigeing a meaits. It is só long sins thi did an anasth dea's bhorc dat thí thinks 'manuil leabear' is de neim obh of a Portuguis arditeitear" (263).

9—The 1970s: *Plunkett, Dillon, Flanagan*

1. Eilís Dillon, letter to author, May 11, 1981, reprinted here by kind permission of Ms. Dillon. I am very grateful to Ms. Dillon for taking the time to write me three letters in answer to my inquiries. Subsequent quotations from these letters are cited parenthetically by date in the text.

2. Georg Lukács, *The Historical Novel*, trans. Hannah and Stanley Mitchell (London: Merlin Press, 1962), 17.

3. For an overview of Plunkett's whole career, see my entry, "Plunkett, James," in *Dictionary of Irish Literature*, ed. Robert Hogan (Westport, Conn.: Greenwood Press, 1979), 554–60.

4. It is significant that a large proportion of Plunkett's other efforts during these years, which must escape our attention here, were of a historical bent. "Farewell Harper" (1956) is a remarkable radio play that penetrates the Irish 1940s in powerful and subtle ways. The short story "The Plain People" (1960) deals with the labor union world of Plunkett's own period of involvement, as *Strumpet City* deals with his father's time; the picture is again quite compelling yet quite different. "When Do You Die, Friend?" (1966) is a television play that recreates the events of 1798, using William Farrell's journal as a guidebook.

5. For a detailed examination of this transformation, see my article "The Making of *Strumpet City*: James Plunkett's Historical Vision," *Éire-Ireland: A Journal of Irish Studies* 13, no. 4 (1978): 81–100.

6. James Plunkett, interview with Eavon Boland, "Dublin's Advocate," *This Week* (Dublin), October 12, 1972, 40.

7. Plunkett, "Jim Larkin," in *Leaders and Workers*, ed. J. W. Boyle (Cork: Mercier Press, n.d.), 80.

8. Lukács, *Historical Novel*, 52–53. When asked in 1976, Plunkett told me that he had never read Lukács, but he agreed with Lukács's thesis when I summarized it to him.

9. Plunkett, *Big Jim: A Play for Radio* (Dublin: Martin O'Donnell, 1955), 7.

10. Plunkett, letter to author, January 17, 1981. As always, I am deeply indebted to Mr. Plunkett for his generous help. Plunkett, "Dublin's Advocate," 42.

11. Plunkett, interview in *The Times* (London), December 6, 1968; cited by Godeleine Carpentier in "Dublin and the Drama of Larkinism: James Plunkett's *Strumpet City*," in *The Irish Novel in Our Time*, ed. Maurice Harmon and Patrick Rafroidi (Lille: Lille University Press, 1976), 213. In "Dublin's Advocate," Plunkett comments that "there was this social question which Joyce never bothered with. So I felt between the world of Joyce or

socially a little above the world of O'Casey—I thought this would give a more total picture of the world I grew up in, the kind of Dublin that created the environment and the way I had to live and the way I had to think, the thing I had to break away from. When I talk about O'Casey and Joyce, I'm not placing myself above them, or even leaving myself out, I just mean that these were enormous influences . . . and that was more or less the basis for beginning the book."

12. Plunkett, "Jim Larkin," 79; Arnold Wright, *Disturbed Dublin: The Story of the Great Strike of 1913* (London: Longmans, Green, 1914), 37.

13. Plunkett, "Yours Respectfully," an address to the Irish Management Institute, *New Realities* (Dublin), 1972, 31.

14. Plunkett, *Strumpet City* (Hertfordshire: Panther Books, 1971), 247. Further quotations are cited parenthetically in the text.

15. Plunkett, "Dublin's Advocate," 41–42.

16. Lukács, *Historical Novel*, 45.

17. Plunkett, "Yours Respectfully," 30; James Connolly, *The Irish Worker*, November 28, 1914; cited in Carpentier, "Drama of Larkinism," 213.

18. Plunkett, "Yours Respectfully," 30; Wright, *Disturbed Dublin*, 37.

19. Carpentier, "Drama of Larkinism," 213.

20. Dillon, *Across the Bitter Sea* (London: Hodder Fawcett, 1975); Dillon, *Blood Relations* (New York: Fawcett Crest, 1977). Further quotations from each of the novels are cited parenthetically in the text using the abbreviations *ABS* and *BR*. It should be added that Dillon's earlier novel *The Bitter Glass* (London: Faber and Faber, 1958; pbk. Swords, County Dublin: Wand River Press, 1981), like *Blood Relations*, attempted to use a frustrated love story to reflect the civil conflict—but both its characterizations and its use of history are much thinner, almost too thin to call it a historical novel.

21. Wayne Hall, "*Trinity:* The Formulas of History," *Éire-Ireland: A Journal of Irish Studies* 13, no. 4 (1978): 144.

22. See Leon Uris, *Trinity*, (New York: Bantam, 1977), 99. for other examples of this error, see pp. 50, 329, 349, 370, 379, 438, 637, 721, and 791.

23. Thomas Flanagan, *The Year of the French* (New York: Pocket Books, 1979). Further quotations are cited parenthetically in the text.

24. "Flanagan, Thomas James Bonner," *Dictionary of American Scholars: English, Speech, and Drama*, ed. James Cattell Press (New York: R. R. Bowker, 1978), 2: 214.

25. Flanagan, *The Irish Novelists, 1800–1850* (New York: Columbia University Press, 1958), 189; Flanagan following "Fact and Imagination in Ireland," talk presented in the Boston College Humanities Series, October 9, 1980, recorded with permission of Professor Flanagan. My question was, "I wonder if we might get you to comment at all on your own novel in relation to the tradition of historical novels the pitfalls of which you have traced a little. Does yours escape those pitfalls? Did you feel haunted by writers like Banim and others, when writing your own novel?"

26. See Thomas Pakenham, *The Year of Liberty: The Story of the Great Irish Rebellion of 1798* (London: Panther Books, 1969), 407–17.

27. Emily Lawless and Shan F. Bullock, *The Race of Castlebar* (London: John Murray, 1913). See Steven J. Brown, *Ireland in Fiction* (1919; reprint, Shannon: Irish Universities Press, 1969), 163.

28. Joseph Stock, *A Narrative of What Passed at Killala in the County Mayo, and the Parts Adjacent, During the French Invasion in the Summer of 1798* (Limerick: John and Thomas McAuliff, 1800), 1; Sir Jonah Barrington, *The Ireland of Sir Jonah Barrington*, ed. Hugh B. Staples (Seattle: University of Washington Press, 1967), 302.

Conclusion

1. Tim Pat Coogan, *On the Blanket: The H Block Story* (Dublin: Ward River Press, 1980), 4, 241–42, 244–45.

2. Thomas Flanagan, "In Troubled Ireland, the Enemy Is History," *The Boston Globe*, May 11, 1981, 15.

Bibliography

Primary Sources

For novels with more than one edition, the more recent (and thus more accessible) edition is given, listed at the end of those entries. Original publication data are also listed below, appearing first.

Banim, John. *The Boyne Water; A Tale by the O'Hara Brothers.* London: W. Simpkin and R. Marshall, 1826. 3 vols. New York: D. and J. Sadlier, 1866. Reprint. New York: Garland Publishing, 1979. 3 vols.

———. *The Denounced.* 3 vols. 1830. Reprint. New York: Garland Publishing, 1979. (Consisting of the two novels *The Last Baron of Crana* and *The Conformists.*)

Banim, Michael. *The Croppy; A Tale of the Irish Rebellion of 1798.* London: H. Colburn, 1828. Dublin: James Duffy, 1865.

Buckley, William. *Croppies Lie Down: A Tale of Ireland in '98.* London: Duckworth, 1903.

Carleton, William. "The Late John Banim." *The Nation* (Dublin), September 23, 1843, 794–95.

———. *Redmond Count O'Hanlon, the Irish Rapparee.* 1862. Reprint. Dublin: James Duffy, 1886.

Dillon, Eilís. *Across the Bitter Sea.* London: Hodder and Stoughton, 1973. London: Hodder Fawcett, 1975.

_____. *The Bitter Glass.* London: Faber and Faber, 1958. Swords, County Dublin: Ward River Press, 1981.

_____. *Blood Relations.* New York: Fawcett Crest, 1977.

Flanagan, Thomas. "In Troubled Ireland, the Enemy Is History." *The Boston Globe,* May 11, 1981, 15.

_____. *The Year of the French.* New York: Pocket Books, 1979.

Le Fanu, Joseph Sheridan. *The Cock and Anchor; A Chronicle of Old Dublin.* 3 vols. 1845. Reprint. New York: Garland Publishing, 1979.

_____. *The Fortunes of Colonel Torlogh O'Brien: A Tale of the Wars of King James.* Dublin: James M'Glashan, 1847.

Macken, Walter. *The Scorching Wind.* London: Macmillan, 1964. London: Pan Books, 1966.

_____. *Seek the Fair Land.* London: Macmillan, 1959. London: Pan Books, 1962.

_____. *The Silent People.* London: Macmillan, 1962. London: Pan Books, 1965.

MacManus, Francis. *After the Flight; Being Eyewitness Sketches from Irish History from A.D. 1607 to 1916.* Dublin: Talbot Press, 1935.

_____. "Arrows for the Target." *The Irish Monthly* 62 (1934): 541–47.

_____. "The Artist for Nobody's Sake." *The Irish Monthly* 63 (1935): 175–80.

_____. "The Background of the Catholic Novel." *The Irish Monthly* 62 (1934): 433–40.

_____. *Candle for the Proud.* Dublin: Talbot Press, 1936. Cork: Mercier Press, 1964.

_____. "Communism: The Monstrous Parody." *The Irish Monthly* 63 (1935): 79–85.

_____. "The Conflict and the Hidden Enemy." *The Irish Monthly* 64 (1936): 216–23.

_____. "History with Tears." *The Irish Monthly* 65 (1937): 245–49.

_____. "The Literature of the Period." In *The Years of the Great Test, 1926–39,* 115–26. Cork: Mercier Press, 1967.

_____. *Men Withering.* Dublin: Talbot Press, 1939. Cork: Mercier Press, 1972.

_____. "The Novelist of Vast Landscapes. A Note on Sigrid Undset." *The Irish Monthly* 62 (1934): 361–67.

_____. "The Shape of Nonsense to Come." *The Irish Monthly* 65 (1937): 181–85.

_____. *Stand and Give Challenge.* Dublin: Talbot Press, 1934. Cork: Mercier Press, 1964.

Murdoch, Iris. *The Red and the Green.* New York: Viking Press, 1965.

Ó Faoláin, Seán. *The Irish: A Character Study.* New York: Devin-Adair, 1956.

_____. *A Nest of Simple Folk.* London: J. Cape, 1933. New York: Viking Press, 1934.

_____. *Vive Moi!* Boston: Little, Brown, 1964.

O'Flaherty, Liam. *Famine*. London: V. Gollancz, 1937. Reprint. London: Readers' Union, 1938. Reprint. Boston: David R. Godine, 1982.

_____. *Insurrection*. London: V. Gollancz, 1950. Boston: Little, Brown, 1951.

_____. *Land*. New York: Random House, 1946.

_____. *Shame the Devil*. London: Grayson and Grayson, 1934.

_____. *Two Years*. London: J. Cape, 1930.

_____. "Writing in Gaelic." *The Irish Statesman*, December 17, 1927, 348.

O'Grady, Standish James. *The Crisis in Ireland*. Dublin: Ponsonby, 1882.

_____. *The Flight of the Eagle*. 1897. Reprint. Dublin: Talbot Press, 1945.

_____. *Hugh Roe O'Donnell: A Sixteenth Century Irish Historical Play*. Belfast: Ardrie, 1902.

_____. "Pacata Hibernia." In *Standish O'Grady: Selected Essays and Passages*, 151–64. Dublin: Talbot Press, 1918. (From the "Preface" to *Pacata Hibernia*, 1896.)

_____. *Red Hugh's Captivity: A Picture of Ireland, Social and Political, in the Reign of Queen Elizabeth*. London: Ward and Downey, 1889.

_____. *Toryism and the Tory Democracy*. London: Chapman and Hall, 1886.

_____. *Ulrick the Ready; or, The Chieftains' Last Rally*. London: Downey, 1896.

Ó Tuairisc, Eoghan. *L'Attaque*. 1962. Cork: Mercier Press, 1980.

Plunkett, James. *Big Jim: A Play for Radio*. Dublin: Martin O'Donnell, 1955.

_____. "Dublin's Advocate." *This Week* (Dublin), October 12, 1972, 40–42. (An interview with Eavon Boland.)

_____. "Jim Larkin." In *Leaders and Workers*, edited by J. W. Boyle, 77–86. Cork: Mercier Press, n.d.

_____. *The Risen People*. Dublin: The Irish Writers' Co-operative, 1978. (First performed in 1958.)

_____. *Strumpet City*. London: Hutchinson, 1969. Hertfordshire: Panther Books, 1971.

_____. "Yours Respectfully." *New Realities* (Dublin), 1972, 29–34.

Secondary Sources

Anderson, James. "Sir Walter Scott as Historical Novelist." *Studies in Scottish Literature* 4 (1967): 29–41, 63–78, 155–78; 5 (1968): 14–27, 83–97, 143–66.

Baldanza, Frank. *Iris Murdoch*. New York: Twayne, 1974.

Bayerschmidt, Carl. *Sigrid Undset*. New York: Twayne, 1970.

Beckett, J. C. *The Making of Modern Ireland, 1603–1923*. New York: Alfred A. Knopf, 1966.

Begnal, Michael H. *Joseph Sheridan Le Fanu*. Lewisburg, Pa.: Bucknell University Press, 1971.

Bernbaum, Ernest. "The Views of the Great Critics on the Historical Novel." *PMLA* 41 (1926): 424–41.

Boyd, Ernest. *Ireland's Literary Renaissance*. 1922. Reprint. New York: Barnes and Noble, 1968.

Brown, David. *Walter Scott and the Historical Imagination*. London and Boston: Routledge and Kegan Paul, 1979.

Brown, Malcolm. *The Politics of Irish Literature: From Thomas Davis to W. B. Yeats*. London: George Allen and Unwin, 1972.

Brown, Steven J. *Ireland in Fiction: A Guide to Irish Novels, Tales, Romances, and Folk-lore*. 1919; Revised and enlarged from the original 1911 edition. Reprint. Shannon: Irish University Press, 1969.

――――. "Irish Historical Fiction." *Studies: An Irish Quarterly Review of Letters, Philosophy, and Science* 4 (1915): 441–63; 5 (1916): 82–95.

Browne, Nelson. *Sheridan Le Fanu*. London: Arthur Barker, 1951.

Butterfield, Herbert. *The Historical Novel: An Essay*. Cambridge: Cambridge University Press, 1924.

Cahalan, James M. "The Making of *Strumpet City*: James Plunkett's Historical Vision." *Éire-Ireland: A Journal of Irish Studies* 13, no. 4 (1978): 81–100.

――――. "Michael Davitt: The 'Preacher of Ideas,' 1881–1906." *Éire-Ireland* 11, no. 1 (1976): 13–33.

――――. "Plunkett, James." In *Dictionary of Irish Literature*, edited by Robert Hogan, 554–60. Westport, Conn.: Greenwood Press, 1979.

――――. Review of *Farewell Companions*, by James Plunkett. *Éire-Ireland* 13, no. 2 (1978): 127–30.

――――. "Tailor Tim Buckley: Folklore, Literature, and *Seanchas an Táilliúra*." *Éire-Ireland* 14, no. 2 (1979): 110–18.

Carpentier, Godeleine. "Dublin and the Drama of Larkinism: James Plunkett's *Strumpet City*." In *The Irish Novel in Our Time*, edited by Maurice Harmon and Patrick Rafroidi, 209–19. Lille: Lille University Press, 1976.

Chapman, Malcolm. *The Gaelic Vision in Scottish Culture*. Montreal: McGill-Queen's University Press, 1978.

Coogan, Tim Pat. *On the Blanket: The H Block Story*. Dublin: Ward River Press, 1980.

Corkery, Daniel. *The Hidden Ireland: A Study of Gaelic Munster in the Eighteenth Century*. Dublin: M. H. Gill, 1941.

――――. *Synge and Anglo-Irish Literature*. London and New York: Longmans, Green, 1931.

Costello, Peter. *The Heart Grown Brutal: The Irish Revolution in Literature from Parnell to the Death of Yeats, 1891–1939*. Dublin: Gill and Macmillan, 1977.

Cotter, Denis. "MacManus, Francis." In *Dictionary of Irish Literature*, edited by Robert Hogan, 414-15. Westport, Conn.: Greenwood Press, 1979.

Daiches, David. "Scott's Achievement as a Novelist." *Nineteenth Century Fiction* (September 1951). Reprinted in *Scott's Mind and Art*, edited by A. Norman Jeffares, 21-52. Edinburgh: Oliver and Boyd, 1969.

_____. "Sir Walter Scott and History." *Études Anglaises* 24 (1971): 458-77.

Davie, Donald. *The Heyday of Sir Walter Scott*. London: Routledge and Kegan Paul, 1961.

Debeer, Nöel. "The Irish Novel Looks Backward." In *The Irish Novel in Our Time*, edited by Maurice Harmon and Patrick Rafroidi, 105-27. Lille: Lille University Press, 1976.

De Bhaldraithe, Tomás. "Liam O'Flaherty—Translator (?)" *Éire-Ireland* 3 (1968): 149-53.

De Blacam, Aodh. "Who Now Reads Scott?" *The Irish Monthly* 65 (1937): 486-99.

Devlin, D. D. "Scott and History." In *Scott's Mind and Art*, edited by A. Norman Jeffares, 72-92. Edinburgh: Oliver and Boyd, 1969.

Dorson, Richard M. *American Folklore and the Historian*. Chicago and London: University of Chicago Press, 1971.

_____. *Folklore and Traditional History*. The Hague and Paris: Mouton, 1973.

Doyle, Paul A. *Liam O'Flaherty*. New York: Twayne, 1971.

_____. *Liam O'Flaherty: An Annotated Bibliography*. Troy, N.Y.: Whitson Publishing, 1972.

_____. *Sean O'Faolain*. New York: Twayne, 1968.

Edwards, R. Dudley, and T. Desmond Williams, eds. *The Great Famine: Studies in Irish History, 1845-52*. Dublin: Browne and Nolan, 1956.

Edwards, Ruth Dudley. *Patrick Pearse: The Triumph of Failure*. London: Faber and Faber, 1979.

Escarbelt, Bernard. Introduction to *The Boyne Water*, by John Banim. 1865. Reprint. Lille: Lille University Press, 1976.

Fallis, Richard. "'Fiction Is History': Change, Continuity, and the Persistent Mode of the Irish Historical Novel." In *The Modern Irish Novel (Excluding Joyce): Papers Presented before the 1980 American Committee for Irish Studies — Modern Language Association Symposium, Houston, Texas*, edited by Herbert V. Fackler, 25-47. Research Series, no. 50. Lafayette: University of Southwestern Louisiana, December 1980.

_____. *The Irish Renaissance*. Syracuse: Syracuse University Press, 1977.

Feuchtwanger, Lion. *The House of Desdemona; or, The Laurels and Limitations of Historical Fiction*. Translated by Harold A. Basilius. Detroit: Wayne State University Press, 1963.

Flanagan, Thomas. *The Irish Novelists, 1800-1850*. New York: Columbia University Press, 1958.

Fleishman, Avrom. *The English Historical Novel*. Baltimore: Johns Hopkins University Press, 1971.

Forbes, Duncan. "The Rationalism of Sir Walter Scott." *Cambridge Journal* 7 (1953): 17–32.

French, Robert. "Sir Walter Scott as Historian." *Dalhousie Review* 47 (1966): 159–72.

Friedman, Barton. "Fabricating History, or John Banim Refights the Boyne." *Éire-Ireland* 17, no. 1 (1982): 39–56.

Frye, Northrop. *The Anatomy of Criticism*. New York: Atheneum, 1965.

Gerstenberger, Donna. *Iris Murdoch*. Lewisburg, Pa.: Bucknell University Press, 1975.

Gibault, Henri. "Études sur Walter Scott." *Études Anglaises* 24 (1971): 509–17.

Gibert, John. *Cork Historical and Archaeological Society Journal* 19 (1913): 172. (An untitled article on Cork writers, with a reference to William Buckley.)

Gordon, Robert C. *Under Which King? A Study of the Scottish Waverley Novels*. Edinburgh and London: Oliver and Boyd, 1969.

Hall, Wayne E. *Shadowy Heroes: Irish Literature of the 1890s*. Syracuse: Syracuse University Press, 1980.

———. "*Trinity*: The Formulas of History." *Éire-Ireland* 13, no. 4 (1978): 137–44.

Harmon, Maurice. *Sean O'Faolain: A Critical Introduction*. Notre Dame: University of Notre Dame Press, 1967.

Hart, Francis R. *The Scottish Novel: From Smollett to Spark*. Cambridge, Mass.: Harvard University Press, 1978.

———. *Scott's Novels: The Plotting of Historic Survival*. Charlottesville: University of Virginia Press, 1966.

Hawthorne, Mark. *John and Michael Banim (The "O'Hara Brothers"): A Study in the Early Development of the Anglo-Irish Novel*. Salzburg: Institut für Englische Sprache und Literatur, 1975.

Hayden, John O., ed. *Scott: The Critical Heritage*. New York: Barnes and Noble, 1970.

Hayes, Richard. *The Last Invasion of Ireland, When Connacht Rose*. Dublin: M. H. Gill, 1937.

Hegel, Georg Wilhelm Friedrich. *Reason in History: A General Introduction to the Philosophy of History*. Translated by Robert S. Hartman. Indianapolis and New York: Bobbs-Merrill, 1953.

Hillhouse, James T., revised by Alexander Welsh. "Sir Walter Scott." In *The English Romantic Poets and Essayists: A Review of Research and Criticism*, edited by Carolyn Washburn Houtchens and Lawrence Huston Houtchens, 117–54. New York: New York University Press, 1966.

Hillhouse, James J. *The Waverley Novels and Their Critics*. 1936. Reprint. New York: Octagon Books, 1968.

Hogan, Robert. *After the Irish Renaissance: A Critical History of the Irish Drama since "The Plough and the Stars."* Minneapolis: University of Minnesota Press, 1967.

_____. *Eimar O'Duffy.* Lewisburg, Pa.: Bucknell University Press, 1972.

Howarth, Herbert. *The Irish Writers, 1880–1940: Literature under Parnell's Star.* London: Rockliff, 1958.

Johnston, Edith Mary. *Ireland in the Eighteenth Century.* Dublin: Gill and Macmillan, 1974.

Joyce, P. W., ed. *Old Irish Folk Music and Songs.* New York: Cooper Square Publishers, 1965.

Keen, Maurice. "The Outlaw Ballad as an Expression of Peasant Discontent." In *The Outlaws of Medieval Legend.* Toronto: University of Toronto Press, 1977.

Kiely, Benedict. *Modern Irish Fiction — A Critique.* Dublin: Golden Eagle Books, 1950.

_____. *Poor Scholar: A Study of the Works and Days of William Carleton (1794–1869).* New York: Sheed and Ward, 1948.

Le Fanu, W. R. *Seventy Years of Irish Life: Being Anecdotes and Reminiscences.* London: Arnold, 1893.

Levine, George. "Sir Walter Scott: The End of Romance." *Wordsworth Circle* 10 (1979): 147–60.

Lukács, Georg. *The Historical Novel.* Translated by Hannah and Stanley Mitchell. London: Merlin Press, 1962.

Lyons, F. S. L. *Ireland since the Famine.* Glasgow: Fontana/Collins, 1975.

MacArdle, Dorothy. *The Irish Republic: A Documented Chronicle of the Anglo-Irish Conflict, and the Partitioning of Ireland, with a Detailed Account of the Period 1916–1923.* London: V. Gollancz, 1937.

"Macken, Walter." In *Contemporary Authors,* edited by James Etheredge, 13–14. Detroit: The Book Tower, 1965.

Maigron, Louis H. *Le roman historique a l'époque romantique: Essai sur l'influence de Walter Scott.* Paris: Libraire Ancienne Honoré Champions, 1912.

Makem, Tommy, and the Clancy Brothers, eds. *The Irish Songbook: Collected, Adapted, Written, and Sung by the Clancy Brothers and Tommy Makem.* Toronto: Macmillan, 1969.

Marcus, Phillip L. *Standish O'Grady.* Lewisburg, Pa.: Bucknell University Press, 1970.

_____. *Yeats and the Beginning of the Irish Renaissance.* Ithaca: Cornell University Press, 1970.

Marlow, Joyce. *Captain Boycott and the Irish.* London: Deutsch, 1973.

McCormack, W. J. *Sheridan Le Fanu and Victorian Ireland.* Oxford: Clarendon Press, 1980.

McHugh, Roger. "The Famine in Irish Oral Tradition." In *The Great Famine: Studies in Irish History, 1845–52*, edited by R. Dudley Edwards and T. Desmond Williams, 391–437. Dublin: Browne and Nolan, 1956.

McMahon, Sean. "Francis MacManus' Novels of Modern Ireland." *Éire-Ireland* 5, no. 1 (1970): 116–30.

Montgomerie, William. "Scottish Ballad Manuscripts." *Studies in Scottish Literature* 4 (1967): 15–28.

Murison, David. "The Two Languages in Scott." In *Scott's Mind and Art*, edited by A. Norman Jeffares, 206–29. Edinburgh: Oliver and Boyd, 1969.

Murray, Patrick Joseph. *The Life of John Banim*. 1857. Reprint. New York: Garland Publishing, 1978.

O'Brien, James H. *Liam O'Flaherty*. Lewisburg, Pa.: Bucknell University Press, 1973.

O'Connor, Frank. *A Short History of Irish Literature: A Backward Look*. New York: Putnam, 1967. New York: Capricorn Books, 1968.

Ó Danachair, Caoimhín. "Donall Ó Conaill i mBéalaimh na nDaoine." *Studia Hibernica* 14 (1974): 40–66.

O'Donnell, Peadar. Review of *Land*, by Liam O'Flaherty. *The Bell* (Dublin) 12, no. 5 (1946): 442–44.

O'Donoghue, D. J. *The Life of William Carleton*. 2 vols. 1896. Reprint. New York: Garland, 1969.

_____. *Sir Walter Scott's Tour in Ireland in 1825, Now First Fully Described*. Dublin: O'Donoghue and Gill, 1905.

O'Grady, Hugh Art. *Standish James O'Grady, the Man and the Writer: A Memoir*. Dublin: Talbot Press, 1929.

O'Hegarty, P. S. A Bibliography of Standish O'Grady. Dublin: A. Thom, 1930.

Ó Lochlainn, Colm, ed. *Irish Street Ballads*. Dublin: Three Candles, 1939. London: Pan Books, 1978.

_____. *More Irish Street Ballads*. Dublin: Three Candles, 1965. London: Pan Books, 1978.

Ó Súilleabháin, Seán, ed. *Folktales of Ireland*. Chicago and London: University of Chicago Press, 1966.

_____. "The Iveragh Fenians in Oral Tradition." In *Fenians and Fenianism*, edited by Maurice Harmon, 28–39. Seattle: University of Washington Press, 1970.

_____. "Oliver Cromwell in Irish Oral Tradition." In *Folklore Today: A Festschrift for Richard M. Dorson*, edited by Linda Dégh, Henry Glassie, and Felix J. Oinas, 473–83. Bloomington: Indiana University Research Center for Language and Semiotic Studies, 1976.

Pakenham, Thomas. *The Year of Liberty: The Story of the Great Irish Rebellion of 1798*. London: Hodder and Stoughton, 1969. London: Panther, 1972.

Parsons, Coleman O. *Witchcraft and Demonology in Scott's Fiction*. Edinburgh and London: Oliver and Boyd, 1964.

Rafroidi, Patrick. *L'Irlande et le romantisme: La littérature irlandaise-anglaise de 1789 à 1850 et sa place dans le mouvement occidental*. Paris: Éditions Universitaires, 1972.

Shaw, Rose. *Carleton's Country*. Dublin: Talbot Press, 1930.

Sheeran, Patrick F. *The Novels of Liam O'Flaherty: A Study in Romantic Realism*. Atlantic Highlands, N.J.: Humanities Press, 1976.

Sheppard, Alfred. *The Art and Practice of Historical Fiction*. London: Humphrey Toulmin, 1930.

Staples, Hugh B., ed. *The Ireland of Sir Jonah Barrington*. Seattle: University of Washington Press, 1967.

Steger, Anna. *John Banim, ein Nachahmer Walter Scotts*. Erlangen: Karl Döres, 1935.

Stock, Joseph. *A Narrative of What Passed at Killala, in the County Mayo, and the Parts Adjacent, During the French Invasion in the Summer of 1798*. Limerick: John and Thomas McAuliff, 1800.

Thompson, William Irwin. *The Imagination of an Insurrection: Dublin, Easter 1916: A Study of an Ideological Movement*. New York: Oxford University Press, 1967.

Thornton, Weldon E. "Elusive Balance in Iris Murdoch's *The Red and the Green*." In *The Modern Irish Novel (Excluding Joyce): Paper presented before the 1980 American Committee for Irish Studies — Modern Language Association Symposium, Houston, Texas*, edited by Herbert V. Fackler, 59–85. Research Series, no. 50. Lafayette: University of Southwestern Louisiana, 1980.

Welsh, Alexander. *The Hero of the Waverley Novels*. New Haven: Yale University Press, 1963.

Williams, Joan, ed. *Novel and Romance, 1700–1800: A Documentary Record*. London: Routledge and Kegan Paul, 1970.

Wolff, Robert Lee. "The Fiction of the 'O'Hara Family'." Introduction to *The Denounced*, by John Banim. New York: Garland Publishing, 1979.

_____. Introduction to *The Life of John Banim*, by Patrick Joseph Murray. New York: Garland Publishing, 1978.

_____. "The Irish Fiction of Joseph Sheridan Le Fanu (1814–1873)." Introduction to *The Cock and Anchor; A Chronicle of Old Dublin* by Joseph Sheridan Le Fanu. New York: Garland Publishing, 1979.

_____. *William Carleton, Irish Peasant Novelist: A Preface to His Fiction*. New York: Garland Publishing, 1980.

Woodham-Smith, Cecil. *The Great Hunger: Ireland, 1845–1849*. New York: Harper and Row, 1962.

Wright, Arnold. *Disturbed Dublin: The Story of the Great Strike of 1913–14*,

with a Description of the Industries of the Irish Capital. London: Longmans, Green, 1914.

Yeats, William Butler. "Battles Long Ago." *The Bookman* (London), February 1895, 153.

Zellars, W. C. *Scott and Certain Spanish Historical Novels.* Albuquerque: University of New Mexico Press, 1930.

Index

Italicized page numbers refer to extensive discussions of the novels.

233

GREAT HATRED, LITTLE ROOM

was composed in 10-point Digital Compugraphic Palatino and leaded two points,
with display type in Palatino Bold by Metricomp,
with title display type in Linotron 202 Skjald by Utica Typesetting Company, Inc.;
printed by sheet-fed offset on 50-pound acid-free Glatfelter Antique Cream,
Smythe-sewn, and bound over boards in Joanna Arrestox C,
by Maple-Vail Book Manufacturing Group, Inc.;
and published by

SYRACUSE UNIVERSITY PRESS

SYRACUSE, NEW YORK 13210